Second Edition

CASES IN SPECIAL
EDUCATION

McGraw-Hill Higher Education

A Division of The **McGraw-Hill** Companies

CASES IN SPECIAL EDUCATION, SECOND EDITION

Published by McGraw-Hill, an imprint of The McGraw-Hill Companies, Inc., 1221 Avenue of the Americas, New York, NY 10020. Copyright © 2001, 1997 by The McGraw-Hill Companies, Inc. All rights reserved. No part of this publication may be reproduced or distributed in any form or by any means, or stored in a database or retrieval system, without the prior written consent of The McGraw-Hill Companies, Inc., including, but not limited to, in any network or other electronic storage or transmission, or broadcast for distance learning.

Some ancillaries, including electronic and print components, may not be available to customers outside the United States.

This book is printed on acid-free paper.

2 3 4 5 6 7 8 9 0 DOC/DOC 0 9 8 7 6 5 4 3 2 1

ISBN 0–07–232271–3

Vice president and editor-in-chief: *Thalia Dorwick*
Editorial director: *Jane E. Vaicunas*
Sponsoring editor: *Beth Kaufman*
Developmental editors: *Teresa Wise/Kate Scheinman*
Marketing manager: *Daniel M. Loch*
Project manager: *Rose Koos*
Production supervisor: *Enboge Chong*
Coordinator of freelance design: *David W. Hash*
Cover designer: *Joshua Van Drake*
Cover image: © *Tom McCarthy/PhotoEdit*
Compositor: *David Corona Design*
Typeface: *10/12 Palatino*
Printer: *R. R. Donnelley & Sons Company/Crawfordsville, IN*

Library of Congress Cataloging-in-Publication Data

Boyle, Joseph R.
   Cases in special education / Joseph R. Boyle, Scot Danforth —2nd ed.
      p.   cm.
   On previous edition more than three authors were named; Boyle's name appeared first.
   ISBN 0–07–232271–3
   1. Special education teachers—Training of—United States. 2. Case method—United States. 3. Special education—United States—Case studies. 4. Handicapped—Education—United States—Case studies. I. Danforth, Scot. II. Title.

LC3969.45 .B69   2001
371.9'0973—dc21
                                                                00–041830
                                                                CIP

www.mhhe.com

Second Edition

CASES IN SPECIAL EDUCATION

Joseph R. Boyle

Virginia Commonwealth University

Scot Danforth

University of Missouri—Saint Louis

Boston   Burr Ridge, IL   Dubuque, IA   Madison, WI
New York   San Francisco   St. Louis
Bangkok   Bogotá   Caracas   Lisbon   London   Madrid   Mexico City
Milan   New Delhi   Seoul   Singapore   Sydney   Taipei   Toronto

This book is dedicated to:
Carole, my wife and best friend, and
Joshua and Ashley, two wonderful kids.
JRB

• • •

My supportive parents,
George and Betty.
SD

BRIEF CONTENTS

CONTENTS

PREFACE

Teacher educators have long relied upon traditional lecture methods when teaching students how to be effective teachers in preservice programs. We often teach college students with the hope that they will simply absorb the countless facts, strategies, and procedures that we present to them. On written examinations we find that our students can recall and recite the information that we presume will be essential to their livelihood as teachers. As a result of their performance, we, as educators, often continue teaching using this traditional method of dissemination of knowledge. Yet occasionally even the best professor has to pause and ask whether students really understand what he or she is presenting. Every professor has at one time or another wanted to stop in the middle of a lecture and say to students, "If you listen to nothing else that I say, you should now listen to what I am about to say. You will need this crucial 'bit' of information to be a good teacher." The problem with using a traditional method of learning is that, despite good to excellent student performance on written tests, we don't really know if students will ever use the information that we are teaching them. We have seen a number of excellent students who excelled in methods and characteristics courses go on to perform poorly in student teaching. For some reason, they failed to make the connection between theory and practice.

In addition to students' lack of skill transfer, we educators are often up against content coverage and time demands. In many courses, professors sift through essential components and overplan in an attempt to have students overlearn certain bits of information. At other times, professors are forced to move at a quick pace through material to try to cover *all* the essential components. Still in other instances, professors are forced to rush through crucial content to stay on schedule. Whatever the reason students fail to transfer effective teaching skills or knowledge, we know that there are *better ways to teach.* From our experiences, case method teaching represents one of the best ways for college students to apply knowledge and skills.

By using cases, we move one step closer to certainty that students learn, remember, recall, and use those essential "bits" of information from our lectures and textbooks. From our experiences, we have found that cases bring to life much of the information covered in classes. Cases seem to show students how important certain teaching skills are for students with disabilities. Cases get students actively engaged in the task and promote the use of those higher level thinking skills, such as analysis, synthesis, and evaluation.

We are excited to see case method teaching emerging as a popular technique in education. We commonly encounter professors who mention that they are using cases in their courses. In addition, often we see textbook publishers promoting and recommending case method books for education courses. Yet despite the recent fanfare for case method teaching, we hope that this technique does not die as quickly as it has emerged. We, in the field of education, have seen many innovative teaching techniques become popular only to fizzle out after the initial boom. Despite many of these techniques being effective tools, they have fallen by the wayside as newer, but not necessarily better, techniques become the latest fad. Will case method teaching endure to become a standard tool that is used by professors in education courses? We can only hope that this technique will continue to supplement traditional college lectures.

If you have used cases in your courses, then you are probably aware that case method teaching is a valuable tool. If you are new to case method teaching, we hope that you will give it a chance. Although not for everyone to use everyday, case method is a tool that instructors can use at least occasionally in their courses. Using case method teaching requires that you be somewhat adventurous and willing to try something new. Keep in mind that not every student will like using cases and you will not be successful 100 percent of the time. However, as you use case method teaching more frequently, we hope you will become excited by its potential. If you find that a particular case was not successful, try to reflect on what occurred and try a different approach the next time. Learn from your experiences.

As you use the cases in this book, we anticipate that your students' understanding of special education will change. Anticipate new questions and novel responses to the problems and issues raised when discussing topics about students with disabilities. Try to understand how students developed their responses and try to help them use their knowledge from previous courses. We hope that you will find this book to be a valuable tool to engage students during classes and to help them connect knowledge with practice.

We would like to thank the following reviewers for their helpful comments in revising this text: Kim Beloin, Cardinal Stritch University; Ronilue Garrison, William Jewell College; Bruce Marlowe, Johnson State College; Sandra Squires, University of Nebraska, Omaha; Colleen Thoma, University of Nevada, Las Vegas; and Sue Thorson, University of Main at Farmington.

Joseph R. Boyle
Virginia Commonwealth University

Scot Danforth
University of Missouri—St. Louis

CHAPTER 1

USING CASES IN SPECIAL EDUCATION

In this chapter we describe cases and discuss how cases can be used in college classrooms to expand the reader's knowledge of persons with disabilities. We initially define cases and discuss how we developed these cases. Next, we describe the case questions, the purpose of the questions, and the different types of questions included with the cases. Following this information, we delve into case method teaching. In this section of the chapter, we describe how it is used in other fields and how it could be used in special education. We then report on what others have found using case method teaching as part of a teacher training program. Finally, we describe how instructors can directly incorporate case method teaching into their classes.

WHAT ARE CASES?

Cases are short narratives used by instructors to help students understand some of the issues and problems that individuals with disabilities encounter in their daily lives. The cases presented in this book are meant to reflect those common characteristics associated with students within each categorical area. Furthermore, we have designed the cases to cover a wide range of ages, from infants to adults. While some events that occur in cases may seem to be embellished, the events or incidents presented in the cases come from individuals we have known over the years. Despite our firsthand knowledge of these individuals, we have chosen to use fictitious names for the students and places where the incidents occurred to protect the confidentiality of those individuals. Each case contains student information and data, observational data, or technical information (i.e., testing information, drug information, etc.) derived from actual student data. The cases are meant to be used as tools by college students to help them better understand the complexities in the lives of individuals with disabilities and to assist them at more fully understanding how, as a person with disability interacts with others, changes occur in the lives of those around the individual with disabilities.

Case Questions

The questions that follow each case can be used by the reader in several ways. First, the questions will help the reader better understand the characteristics of a disability. Second, the questions were specifically designed to help the reader more fully comprehend how the social systems perspective can provide different points of view for learning about students with disabilities. Third, the questions are centered around conflicts that occur in an individual's life, conflicts often exacerbated by a disability. Fourth, some questions focus on reoccurring issues, such as behavior management, collaboration/consultation, transition, and others. We purposefully developed the cases with at least one particular reoccurring issue (collaboration/consultation, transition, instructional methods/techniques, etc.) so the reader can practice dealing with and resolving one particular issue over several cases. Table 1.1 shows each reoccurring issue per case.

TABLE 1.1

Issues and Cases

Issue	Name and Case Number
Behavior Management	Edward, 1; Lawrence, 2; Julian, 9; Gabrielle, 13; Isaac, 17; Kimika, 18; Todd, 36; Phillip, 38; Dixon, 40; Latasha, 48; Nghia, 51
Collaboration/Consultation	Kelly, 3; Simon, 16; Adam, 19; Anita, 25; Sammy, 29; Anthony, 35; Raymond, 39; Darlene, 43; Elizabeth, 50; Angela, 54; Todd, 58
Educational Goals/Objectives	Sean, 4; Toby, 12; Jose, 14; Kimika, 18; Rita, 24; Kim, 27; Tiffany, 32; Phillip, 38; Luis, 41; Warren, 42; Eugene, 53
Inclusion	Edward, 1; Jose, 14; Simon, 16; Bertha, 26; Kathy, 37; Eric, 49
Instructional Methods/Techniques	Nyasha, 6; Loretha, 7; Donald, 11; Toby, 12; Gabrielle, 13; Randie, 20; Telsa, 21; Angie, 22; Marvin, 23; Rita, 24; Anita, 25; Juan, 28; Ladonna, 31; Dudley, 47; Takia, 52; Steve, 57
Social Diversity	Cesar, 8; Jose, 14; Emily, 33; Hari, 34; Anyssa, 44; Cynthia and Unborn Child, 56; Guillarmo, 59
Transition	Jason, 5; Kenny, 10; Bill and Lisa, 15; Isaac, 17; Adam, 19; Angie, 22; Marvin, 23; Winston, 30; Todd, 36; Janice, 45; Jean, 46; Dudley, 47; Eric, 49; Sally, 55; Talia, 60

The issues listed were chosen because they are meant to represent skills or information that teachers, parents, and other service personnel can use as they work with and care for students with disabilities. For example, knowledge of behavior management techniques, skills in collaboration/consultation, and knowing how to write appropriate educational goals/objectives, represent basic teacher training skills. Moreover, as classrooms become more integrated, teachers are in need of knowledge about inclusion and effective instructional methods for working with students with disabilities. Finally, we included the issues of social diversity and transition to expose the reader to crucial, but often overlooked, issues. We hope that the seven key issues represented in this casebook will invoke the reader to reflect more deeply on how these issues affect the lives of students with disabilities.

BACKGROUND ON CASE METHOD TEACHING

Case studies or cases have been used for some time in a number of disciplines—medicine, nursing, law, and business being the most notable (Kagan, 1993). In medicine, college students learn general principles as part of their knowledge base and then apply that knowledge to cases. For example, during the premedical and preclinical phases of their education, the typical medical student is instructed in general principles that help to guide the decision-making process (Shulman, 1986). Once these principles have been acquired and demonstrated through exams and projects, students receive opportunities to demonstrate their knowledge during supervised residency and clinical trials. Similarly, cases have been used in nursing to help students make decisions and apply their knowledge, all while in a controlled paper/pencil environment (Jones & Sheridan, 1999).

In law school, college students reason facts from previous court cases and apply precedents to their own case. Learning the knowledge base of law requires repeated opportunities to practice the general principles of law and the opportunity to generalize laws and principles to new and different cases (Shulman, 1986).

Likewise in business, cases are used to help college students tackle the complex issues of business management. Using cases of fictional businesses, students have to manage the business while the instructor changes variables in the environment so that students can practice applying knowledge of business to simulated situations. For example, as changes occur, such as periods of high unemployment, tight fiscal spending, and recession, business students decide what appropriate actions to take to ward off business failure (i.e., what products to sell, how high [or low] to set prices, or whether to sell off excess inventory). Following the use of these "paper" cases, it may be possible to use field-based projects so that students can apply their knowledge to "living cases" (Richardson & Ginter, 1998).

In education, some professionals have argued that similar methods should be used in teacher training programs. Fenstermacher (1986) feels that educating a teacher involves more than teaching a set of skills and competencies; instead, teacher training programs should encourage students to generalize principles from research to make better educational decisions. Similarly, we feel that case method teaching can greatly enhance the knowledge base of future teachers, providing them with important reasoning and decision-making skills. By doing so, college students can learn to apply the principles and theory derived from their courses to make sound decisions. Some educators feel that cases "bring to life" much of the factual knowledge that students have learned throughout their education and that this process enables students to begin to "think like teachers" (Harrington & Garrison, 1992). Others argue that cases develop higher order thinking skills in students, and using these higher order skills often results in learning that continues long after discussion of the case has ended (Kuntz & Hessler, 1998).

CASE METHOD TEACHING

Case method teaching is a method to "connect" theory with practice, particularly when problems from cases are explored in an environment of "shared inquiry" (Harrington & Garrison, 1992). In this environment, the instructor guides the "knowledge to application" process of students through particular examples derived from cases. During shared inquiry, it is of utmost importance that everyone involved has a clear understanding of the case, problems, and how solutions are derived.

Case method teaching involves a number of components and steps (Martin, Glatthorn, Winters, & Saif, 1989; Wassermann, 1994a, 1994b). First, cases such as the ones presented in this book, should be explored one case at a time. In doing so, college students are able to focus on important issues or concepts of each case. To assist you at this, we have limited the number of variables used in each case to prevent students from losing sight of the important theme of each case. Second, the cases were written at different levels of difficulty. This was done so that the cases can then be used with a variety of courses or they can be used at specific junctures in a course (i.e., serving as a review of a certain concept, such as "inclusion").

To further eliminate confusion of case themes or issues, some instructors may find it useful to discuss the case in class prior to allowing students to work on the questions. In this way, the instructor can further define specific terms or set limits for the amount of liberty that students can take at filling in the gaps of each case. Assumptions about different aspects of the case can also be discussed at this time. For example, some instructors may want to tell students to make assumptions about the character in the case, provided they explain their assumptions before responding to questions.

Wassermann (1994b) suggests several steps for orienting students to the case method process. In terms of preparing students to use cases, the instructor should discuss how to examine the cases and how to answer questions, focusing not so much on answering the questions, but noting how they came up with a particular solution. Orientation should include describing to students how they will be evaluated throughout this process (i.e., Will their responses from the small group discussion be graded? Their responses during the case discussion? Or, will a written assignment be graded?). Wassermann also recommends that the instructor be explicit about how students should prepare for class and what should occur during out-of-class assignments or during small group discussions. Case method teaching represents a different mode of learning for students, many of whom may be unfamiliar with it, therefore instructors should do their best to ease student anxiety and encourage class participation by reviewing these different aspects of case method teaching prior to using the cases.

Second, study or discussion questions have been included with each case to assist the reader at understanding or elaborating on the issues and problems from the case. The *issues* of the questions have been described earlier in this chapter. The questions are framed to engage students in multiple levels of thinking, from low-level factual skills to more complex problem-solving skills. Many of the low-level (factual) questions will require students to state only minimal information derived directly from the cases. Other questions will require that students think through their responses and support their responses with specific details.

The third component of case method teaching involves preparing students to work in small groups. Through small group discussion, students can deliberate and discuss different aspects of the case. The small groups must be arranged so that students will feel free to express their opinions in front of other students and not feel intimidated by the process. Prior to using a case, it may be helpful to discuss the different aspects of collaboration and let students practice a collaborative problem-solving task. Taken from special education, collaboration is meant to include the aspects of partnership building skills, communication skills, knowledge about effective teaching practices, and knowledge about how to problem solve (Robinson, 1991). Having previously taught collaboration to students, we know these techniques help students better understand group dynamics or at least make them realize that their interactions with fellow students have both positive and negative influences.

Once students can communicate with one another and the group has established productive group dynamics, the instructor might recommend a problem-solving procedure. Martin et al. (1989) have suggested six steps to analyze cases. They suggest that the student list the underlying issues of the case, propose solutions to resolve the issues, present a rationale for their proposed solutions, list several possible consequences for each proposed solution, rank the possible solutions based upon the likelihood of their success, and present the proposed solution to the class. While this procedure would help some students navigate through certain issues in a case, an alternative procedure would be to have students use "collaborative problem solving." Taken from Knackendoffel (1996), collaborative problem solving involves having educators work together to solve problems and resolve issues involving children with learning problems. In brief, the steps for this process are as follows: define the problem, identify possible solutions, select the best possible solution, develop an implementation plan, and specify a criteria for success (Knackendoffel; Robinson, 1991). Using educational cases, preservice teachers can easily collaborate with one another to develop (and agree upon) possible solutions to problems.

Fourth, the role of the instructor in case method teaching should be to facilitate a discussion of the case, sometimes referred to as debriefing a case or discussion teaching (Wassermann, 1994a, 1994b). This component involves more than leading a discussion. It involves having the instructor establish an environment in which students are free from ridicule or rejection of their ideas. Students should feel that their responses will be respected by all and, at times, judgment of their responses will be temporarily suspended until the response has been extensively discussed. During the case discussion, the instructor should do a number of things to facilitate discussion and keep students directed to the issues of the case. At times the instructor should paraphrase and summarize student responses so that the meaning of their statements are clear and understood. At other times, the instructor should introduce questions and statements to redirect talk back to the main issues. In addition, it may be necessary for the instructor to point out events from the case that may have gone unnoticed, yet be problematic. Finally, the instructor should refrain from expressing their opinion about issues during the discussion, unless it is necessary to prevent students from learning erroneous material. By having an instructor suspend his or her opinion about the issues, an atmosphere is created in which students feel free to express their ideas because they know that their responses will not be judged against those of the instructor.

Once the discussion ends, there will still be many unanswered questions about the issues, yet the instructor may not have time to address them. Therefore the fifth component that we recommend with the cases (to assist students with closure on certain issues) would be the use of follow-up activities. Although we provide activities in the casebook, the instructor may want to develop or tailor activities so that they are centered on specific issues in the case. For example, if students are having difficulty with the concept of "inclusion," the instructor may want to develop or use activities that will help the student more fully grasp the concept of inclusion. These activities could come in a variety of forms, such as videos, readings, observations, or out-of-class discussions. In some instances, it may be necessary to revisit issues to insure that students fully understand them.

SUPPORT FOR CASE METHOD TEACHING

Case method teaching is a technique with a record of success in other professional programs and offers considerable promise for the field of education (Wassermann, 1994a). For example, Cruickshank and Broadbent (1968) found that students who used cases (simulated experiences) during preservice training, experienced fewer problems in the classroom. A number of other leading educators also report similar benefits from using cases in college courses (Shulman, 1986; Wassermann). For example when used with preservice teachers, a case method approach (that included discussion) is believed to be responsible for teachers' increasing sensitivity toward culturally diverse students. Through case discussions, Dana and Floyd (1993) found that teachers are able to examine and understand their beliefs, subjectivity, and biases for culturally diverse students in learning environments.

There are many advantages for using cases to teach preservice teachers about students with disabilities. The biggest advantage of using cases is that cases require college students to be actively engaged during instruction. Cases require that students attend to and focus on discerning important facts of the case from the extraneous material. Cases also require that students focus on and link important issues to their knowledge base on teaching. Using cases requires students to analyze, interpret, and use data to develop solutions to complex issues (Wassermann, 1994a). In addition, through case method teaching, students learn that at times there are no clear answers to complex educational issues. Sometimes there may be no one acceptable solution, only a choice of "least detrimental alternatives." Finally, case method teaching promotes self-learning. As students resolve issues, we have found that they look for supplemental materials to better understand terms or concepts used in the cases (e.g., petit mal seizures, HIV, or collaboration), and they often use reference resources to resolve case problems.

From our experience using cases in our courses, we have found that students become more aware of the personal issues related to having a disability. Rather than only studying unrelated facts and figures about students with disabilities, the student can now apply their tacit knowledge base of special education to simulated experiences. As summed up by Harrington and Garrison (1992), case method teaching allows students "opportunities to generate *better* solutions and to see the possibilities by viewing connections between theory and practice through normative lenses" (p. 271) [emphasis added].

USING CASES IN COURSES

The cases in this book were designed to present a broad overview of individuals with disabilities from numerous categorical areas. Moreover, we designed the cases so that they could be used to supplement learning after reading about the different categorical areas. They could also be used during instruction to further elaborate on new knowledge about disabilities. The cases are meant to complement instruction in a variety of classes such as a survey course about disabilities, a characteristics course, a methods course, a behavior management course, or a parenting course. In addition, because inclusion has become such a topical issue in the field of special education, the cases presented in this book will allow students to deal with this issue in a number of ways.

ASSIGNING CASES TO STUDENTS

From a practical standpoint, instructors can use the cases in their courses in one of three ways. First, the cases can be used as individual assignments, allowing students to progress at their own pace. These out-of-class assignments can allow preservice teachers to supplement their knowledge from classes. After students have written their responses, they would then come to class prepared to discuss the case.

In a second way, the cases can be used as in-class discussion topics, allowing the reader to become exposed to different points of view about the topic. Perhaps in advanced education classes, instructors could use a case to assess student learning of previously covered topics (i.e., writing objectives, a behavioral management plan, etc.). Rather than have students prepare on their own, they would discuss the cases and respond to questions. This method would be useful at certain junctures in the course, after the student has acquired sufficient background knowledge about methods, techniques, or characteristics. This method may be useful to check students' ability to apply knowledge to a simulated situation from the case.

Third, each case could be presented to students in cooperative learning groups, allowing them to collaborate with other students and develop group solutions or responses. This method may be useful particularly when students may not have in-depth knowledge about certain issues or problems from the case. From our experiences, when students are assigned to cooperative learning groups and allowed to work on projects, the result is a superior product brought about from the numerous voices of experience. After students have responded to case questions, the entire class could then be brought together to review and evaluate group responses.

In conclusion, case method teaching has been used, in one form or another, for over fifty years (Kagan, 1993), yet it is probably one of the most underused methods in teacher training programs. If effectively carried out, case method teaching can offer students the opportunity to examine how their beliefs interact with their knowledge of education and can help students understand effective teaching principles (Wassermann, 1994a). So often students can describe a specific technique or method, but are unable to explain why they are applying the technique because they are unable to *connect* theory with practice. A firm understanding of effective teaching principles is needed for special education teachers, therefore case method teaching appears to be a valuable tool to allow them to practice what they have learned. More specifically, case method teaching can serve as an effective tool to use during the stage between acquiring knowledge and using that knowledge in the classroom.

WHAT'S NEXT?

As explained in this chapter, the case questions constantly reference different aspects of the social systems perspective. In the next chapter, we discuss the social systems perspective as it pertains to the lives of individuals with disabilities. In Chapter 2, we will compare the social systems perspective with other educational and psychological perspectives of education. Moreover, from reading about the social systems perspectives (i.e., school, community, and society), the reader will gain an insight into how a disability affects others who interact with the individual. As a stone cast into a pool of water will produce ripples throughout the pool, so too will a disability produce ripples in the social fabric of the lives of those around them.

REFERENCES

Cruickshank, D. R., & Broadbent, F. (1968). *The simulation and analysis of problems of beginning teachers* (Final report, Project No. 5-0798). Washington, DC: Department of Health, Education, and Welfare. (ERIC Document Reproduction Service No. ED 024 637).

Dana, N., & Floyd, D. (1993, February). *Preparing preservice teachers for the multicultural classroom: A report on the case study approach.* Paper presented at the Annual Meeting of the Association of Teacher Educators, Los Angeles, CA.

Fenstermacher, G. D. (1986). Philosophy of research on teaching: Three aspects. In M. C. Wittrock (Ed.), *Handbook of research on teaching* (3rd ed., pp. 37–49). New York, NY: Macmillan Publishing Company.

Harrington, H. L., & Garrison, J. W. (1992). Cases as shared inquiry: A dialogical model of teacher preparation. *American Educational Research Journal, 29*(4), 715–735.

Jones, D. C., & Sheridan, M. E. (1999). A case study approach: Developing critical thinking skills in novice pediatric nurses. *Journal of Continuing Education in Nursing 30*(2), 75–78.

Kagan, D. M. (1993). Contexts for the use of classroom cases. *American Educational Research Journal, 30*(4), 703–723.

Knackendoffel, E. A. (1996). Collaborative teaming in the secondary school. In D. D. Deshler, E. S. Ellis, & B. K. Lenz (Eds.), *Teaching adolescents with learning disabilities: Strategies and method* (2nd ed., pp. 579–616). Denver, CO: Love Publishing Company.

Kuntz, S., & Hessler, A. (1998, January). *Bridging the gap between theory and practice: Fostering active learning through the case method.* Paper presented at the Annual Meeting of the Association of American Colleges and Universities, Washington, DC.

Martin, D. S., Glatthorn, A., Winters, M., & Saif, P. (1989). *Curriculum leadership: Case studies for program practitioners.* Alexandria, VA: Association for Supervision and Curriculum Development.

Richardson, W. D., & Ginter, P. M. (1998). Using living cases to teach the strategic planning process. *Journal of Education for Business, 73*(5), 269–273.

Robinson, S. M. (1991). Collaborative consultation. In B. Y. L. Wong (Ed.), *Learning about learning disabilities* (pp. 441–460). San Diego, CA: Academic Press.

Shulman, L. S. (1986). Paradigms and research programs in the study of teaching: A contemporary perspective. In M. C. Wittrock (Ed.), *Handbook of research on teaching* (3rd ed., pp. 3–36). New York, NY: Macmillan Publishing Company.

Wassermann, S. (1994a). Using cases to study teaching. *Phi Delta Kappan, 75*(8), 602–611.

Wassermann, S. (1994b). *Introduction to case method teaching: A guide to the galaxy.* New York, NY: Teachers College Press.

CHAPTER 2

THE SOCIAL SYSTEMS APPROACH

This casebook is about individuals with disabilities and the special education system. Children, adolescents, and adults with disabilities are individuals often seen by others as "different" for various reasons. They may vary
from their peers in appearance, in their behavior, in how they communicate,
in the rate and manner in which they learn, or in their mobility.

In the traditional sense, special education is essentially a subsystem of
general education. It supports the education of students with disabilities. In
other words, special education is the part of general education that provides
services for individuals who do not fit into the standard educational system
(i.e., children who are significantly different from the norm). Individuals with
disabilities are a challenge to an educational system designed to teach to the
"norm." Unlike the majority of children, students with disabilities often do
not move as quickly and unobtrusively through the system as their peers.
Typically, these students are tested (via standardized tests); compared to a
norm group; determined that their scores or measures fall below the normal
population; classified with a federal categorical label such as specific learning
disability, mental retardation, serious emotional disturbance, or other labels;
and placed in a special setting that provides a prescriptive educational plan.
Ysseldyke, Vanderwood, and Shriner (1997) would argue that it is an "automatic" or "slam dunk" process. In other words, from their research, approximately 91 percent of those students referred to special education were tested
and 72 percent of those tested were declared eligible for special education.

While this traditional system of educating students with disabilities
worked well in the past, it was seen by some as having many shortcomings.
Perhaps, the biggest pitfall of this traditional system has been the affects of a
label on an individual. While the label is needed to gain access to federal
funding, it comes with a cost. For some students with disabilities the "cost"
can be found in the perceptions of those individuals interacting with them
(Ysseldyke, Algozzine, & Thurlow, 2000). In some cases, the label may evoke
negative perceptions and lower expectations. In other cases, the label may
serve as a template that supposedly explains how and why an individual
behaves as he or she does. It is in this latter case that the label prevents people
from fully understanding the complex strengths and needs of a child with a
disability. Growing up, one of the authors came to be friends with a neighbor,
a boy three or four years older than himself. Despite his label (moderate mental
retardation), he was a great kid to play with. Ninety-nine percent of the time,
we "forgot" about his label and played like other kids play together—running

after each other, building models, having fun. It was only when the other children in the neighborhood would torment him with cruel names that we were reminded of the harsh effects of labels.

The point is that "students with disabilities" are first and foremost individuals. These individuals often live lives similar to ours (i.e., they go to school, work, church, etc.); however, during learning they often vary from their peers to such an extent that "something," beyond that which usually occurs in the classroom, at home, and in the community, must be provided to them if they are to be successful. In the educational system, that "something" is provided via special education services. In the home and community, that "something" may be any one of a broad range of educational, therapeutic, and rehabilitation services offered by public and private medical and human service agencies.

For some people in special education, how these services are provided in and out of school became the issue. During the middle to late 1980s for some, "inclusion" became a more appropriate method to deliver special education services, rather than the traditional model of pulling students out of their regular education class. Now, in many public schools across the country, students with disabilities are receiving special education services in their regular education (or inclusion) classroom. For many students, receiving services in this method has helped to reduce the stigma associated with the label. Inclusion, like other issues in special education, can be viewed from many angles and through the social systems model we hope to provide a framework for understanding the child and the issues associated with disabilities, as well as other issues in special education. Others have also provided this perspective by looking at inclusion in early childhood programs through a "systems" approach (Odom & Diamond, 1998).

In this book, the social systems perspective is meant to provide a broader understanding of the issues that individuals with disabilities face. A social systems perspective is one in which the individual is seen as developing in a dynamic relationship with and as an inseparable part of the settings in which the individual functions over his or her life span. The perspective we apply is based on Bronfenbrenner's ecology of human development (1979). It may be referred to as an ecological perspective in that it is based on the relationship between humans and their environment (Thomas & Marshall, 1977).

The social systems perspective is not the only perspective through which human development and individuals with disabilities can be viewed (D'Amato & Rothlisberg, 1992). There are many others, a few of which will be discussed briefly. However, it is important to understand that social systems theory was selected as the framework because it is broad in scope and allows the integration of information derived from other theories. It is a perspective that allows us to study and use all facets of the individual and the environment when explaining the development of individuals with disabilities. The selection of a more restrictive theory would have limited our discussion of various individual, behavioral, and environmental factors.

Among the other perspectives available for the study of individuals with disabilities are the behavioral, psychoeducational, and biophysical theories.

From the behavioral perspective, an individual's behavior is viewed as being maintained by the stimuli in the immediate environment in which the individual is functioning. Teaching involves manipulating those stimuli and managing the contingencies in the immediate environment to facilitate change in the individual's behavior. In this perspective, little consideration is given to factors within the individual and factors in the individual's extended environment. For example, using the behavioral perspective, if a student fails to turn in his homework assignments, the teacher would arrange for a reward each time an assignment is turned in.

From the psychoeducational perspective, factors within the individual are seen as the primary cause of behavior. Emphasis is focused on the dynamic equilibrium of intrapsychic phenomena such as the id (basic instinct), ego (manager), and the superego (conscience). In addition, emphasis is placed on the impact of the immediate and extended environments. Teaching involves accepting and interpreting the individual's behavior and encouraging new and more effective modes of interacting. Using the psychoeducational perspective, an interview would be held with the student who fails to bring in homework assignments to explore the reasons why the work was not returned. The student's feelings about the work and the relationship with the teacher and those who supervise the students would be examined in an attempt to explain the student's inappropriate behavior.

The biophysical perspective emphasizes neurological and other organic factors as possible causes of behavior. Teaching involves providing ordered, controlled environments to assist the individual to neurologically process stimuli. In addition, this perspective involves concern for nutrition, medication, and other medical interventions. Using this perspective, failure to bring in homework assignments may be viewed as a short-term memory problem and strategies to improve retention may be employed.

While these competing theories make a significant contribution to the understanding of human development and the individual with disabilities, they are limited in scope and restrict our view of human development of individuals with disabilities as it pertains to learning and education. The systems perspective does not rule out information derived from work regarding these theories, but rather provides a context for organizing vast amounts of information about individual diversity.

THE SOCIAL SYSTEMS PERSPECTIVE

In the systems perspective, development is viewed as the continual adaptation or adjustment of the individual to new and ever-changing environments. It is a progressive mutual accommodation that takes place throughout the life span between growing individuals and their changing environments. It is based on "the person's evolving conception of the ecological environment and his [or her] relationship to it, as well as the person's growing capacity to discover, sustain, or alter its properties" (Bronfenbrenner, 1979, p. 9). Thomas and Marshall (1977) relate this continual adaptation or development to the function of special education, in stating that:

The environment seldom adapts, and never completely to the specific
needs of an individual with a handicap. Therefore, the ultimate purpose
of any special education program is to assist that individual in adapting
to the environment to [her or] his maximum capacity. (p. 16)

Behavior is the expression of the dynamic relationship between the individual
and the environment (Marmor & Pumpian-Mindlin, 1950). Behavior occurs in
a setting that includes a specific time, place, and object "props" and previously
established patterns of behavior (Scott, 1980). By "previously established
patterns of behavior," we mean those ways of behaving that are characteristic
of an individual, as he or she develops, and those experiences that the individual brings to the setting in which the behavior is occurring. Understanding
behavior requires more than the observation of an individual's behavior by
one or two persons in a specific setting; it requires an examination of the
systems of interaction surrounding the behavior and is not limited to a single
setting. In addition, to understand behavior one must take into account those
aspects of the environment *beyond* the immediate situation in which the individual is functioning that may impact on the behavior (Bronfenbrenner, 1979).
    Congruence is the "match" or "goodness of fit" between the individual
and the environment. Thurman (1977) suggests that individuals whom we
judge to be normal are operating in an ecology that is congruent. The "normal"
individual's behavior is in harmony or congruence with the norms of the environment. Thurman further maintains that when there is a lack of congruence, the individual is viewed as either deviant (being out of harmony with
the norms) or incompetent (lacking the necessary behaviors). Congruence
between the individual and the environment results in maximum competence
and acceptance. According to Poplin and Stone (1992), an individual may be
identified as disabled when there is a mismatch between past and present
experiences. In summary, from the social systems perspective, human development is the progressive, mutual accommodation (adaptation and adjustment) between an active, growing human being and ever-changing settings in
which the individual functions, as well as the relationships between those
settings and the broader ecological contexts (the environments in which the
individual develops) in which they are embedded. The reader is urged to refer
to this chapter to understand how the cases fit within the social systems
perspective.
    The social systems approach is distinguished by its concern with the
ongoing and progressive accommodation between the individual and his or
her immediate environment and the way in which this relationship is established and maintained by forces coming from more distinct aspects of the
individual's social milieu (i.e., the individual's social surroundings).

Human Development from a Social Systems Perspective

Bronfenbrenner suggests that the ecological contexts, or settings, in which an
individual develops are nested, one inside the other, like a set of Russian dolls.
He argues that the nested nature of the contexts is decisive in the individual's

development as events take place within them. For example, he suggests that a child's ability to read may be related to the nature of the relationship between the child's home and school and the methods used in school to instruct reading.

Any individual change must be viewed within the context of the larger social and cultural system (Riegel, 1975). From a special education perspective, the specific settings of most relevance to the development of the individual with disabilities are family, school, neighborhood, community, and society.

In the systems perspective, all individuals are viewed as growing, dynamic persons who progressively move into and restructure the settings in which they find themselves. As previously stated, these systems are nested (see Figure 2.1) and dynamic. Bronfenbrenner refers to these contexts as the microsystem, the mesosystem, the exosystem, and the macrosystem. For our

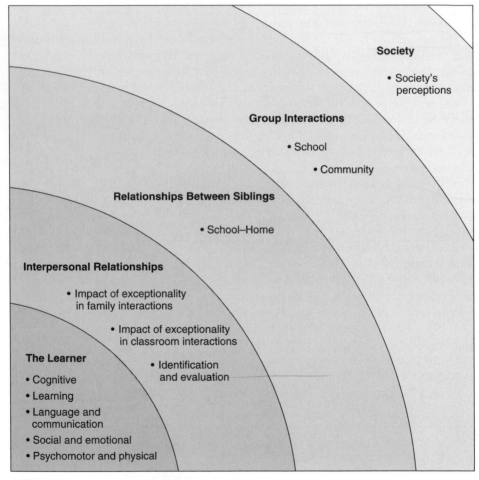

FIGURE 2.1 *The Social Systems Model*
From Shea, T. M., and A. M. Bauer. *An Introduction to Special Education: A Social Systems Perspective.* McGraw-Hill, 1997. Reproduced with permission of The McGraw-Hill Companies.

purposes, we will refer to these contexts as the individual, interpersonal relationships, relationships between settings, group interactions, and society.

Interpersonal Relationships

In the home, relationships occur between either parent and the child, the child and each sibling, and between other pairs of family members. In the school, relationships occur between the child and teacher, and the child and each of her or his peers. Referral to special education usually begins when there is a problem or lack of congruence in child-teacher or child-peer interaction within these interpersonal relationships.

Relationships Between Settings

Relationships between settings may include the interrelations among home and school, home and service agency, home and neighborhood, and school and peer group. For example, students from diverse cultural, ethnic, and linguistic groups may be challenged by the interrelationships between their home culture and the school culture and, as a consequence, be overrepresented as a group in special education. Parent-teacher collaboration and family-community service involvement are included within this system. Relationships between settings include consideration of transitions or the movement of the individual with disabilities between settings.

Group Interaction

Group interaction settings do not involve the individual directly, however, events affect, or are affected by, what happens to the individual. These settings include a parent's workplace, a sibling's classroom, and the school system. Factors such as the availability of special education service programs, the goals of educational programs in the community, and the selection of school systemwide instructional materials and textbooks are examples that can be found within group interaction settings.

Society

The nature of society often depends upon the belief system of the dominant population. These beliefs are broad social factors that impinge upon the settings within which the individual functions. Society's general perspective of individuals with disabilities, teachers, special education, the social role of students, and community values, for example, impact on each student's education (Riegel, 1975).

The Learner

Belsky (1980) suggests that though Bronfenbrenner's ecological contexts provide an essential recognition of the complexity of human development, using only those contexts fails to take into account the individual differences or variations that each individual brings to his or her primary interpersonal relationship settings. He argues for the inclusion of the ontogentic system, suggested by Tinbergen (1951), within the social systems perspective. We refer to this system as "the learner."

The learner includes the personal characteristics of the individual. Among these characteristics are the cognitive, communicative, social, and physical competencies that the individual brings to the settings in which they are functioning. Each individual has personal factors for coping with the environment including personality attributes, skills, abilities, and competencies. As Gatlin (1980) suggests, people do not deliberately make inappropriate behavioral decisions, but "attempt to satisfy their needs as they best understand them, while attempting to maintain some sense of personal and social integrity" (p. 252).

By including the learner in our perspective, we are forced to look at human development not as a series of cause and effect relationships between this individual and the environment, but as interactions between the individual and the environment. Sameroff (1975) contends the contact between the individual and the environment is a transaction (or communicative exchange) in which each is altered by the other. For example, the infant is influencing her or his caregiving environment at the same time that the caregiving environment is influencing the infant. Parents with similarly behaving children may vary in their responses toward each child and thus cause different developmental outcomes. Moreover, a child's development cannot be explained entirely by either biological or environmental factors. Rather, developmental and behavioral outcomes are due to the ongoing reciprocal interactions between the individual and the environment (Sameroff & Chandler, 1975).

IMPACT OF THE SOCIAL SYSTEMS APPROACH

The use of the social systems framework forces us, as professionals, to look beyond the education system and consider the complexities of human growth and development within a larger framework (i.e., home, school, community, and society). In addition, the social systems perspective insists that we recognize the complexity of the many issues related to individuals perceived as varying from their peers. Taking into account the transactions between the developing child and the environment, we can recognize how predictions resulting from the child's early assessment may be inadequate (Sameroff, 1975). For example, if a child is identified as demonstrating a disability, the parents may reduce their expectations for the child, thus limiting the child by their subconscious interaction style. Parents' perceptions of their child influence their behavior toward their child. Parents who perceive the child as "limited" interact with the child in a way that supports their perception. The same is true of the influence of teachers' perceptions of individuals with and without disabilities.

The social systems perspective also has an impact on professional practice. For example, an effective assessment of a student should go beyond mere test scores; instead, it should include observations and records of the individual's interactions with others within a variety of settings. The social systems perspective recognizes that changes in one setting may influence another setting, therefore understanding these changes is essential for the professionals with whom the individual is working. The systems perspective requires the professional to view the individual as a unique learner rather than a person with whom the automatic use of certain assessment techniques is appropriate (Fine, 1992).

SUMMARY

In this chapter, individuals with disabilities and special education were defined and discussed. Individuals with disabilities are those persons perceived by others as varying from their peers. They may differ in appearance, how they communicate, and how they move. They may vary in the ways in which they interact and relate to others, gain access to the environment, or the rate and manner in which they learn. In this chapter, the authors emphasize that individuals with disabilities are unique individuals, and these individuals vary from their peers in some manner. Individuals with disabilities are those persons who challenge the general education system, designed primarily for individuals who can move quickly and unobtrusively through the system.

The social systems perspective of disabilities and several terms essential to effective communication between the reader and authors were presented. The social systems approach was defined as a perspective in which the individual is seen as developing in a dynamic relationship with and as an inseparable part of the social contexts in which the individual functions over his or her life span. The implications of this perspective for the study of individuals with disabilities and special education were discussed. The social system perspective requires the recognition of the complexity of the many issues related to individuals seen as differing from their peers. Using this systems approach allows the reader to view the individual as more than a static component of the system; instead, the individual can be viewed from different perspectives (or systems) and seen as a dynamic factor within each system. We hope that by using this perspective the reader will gain a broader understanding about how the affects of a disability are felt beyond an individual's immediate environment. In doing so, we hope the reader will gain better insight into how the affects of a disability reverberates throughout the entire system.

REFERENCES

Belsky, J. (1980). Child maltreatment: An ecological integration. *American Psychologist, 35,* 320–335.

Bronfenbrenner, U. (1979). *The ecology of human development.* Cambridge, MA: Harvard University.

D'Amato, R. C., & Rothlisberg, B. A. (Eds.). (1992). *Psychological perspectives on intervention: A case study approach to prescriptions for change.* New York: Longman.

Fine, M. J. (1992). A systems-ecological perspective on home-school intervention. In M. J. Fine & C. Carlson (Eds.), *The handbook of family-school intervention* (pp. 1–17). Boston: Allyn & Bacon.

Gatlin, H. (1980). Dialectics and family interaction. *Human Development, 23,* 245–253.

Marmor, J., & Pumpian-Mindlin, E. (1950). Toward an integrative conception of mental disorders. *Journal of Nervous and Mental Diseases, 3,* 19–29.

Odom, S. L., & Diamond, K. E. (1998). Inclusion of young children with special needs in early childhood education: The research base. *Early Childhood Research Quarterly, 13*(1), 3–25.

Poplin, M. S., & Stone, S. (1992). Paradigm shifts in instructional strategies. In W. Stainback & S. Stainback (Eds.), *Controversial issues confronting special education.* Boston: Allyn & Bacon.

Riegel, K. F. (1975). Toward a dialectical theory of development. *Human Development, 18,* 50–64.

Sameroff, A. (1975). Transactional models in early social relations. *Human Development, 18,* 65–79.

Sameroff, A., & Chandler, M. J. (1975). Reproductive risk and the continuum of care-taking causality. In F. D. Horowitz, M. Heatherington, S. Scarr-Salapatek, & G. Siegel (Eds.), *Review of child development research: Volume IV.* Chicago, IL: University of Chicago Press.

Scott, M. (1980). Ecological theory and methods of research in special education. *Journal of Special Education, 4,* 279–294.

Thomas, E. D., & Marshall, M. J. (1977). Clinical evaluation and coordination of services: An ecological model. *Exceptional Children, 44,* 16–22.

Thurman, S. K. (1977). Congruence of behavioral ecologies: A model for special education programming. *Journal of Special Education, 11,* 329–333.

Tinbergen, N. (1951). *The study of instinct.* London: Oxford University Press.

Ysseldyke, J. E., Algozzine, B., & Thurlow, M. L. (2000). *Critical issues in special education.* Boston: Houghton Mifflin Co.

Ysseldyke, J. E., Vanderwood, M. L., & Shriner, J. G. (1997). Changes over the past decade in special education referral to placement probability. *Diagnostique, 23*(1), 193–201.

CHAPTER 3

INDIVIDUALS WITH EMOTIONAL OR BEHAVIORAL DISORDERS

DEFINITION

Individuals with Disabilities Education Act (IDEA)* defines an emotional or behavioral disorder as:

"(i) . . . a condition exhibiting one or more of the following characteristics over a long period of time and to a marked degree, which adversely affects educational performance:

(a) an inability to learn which cannot be explained by intellectual, sensory, and health factors;

(b) an inability to build or maintain satisfactory interpersonal relationships with peers and teachers;

(c) inappropriate types of behavior or feelings under normal circumstances;

(d) a general pervasive mood of unhappiness or depression;

or

(e) a tendency to develop physical symptoms or fears associated with personal or school problems."

KEY TERMS

attention deficit hyperactivity disorder (ADHD) A complex neurobehavioral childhood syndrome characterized by problems with attention, impulsivity, hyperactivity, and distractibility.

diagnostic evaluation A process whereby school professionals gather relevant data and make decisions concerning an individual's eligibility for special education services.

least restrictive environment As required by law, an educational placement for a student with a disability that places that student with nondisabled peers to the greatest extent possible.

---

* *Individuals with Disabilities Education Act Amendment of 1997*, 105th Cong., 1st Sess. (1997).

manic depressive disorder   A psychological condition characterized by moods that swing between two opposite poles, alternating between periods of mania (exaggerated euphoria) and depression.

psychostimulant medication   A group of psychiatric drugs—including Ritalin, Cylert, and others—typically prescribed for children with ADHD.

schizophrenia   A chronic, severe psychological condition consisting of delusions and hallucinations; often terrifying symptoms such as hearing internal voices not heard by others, or believing that other people are reading their minds, controlling their thoughts, or plotting to harm them.

school phobia   A psychological condition marked by severe anxiety, fear, and avoidance behavior in relation to attending school.

Stanford-Binet Intelligence Scale   A norm-referenced measure of general cognitive functioning.

Woodcock-Johnson Psychoeducational Battery   A series of norm-referenced instruments used to measure level of academic achievement in key skill areas such as reading, writing, and mathematics.

 CA**S** E 1. EDWARD

Issues: Behavior Management/Inclusion

Edward is a preschool student whose aggressive behavior has challenged his teacher and his parents. Gwen and Bill, Edward's parents, tell about their efforts to find solutions to their son's outrageous behavior. They seek counseling. Edward is diagnosed with ADHD and takes medication.

Edward is a 4 1/2-year-old preschool student. Three months ago, his teacher referred him for a diagnostic evaluation due to his disruptive and violent behavior in school. He was often cruel to his peers, pushing them down on the playground and grabbing toys or crayons from their hands. Brief, 2-minute time-outs had been an effective intervention for a short time. Then Edward suddenly refused to go to the time-out chair. If his teacher placed her hands on him to move him to the chair, he would struggle, kick, and bite at her hands. The teacher said that Edward was becoming unmanageable. The school evaluation recently produced an educational diagnosis of behavioral disorder. Edward is slated to attend a special kindergarten class for students with behavior disorders next fall.

Two months ago, Edward was diagnosed by the county mental health center psychiatrist as having attention deficit hyperactivity disorder (ADHD). His parents took him to the doctor soon after his behavior at home became too much for his mother to handle.

Edward's mother, Gwen, recalls Edward's rough and hyperactive behavior even in infancy:

"Even as a baby, he was a rambler. I called him that. Rambler. Constantly moving around the house. Either running away from something, into something, or through something. Boom! Eight stitches in the forehead from running full steam into the television screen. And he'd move from one thing to another in the house. He'd mess up one thing, or break it, then ramble on to something else.

"I remember my husband Bill asking me, 'Are babies supposed to do this?' I said, 'Ours is!' I had no idea whether Edward was OK or if he was crazy or if we were crazy or what. You couldn't turn your back a minute or Edward would be out the door. I can't count the times I had to run out and snatch him out of the busy street.

"As he's gotten older and he's gone to day care and school, I got to feeling like I'm always doing something wrong. I mean, I'm the mother and its my kid who knocks down all the G.I. Joes at the toy store. It's my kid who tries to throw an electric train through the neighbor boy's face. It's my kid who stuffs the sandbox sand down a little girl's mouth. The day care lady calls me and asks me why my kid did it. I don't know. One minute I'm at work, just doing my job; the next minute I'm on the phone hearing about my son, Atilla the Hun. I had to give up the job and stay home with Edward. But I'm the mother. They kick him out and it's my fault, right?"

Edward's father, Bill, recalls coming home from a stressful day at the plant to an even more stressful home:

"I always thought Gwen was born to be a mother. She just sees a baby and her eyes light up. And when we had Edward, I figured this would make her happy. This would give her something. I've got my work at the plant. I'm a shift foreman and I have a lot of responsibility. This baby would give her something of her own.

"Things went great for a while. Then, starting when Edward was maybe 16 months old, I'd come home to hear about what a handful the kid is. I was getting home at maybe 7:30 at night, dead tired, and there's Gwen crying and going on about the kid tearing up his toys and making a mess. I was worn out, so I'd just say, 'Yeah. Yeah. He's full of beans. He's adventuresome.' I'd say things like that to try to keep a lid on this whole thing, try to keep the family calm and together.

"Finally, I'm doing overtime on a Saturday and I come home from work to find the kid locked in the hall closet screaming his head off. Gwen's asleep, drunk as can be, on the couch with ZZ Top blasting at 200 decibels. I shook Gwen awake and yelled, 'What are you doing?' She cried and kept saying, 'I can't take it no more. I can't take it no more.' That's when we went to the mental health center. My mother was a drinker. I would be damned if my wild kid was gonna push my wife to the bottle, too."

When the psychiatrist diagnosed the ADHD, he prescribed Ritalin, a common stimulant medication given to hyperactive children. Bill and Gwen hesitated at the thought of putting their four-year-old on medication. Gwen recalls the difficult decision:

"We saw a report on TV about all the schoolchildren lining up for their Ritalin. I remember telling Bill how terrible it was that they're giving the little ones pills instead of love. And then there we were with our own kid with a behavior problem and a prescription for Ritalin. I put that prescription paper in Bill's sock drawer for three days. I didn't want to fill it. But Bill said, 'Gwen, maybe this'll help. Maybe Edward will be less of a monster and more of a little boy.' And didn't that medicine do just that? Or at least it seemed to. Right away Eddie was less aggravating, calmer, more even-tempered, like he had been put into slow motion. The pill didn't solve everything. He still mistreats the other children at school. But the pill seems to have taken the edge off a dangerous situation."

In addition to the Ritalin, a psychostimulant medication, the county mental health center provides family therapy. In the therapy sessions, Gwen and Bill are learning how to manage Edward's behavior. They are also beginning to explore themselves and their marriage. Bill tells of his surprise at the value of the therapy:

"When we first went, you know, to the counselor, it was for Edward. Once we started to get him under control, we started to talk about us. I was surprised to find myself doing this therapy thing. You know, like I'm gonna tell the guys at the plant that I'm expressing my feelings effectively with I-messages. But we started to look at our marriage and we started to see that the kid wasn't the whole story. We had a lot of holes in our marriage that needed and still need filling. We're working on it, and that's good."

The medication and the family therapy have produced results. Edward's behavior in school has improved. Gwen has recently had doubts about placing Edward in a special education class next fall. While she admits that Edward still has behavior problems in school, she wants him to spend his day with peers who model good behavior. She heard about an inclusive elementary school in her district and she has scheduled a visit to see this program.

QUESTIONS

1. Attention deficit hyperactivity disorder (ADHD) has received much "attention" in the media. How have television and the print media described this problem and its solutions? Do you agree with these depictions?
2. What behavior management techniques could be used with Edward?
3. ADHD, like all diagnoses of individual disorders or disabilities, focuses exclusively on the self or individual system. In this case, what do we learn about other systems (family, classroom) that improves our understanding of Edward's behavior difficulties?
4. ADHD and the medication Ritalin have gained prominence in recent years within the field of psychiatry and within educational circles. Why has ADHD become one of the primary explanations for misbehaving schoolchildren in our society?
5. Edward's mother is interested in placing her son in an inclusive kindergarten. Is this the least restrictive environment for this student? How can an inclusive program successfully include Edward?
6. *Activity:* Visit a successful inclusive kindergarten program. Observe and interview the teacher. How many exceptional students are in the class? How are these students successfully, or not so successfully, included in the kindergarten setting?

 C**A**S E   2. LAWRENCE

Issue: Behavior Management

By the second grade, due to a number of violent assaults at home and school, Lawrence had already been shifted to a special school for students with emotional-behavioral disorders. His family life is filled with stress and conflict. His parents have sought psychiatric treatment for Lawrence and family therapy to try to heal their emotionally trying family situation.

L awrence is a fourth grade student at Jeremy Bentham Exceptional Center, a special school for students given the school categorization of emotional-behavioral disorder. He has been a student there since second grade when he was transferred from a self-contained special education class at his neighborhood elementary school.

Lawrence was initially referred for special education services by his first grade teacher. She observed him to be disruptive in class, often shouting and hitting peers. His mood often appeared gloomy and depressed. He responded well to teacher directions and seemed to want to meet the behavioral expectations of the classroom, yet he seemed unable to get along with other students. Most significantly, his teacher was concerned with the seriousness of his assaults on the other children. Twice he struck classmates in the head with solid objects, once with a rock on the playground and once with a stapler in the classroom.

After being placed in the self-contained class for students with emotional-behavioral disorders, Lawrence's behavior improved, but only temporarily. For three months, his special education teacher wondered why he had been sent to her class. He was cheerful, compliant, and on task. He seemed to enjoy the small class and the increased amount of attention from the teacher. In the spring of his second grade year, Lawrence's mood and behavior tumbled. His teacher observed him becoming sometimes lethargic and withdrawn. The next day he would be angry and loud. He began having prolonged temper outbursts, screaming at his peers and his teacher. Although he seemed to intentionally avoid hurting anyone, he stormed around the classroom, bellowing in protest, refusing to go to the time-out area as directed by his teacher. Two or three days a week his teacher and the teacher aide held him on the floor until he calmed down, exhausting episodes that sometimes lasted over an hour. Concerned that she was unable to control him within the self-contained classroom, his teacher referred him to the staffing team. Due to the severity of his school behavior difficulties, Lawrence's school placement was changed in May of his second grade year to Bentham Exceptional Center.

Throughout his school career, Lawrence's academic abilities have been average. Teachers at each grade level have worked with him on grade-appropriate activities in all subject areas. Likewise, standardized testing has placed him in the average range in terms of general intelligence, reading, mathematics, and writing. There is no evidence of a learning disability.

Currently, in his fourth grade class at Bentham, Lawrence's behavior seems to go in waves, improving for a few months and then declining again. The school maintains a point and level system to reward good behavior and discourage misbehavior. Students who are compliant work their way up through the four levels gradually over three to four months. At the highest level, students may begin a gradual transfer to a self-contained classroom in a regular school. Lawrence's interest in earning points has dwindled. He rose to the top level once but fell back down when he got into a fight with a classmate.

Recently, Lawrence has become withdrawn and depressed. He has taken to curling up in a ball on the floor under his desk. Regardless of the intervention tried by his teacher, he has remained passive, only mumbling dully, "I don't care. Do what you want."

Lawrence lives with his mother, Gloria; his father, Phil; and younger brothers, Sam and Louis. Sam is a first grade student and Louis a third grader, each doing well at a local elementary school. The family lives in a suburban middle-class neighborhood. Phil owns a small restaurant and works long hours. Gloria stays at home, taking on almost all of the responsibilities for maintaining the household and raising the three boys. Gloria and Phil view themselves as struggling to live a traditional family life.

Gloria says that Lawrence was a demanding infant, often crying and always seeming to be uncomfortable and dissatisfied. During his first year, he was often sick with respiratory and skin problems. Gloria was an admittedly nervous and overattentive mother. When Lawrence was a year old, Gloria had her second child, Louis. Lawrence was obviously very upset over the birth of a sibling. To this day, he claims that his life would be great if only his parents would get rid of his brothers so he could have his mother to himself.

This family continues to contend with frequent and deep conflict, nearly always having to do with the bizarre and even dangerous behavior of Lawrence. For example, when his mother told him she would not buy him a toy he wanted (after she had recently purchased a special toy for brother Sam), Lawrence raced around the store, screaming "I hate you!" and knocking toys off the shelves. The three boys constantly squabble and fight. Lawrence has twice hurt his brother Sam badly enough that Sam had to be rushed to the emergency room.

Gloria reads books, attends parenting workshops, and seeks the advice of psychologists. She is a virtual encyclopedia of knowledge on behavior management techniques, yet she is often unable to control Lawrence or his siblings. Recently she had Lawrence hospitalized in a child psychiatric facility after he chased Sammy around the backyard with a knife. The psychiatric hospital kept Lawrence for four days and released him once the staff felt that the imminent danger of Lawrence harming his brother had passed.

Gloria has repeatedly sought psychotherapy and medication for Lawrence. He was diagnosed with attention deficit hyperactivity disorder (ADHD) at age six by a psychiatrist. Recently a second psychiatrist diagnosed Lawrence as having a manic-depressive disorder. Medications prescribed for each of these disorders have provided little or no improvement in behavior or mood.

In family therapy, Gloria and Phil maintain firmly that "Lawrence is the problem" and deny any family difficulties beyond those caused by Lawrence's behavior. Notably, Gloria was raised in a chaotic and abusive family. She admits that her father has schizophrenia and her mother is an alcoholic. Also, she was raped by an uncle at age 12. She claims that her painful history has no impact upon her current family life. Phil's family history remains unknown. He seems like a gentle, hard-working, somewhat distant father.

The quality of the working relationship between the family, the public school personnel, and the mental health professionals has been good. Gloria serves as the primary family contact person. She typically does whatever is necessary to support the work of the teachers and therapists. She attends school meetings and often calls Lawrence's teacher to discuss important issues. Yet one requirement she holds is that the teachers and mental health professionals join her in viewing Lawrence as the source of the problem. Due to the individualized nature of special education, the teachers have tended to agree with her. As a result, school-family relations have been good. In contrast, some therapists have viewed this as a family problem requiring in-depth family therapy instead of individual treatment for Lawrence. These professionals have quickly fallen out of Gloria's favor and she has moved on to seek other mental health providers.

One of the major difficulties for Lawrence and his family has been the struggle to find suitable mental health services that the family can afford. Due to their middle-class income, they do not qualify for a number of therapeutic intervention programs reserved for nonpaying clients. As a small business owner, Phil purchases an expensive health insurance policy for his family. This policy provides limited mental health benefits including a lifetime expenditure cap that the family has already reached. They now have to pay high out-of-pocket fees for psychotherapy, medication, and hospitalization.

In their middle-class community, the family strives to be viewed as "normal," as just another family with three kids and a minivan. Yet their family conflicts are viewed with fear and disdain by neighbors. Recently one neighbor called the state toll-free child abuse hot line claiming that Gloria was leaving her children unattended for hours. A social service investigator interviewed the family members. While the investigation turned up no evidence of such neglect, Gloria and Phil feel angry and betrayed. They feel they are being unjustly judged by neighbors while the community is failing to help them handle Lawrence. They are considering a move to a different neighborhood to get a fresh start.

QUESTIONS

1. Currently, Lawrence is often curling up under his desk and refusing to participate in classroom activities. What are some possible actions his teacher can take to help Lawrence?

2. It seems that Lawrence's school behavior greatly depends on his mood, whether that be depressed or positive. How could his teacher use this knowledge in working with Lawrence on improving classroom behavior?

3. Three ecological systems—family, school, and mental health— influence Lawrence's development and learning. How do these systems differ in the way they view Lawrence and in their goals for Lawrence's growth?

4. Common cultural attitudes and beliefs may be seen to influence the actions of those involved in Lawrence's life. Examine the many participants in the Lawrence drama (family members and professionals) and describe the common beliefs or attitudes that influence the behavior of these many persons in Lawrence's life.

5.   Here's a classroom problem situation to puzzle over: As Lawrence's teacher, you have all of your students write daily in personal journals. Lawrence and his classmates typically take fifteen minutes or so each morning to write a paragraph about any topic they choose. One morning Lawrence writes a short story in which he murders his mother with a knife. Explore possible options. What might you do? Why?

6.   Lawrence's school has a point and level behavior management system that is standard for all students. Lawrence seems to have lost interest in the rewards and punishments of this system. If this program is ineffective in helping Lawrence, what interventions or changes might be tried to bring about behavior improvement?

7.   We might say that it seems too easy for Lawrence to end up being blamed for his family's internal conflicts. On the other hand, we might say that it is important that all adults consistently hold Lawrence responsible for his misbehavior. Is Lawrence being unjustly blamed or is he being held responsible? Is there a difference between blame and responsibility? If so, what is it?

 C A S E 3. KELLY

Issues: Consultation/Collaboration

Kelly is a seventh grade student returning to public school after a suicide attempt and psychiatric hospitalization. Mrs. Hobbes, Kelly's homeroom teacher, and Mrs. Lee, a special education teacher, meet to discuss ways of supporting Kelly when she returns to school.

When Kelly's seventh grade teacher, Mrs. Hobbes, got off the phone with the social worker from Vineland Hospital, she immediately went to talk to Mrs. Lee, the teacher in the behavior disorders class. The psychiatric hospital had informed Mrs. Hobbes that Kelly would be discharged at the end of the week. After a suicide attempt and a brief hospital stay, the girl would be back in class on Monday. A flood of questions hit Mrs. Hobbes. How would she teach a seriously depressed, possibly suicidal girl? Should they talk about the suicide attempt? Should they avoid the topic? What should be said to her classmates? By law, Kelly's hospitalization was confidential. The students had not been officially told of it, yet rumors had spread.

Luckily, Mrs. Lee was an experienced teacher who had answers to many of these questions concerning suicide and depression. She had been teaching the middle school behavior disorders class for over ten years. She had seen quite a few students enter and return from the psychiatric hospital. Although she did not know Kelly yet, she did have the knowledge and ability to begin to provide support to her general education colleague. Before giving advice though, she asked Mrs. Hobbes to tell her about Kelly.

Mrs. Hobbes told of a timid yet cheerful little girl, pretty and well-liked by other students. Kelly was a student of average academic skills who was frequently absent. She had missed thirty-eight school days in sixth grade and thirty-two in the first three months of grade seven. When she was present, she seemed to be merely muddling through, pretending she knew what was going on despite missing so much material.

When Mrs. Hobbes had met with Kelly's mother and the school guidance counselor, they reached the conclusion that Kelly suffered from school phobia. She had an extreme and overwhelming fear of school. Despite her abilities, the academic tasks made her feel stupid and inadequate. Perhaps more importantly, the heightened social environment of adolescence pressured her in ways she felt unprepared to handle; how to fit in, be cool, be attractive, be sexual. Given the crushing weight of her anxieties about school, Kelly often skipped school as a quick solution. Unfortunately her solution only increased her level of fear. Staying away from school created a distance that further fostered her sense that school was a scary place to be avoided.

In that meeting, Kelly's mother expressed concern not only that her daughter was skipping school but that she was spending her free days with an older boy, an 18-year-old with a reputation of abusing drugs and alcohol. Forbidden to see this boy by her mother, Kelly often arranged for him to pick her up as soon as her school bus dropped her off at school in the morning. With no father in the family picture, Kelly's mother was frustrated at her own inability to control her daughter.

Since that meeting, the unauthorized boyfriend had broken up with Kelly, sending her into a depressive tailspin and spurring the subsequent suicide attempt with an overdose of sleeping pills. At Vineland Hospital, the psychiatrist diagnosed Kelly as suffering from a major depressive episode. She received antidepressant medication and group and individual therapy during her 3-week hospital stay.

After telling this story of Kelly, Mrs. Hobbes anxiously asked Mrs. Lee, "How do I prepare for her return? She'll be in next week, that is, if she doesn't skip."

"Does she have an outpatient therapist we can consult with?" Mrs. Lee queried in response, "Usually the hospital lines up a therapist on the outside."

"Yes. A Dr. Maria Cottone. I have her number."

"Great. I suggest we call her and find out specifically how to work with Kelly. From my knowledge of depressed teenage girls, I think we'll need to make her feel comfortable. It's hard to come back to school after something like this. The other students are talking. They either know more about it than we do or they're making up some unbelievable gossip that only a fool would believe." Mrs. Lee paused to consider the situation and continued. "The stigma of a suicide attempt or a psychiatric hospitalization can be powerful. Very powerful. And remember, this is a girl who didn't like school in the first place. Getting her to attend and feel relaxed will be quite a task."

This knowledge didn't alleviate Mrs. Hobbes' anxieties. "The odds are stacked against us. How can we make her like school?"

"Good question. We can probably come up with all sorts of rewards and incentives for her attending school. But I suggest we hold off on all that. Instead, let's sit down with Kelly and pose that question to her: 'How can we help you feel more relaxed and comfortable in school?' That way we'll let her know we care. That'll be crucial. We're on her side during a tough time. Plus we start a dialogue in which she begins to think about how she can make it in school and how we can help her do that. We need to meet with her before she comes back on Monday."

"OK," Mrs. Hobbes agreed hesitantly, "I can set that up . . . but shouldn't we start a referral to move her to your class? She must be emotionally disturbed."

Mrs. Lee paused thoughtfully, then answered. "In a way, you're right. The girl obviously has emotional difficulties that require much special support. But my class is primarily for students whose school behavior is disruptive. Her behavior hasn't been disruptive, has it?"

"No. She's never a problem. Just lots of absences."

"Not all students who attempt suicide or enter a psychiatric hospital or go to therapy need a special class placement. Many or even most make it in the regular class. But we do need to watch out for them in a special way."

Mrs. Hobbes still looked fearful. "OK, but I'm not a psychologist. I'm not trained to do this sort of thing. I . . . I . . . well, will you help me?"

Mrs. Lee smiled and grasped her friend's hand. "Of course. I wouldn't dare let you go through this alone. And we won't let Kelly go through this alone."

QUESTIONS

1. Kelly is not one of Mrs. Lee's special education students. Why does Mrs. Lee consult with the general education teacher on this student while simultaneously discouraging the referral to special education?
2. What makes this the beginning of an effective collaboration between general and special education?
3. A suicide attempt often carries a great social stigma. How does society typically treat a person who attempts suicide? Why? How does society view this act and the person who commits it?
4. The school ecology plays a role in influencing Kelly's mood and behavior. How can this ecology be changed to help alleviate her depression and support a more positive mood?
5. If you heard through the student grapevine that one of your students was considering attempting suicide, what would you do?
6. *Activity:* Visit a child or adolescent psychiatric hospital program. Tour the facility. Talk to staff members to learn about what this type of facility offers.

4. SEAN

Issues: Educational Goals/Objectives

In this abridged psychoeducational assessment report, Sean, a tenth grade student, is described as experiencing adolescent onset of schizophrenia. He is qualified for the "emotional disturbance" categorization. Recommendations include continued treatment with psychiatric medications under the supervision of a psychiatrist and additional academic support in the general education classroom.

The following is an abridged version of the recent psychoeducational evaluation of Sean completed by a school psychologist.

ABRIDGED PSYCHOEDUCATIONAL ASSESSMENT REPORT

Background Information

Sean is a 15-year, 2-month-old tenth grader referred for evaluation following a number of incidents of disruptive, bizarre behavior. A review of records indicates that Sean recently received two in-school suspensions and then a 5-day exclusionary suspension for pulling his pants down and revealing himself in class. Sean's academic achievement has decreased in recent weeks. He fails to turn in homework and he seems to daydream in class. Records indicate no previous serious behavior difficulties or academic problems. Classroom teachers describe Sean as an outcast, a passive, compliant boy viewed by peers as odd or weird. He had one friend with whom he spent all of his time, but that male peer switched to a private high school two months ago.

Sean lives with his parents, Frank and Josephine, and his 4-year-old sister, Wanda. According to Sean's mother, he first reported hearing voices at age 11. The family did not seek professional help at that time as Sean claimed that the voices went away soon thereafter. Presently, Sean reports hearing voices again. His parents have taken him to see a psychiatrist, Dr. Owens, who diagnosed schizophrenia and prescribed Haldol. Sean was medicated with the Haldol during the psychological testing. He seemed a bit sluggish and slow to respond at times.

Results and Interpretations

Stanford-Binet Intelligence Scale, Fourth Edition

Test Composite: 93
Verbal Reasoning: 97
Quantitative Reasoning: 100

Abstract Reasoning: 92
Short-Term Memory: 89

Results of the Stanford-Binet indicate that overall Sean is performing within the average range of cognitive abilities, approximately the thirty-third percentile in comparison to same-aged peers. This may be considered a low estimate of his cognitive functioning due to the possible tranquilizing effect of the medication.

A generally even pattern of development may be seen across areas. Relative strengths (still in the average range) were noted in quantitative reasoning and verbal reasoning skills.

Woodcock-Johnson Psychoeducational Battery—Revised

Mathematics: 94 (grade equivalent 9.6)
Reading Comprehension: 86 (grade equivalent 8.7)
Written Language: 88 (grade equivalent 9.0)

This test indicates academic abilities of average or low average abilities in all areas as expected based on the Stanford-Binet results.

A personality assessment was conducted using projective techniques. Sean's responses on the sentence completion test demonstrated a marked preoccupation with powerful figures, most notably negative personae (demons, werewolves, Hitler), although he also referred to Jesus as both a negative and a positive force. These responses also indicate an extreme amount of hostility and grandiosity and a tendency to act out these hostilities through sexual means. Other responses were tangential and demonstrated grandiose thinking and some paranoia. Additional data from the Draw-A-Person and Kinetic Family Drawing indicate that Sean views himself as empty and lacking. He drew his family as a "demon" and described himself as alternately identified with that demon and then distant from the demon. He seems to be confused about his identity and his attachments to family members and school peers. In discussing auditory hallucinations, Sean reported that the voices are frightening, "evil," and that they sometimes tell him to expose himself to girls. When asked if he is able to ignore the voices or disobey their commands, he spoke of how hard it is to disobey. He does, however, seem hopeful that his new medication will help him hear the voices less. Sean affirmed no other forms of hallucinations. Sean's responses in this evaluation suggest agreement with a diagnosis of schizophrenia.

Summary and Recommendations

Sean is a tenth grade student who has recently experienced a number of behavioral difficulties related to the adolescent onset of schizophrenia. Although he has been placed on antipsychotic medication, it is possible that his illness is in an early stage of progression and will become worse. There are signs that Sean could become more violent and paranoid. He is under the care of Dr. Owen, a psychiatrist.

Classroom behavior problems have centered around issues of sexuality, feelings of hostility, and identity confusion over relational attachment/nonattachment. While this student's behavior difficulties do not seem to warrant a full-time placement in a class for emotionally disturbed students, he could receive great benefits through a resource class and consultative/collaborative model. These two services could be used to:

1. provide academic support and compensatory instruction to help Sean remain focused, on task, and motivated in his general education courses, and
2. provide social skills and self-awareness instruction so that Sean can learn to manage himself and decrease the effects of his mental illness.

Based on this evaluation, this student qualifies for special services under the emotional disturbance categorization. It is recommended by this evaluator that this student receive additional academic support as needed to allow him to continue to receive his education in the general classroom.

QUESTIONS

1. Like most psychoeducational evaluations, this report focuses almost exclusively on the self or individual system. What knowledge of other systems can we gather from this report? What additional information about other systems would be useful to a classroom teacher?
2. If you were Sean's resource class teacher, how might you help Sean control the impulse to expose himself?
3. Keeping in mind that individualized education programs (IEPs) should involve input from students, parents, and family members, write one annual goal and three short-term objectives that might be appropriate for Sean's social development.
4. Using this report and other resources, define schizophrenia. How prevalent is this disorder among school-age youth? What impact does it have on the education of a child?
5. How can mental health and school professionals work together to help Sean?
6. *Activity:* Interview a psychologist about the use of projective testing. How do projective tests provide insight into a person's underlying psychological issues and conflicts? From what theoretical tradition within psychology have these tests been developed?

C**A**S E   5. JASON

Issue: Transition

Mrs. Polanski, a high school special education teacher, goes to a supermarket to supervise Jason, a student working at a vocational training site. She counsels him on solving problems with co-workers and encourages him to plan on attending community college after high school.

M rs. Polanski pulled out of the high school parking lot and turned up Route 109. It was sixth period and she was driving over to the Food Lion store to meet with Jason, a twelfth grade student in her behavior disorders class. Jason had been in her class for the last two years, working his way gradually through the prevocational and vocational programs. He was now spending more time in his supermarket job placement than he spent in Mrs. Polanski's class.

As she pulled in the parking lot at Food Lion, "Mrs. P" (as the students called her) was worrying about Jason's future. She had known that he was a bright student. If not for his behavior, he would have taken college preparatory classes. Instead he had been assigned to Mrs. P and she was understandably unable to replicate the advanced course offerings of the college preparatory curriculum. Jason had recognized this and resigned himself to an immediate future pointed in the direction of stocking the Food Lion produce section. Mrs. P always told him, "Stock the vegetables by day and go to community college at night. Your mind belongs in college."

Mrs. P didn't know if Jason listened to her encouragement. He had been abandoned by his parents as an infant and had grown up in the state foster care system. One morning he sat silent in the back of Mrs. P's class, working feverishly on an important problem. Mrs. P let him work on it, whatever it was. When it was time for lunch, Jason handed her a yellow notepad covered with scribblings, numbers, addition problems, and many names. At the top was the number 42 with a circle around it.

"That's how many, Mrs. P."

"How many what?"

"That's how many foster homes I've lived in. Forty-two."

Jason had been placed originally in a behavior disorders class in fifth grade, after a series of incidents in which he ran out of the school building and eluded school staff members for hours. He ran outside an average of twice a week, each time lingering at the edge of the school property, just beyond the reach of the adults who might foolishly try to catch him. In addition to this pattern of running out, Jason was often rude and disruptive in class. The teacher's authority seemed to mean little to him. Or perhaps it meant too much, for he seemed to often act in stern opposition to that authority.

Through the years, his academic skills have tested at one-to-two years above grade level. His most recent full scale IQ score is 128, well above average but not high enough to qualify him for the gifted program.

Jason's attitude toward school has been lukewarm. He has put in just enough effort to get by. A few times he has become highly interested in academics. For example, in eighth grade he was mainstreamed into an earth science class. He dove head first into studying rocks and dirt and geological formations. He spoke glowingly of his teacher and the experiments they did in class. At the end of the school year, however, his attitude suddenly shifted. He claimed that he never liked the class and that the students and teacher had been mean to him. His behavior deteriorated so much that the school personnel decided to remove him from the class with only two weeks left in the school year.

All this had brought him to complete his public school education by working at a job placement at a supermarket. Mrs. P had arranged the placement and she had supervised his work. The plan was for Jason to work full time in the produce department after the school year. His foster parents would continue to house him until age eighteen when he would move to a supervised independent living program, a small apartment complex where young adults from foster homes live under the supervision of social workers.

As Mrs. P walked into the supermarket to meet with Jason, she quickly flipped through his weekly job performance evaluations to note that he had done well until recently. In the last evaluation, the produce manager had rated Jason's attitude toward work as unsatisfactory. He had scribbled in a note about Jason illegitimately extending his 15-minute break into a half hour.

Mrs. P and Jason sat down in the employee break room to talk about his most recent evaluation. She expressed her concern over the produce manager's comments.

"That guy is no produce manager," blustered Jason, "He wouldn't know a new potato if it hit him in the head. Hey, maybe that'll help him, a few potatoes in the head."

"All right, Jason. Enough with the insults. Just explain to me what's going on here with the half hour breaks. You only get fifteen minutes, right?"

"We're supposed to. Fifteen in the morning. Fifteen in the afternoon. The same for everybody. But I've been timing the ladies on the registers and they take over half an hour every afternoon. Business is so slow then that nobody really cares."

"So you figure that if they get half an hour you should get half an hour?"

"Fair's fair. Don't you think, Mrs. P?"

"Sometimes fair is fair and sometimes it's impossible, Jason. Did you talk to your manager about this?"

"The guy barely speaks English. Last week, I asked him a question about the rutabagas and he-"

"No. No. No. Let's stay on the topic here," Mrs. P. insisted sharply. "Did you talk to your manager or did you just assume that you could take extra long breaks?"

"I just know what's right, so I did it. I don't need to ask this bozo whether I deserve the same break as the cashiers."

"There's the problem then, Jason. I agree with you that everybody should get the same amount of time for break. But you have to ask your manager about it. You can't just take it on yourself to change store policy. Get it?"

"Yeah, I know, but I hate asking that guy questions. Its like he's the expert and I'm the idiot."

"You're not an idiot, but you are below him on the chain of command. You have to ask him before you do something like that. And when you ask him, know ahead of time that you might not get the answer you want. He might tell you that cashiers get half an hour and you get fifteen minutes. No fair, but that's the way it is. At least your job lets you move around a little bit. Those cashiers stand in one place for hours."

"That's true. I wouldn't want their job. I barely want mine."

"What?"

"It's OK, Mrs. P, but there's got to be more to life than fruits and vegetables."

"Remember what I said Jason. Veggies in the daytime and college at night."

"Maybe, Mrs. P. Just maybe."

QUESTIONS

1. Should Jason be in a vocational training program? Would it and should it be possible for him to take a college preparatory curriculum?

2. Jason's family life has consisted of forty-two different foster families over the years. What effect might this have on him? On his self-esteem? On his ability to form relationships? On his sense of direction in life?

3. If you had a student like Jason in your class, a boy or girl bounced around from home to home, how would you win his or her trust?

4. What transition planning has been done for Jason? What additional transition planning do you think would help Jason be successful after high school graduation?

5. Examine the dialogue between Mrs. Polanski and Jason. How would you describe Mrs. Polanski's style in working with him? Is this an effective way to talk and work with him? What is your style in talking to adolescents like Jason?

6. *Activity:* Visit a vocational training program where special education students prepare for jobs in supermarkets, retail stores, restaurants, and so on. Interview the teacher and students about their experiences.

CHAPTER 4

INDIVIDUALS FROM DIVERSE ETHNIC, CULTURAL, OR LINGUISTIC BACKGROUNDS

DEFINITION

Cultural, ethnic, and linguistic diversity are not special education disability categories. This chapter describes students the public schools often do not serve very well. Public schools often operate on middle-class, white values and behavioral norms. Additionally, schools tend to serve a sorting function within the economic marketplace, providing a competitive arena for the distribution of economic futures of varying value. Students of color and/or students of working or lower-class backgrounds have frequently fared worse than their middle-class, white peers. This has motivated some educators to look seriously at these "diverse" populations to understand their needs and other educators to look closely at how schools favor some groups of students.

Increasingly, due to demographic shifts, American youngsters and youths in public schools are not of Euro-white descent. Often English is not their first language.

As family configurations have changed, many or even most students do not go home each afternoon to the Ozzie and Harriet style, two-parent family. Students live with one parent, with grandparents, or with aunts and uncles. They live in group homes or foster homes. They even live on the streets and in homeless shelters.

As the population changes, so do the students, and our schools struggle to figure out how to meet the needs of a widely varied student population. For the purposes of this book, we have included cases describing individuals who struggle with some of the difficulties that can occur when one lives on the economic and cultural margins of the dominant society.

C A s E 6. NYASHA

Issues: Instructional Methods/Techniques

Mr. Perez is an elementary school teacher considered to be the resident expert on the new immigrant children from the Dominican Republic and Africa. Thenjiwe wants to enroll her younger sister Nyasha, a 7-year-old, in school. Nyasha and Thenjiwe are from Zimbabwe and English is their second language. Mr. Perez meets with the two girls to try to figure out the best classroom placement for Nyasha.

"**M**r. Perez? Are you there?" The voice crackled over the classroom intercom. Oh no, thought Mr. Perez. An interruption. The entire school was off on a field trip and he had arranged coverage for his class of special education students. He would stay in his room, sit alone and unbothered, and quietly take on the mountain of IEPs that needed his immediate attention weeks ago. Maybe not. He jumped up from his paperwork and pressed his mouth against the wall to respond to the call.

"Yes, Mrs. Whitman, what do you want?"

"Mr. Perez, there's a young mother here with a student . . . uh . . . from uh . . . Africa. She wants to enroll. Mrs. O'Shea is out. Can you take it?"

"Sure," Mr. Perez answered cheerfully while groaning inside. "Could you please give them one of Mrs. O'Shea's enrollment packets and send them to my classroom?"

"OK."

Mr. Perez knew that with the guidance counselor Mrs. O'Shea out of the building, somebody had to handle this. Why me? he thought to himself. There are others in the building who can do this. He knew the answer. When a large group of Dominican Republic families moved to the district and began sending their children to this elementary school, it was assumed by many that Mr. Perez could not only speak Spanish but that he somehow had some sort of cultural insider knowledge. Despite the fact that he was born and raised in Idaho and only knew enough Spanish to order at the Taco Bell drive-thru window, Mr. Perez took on the job of unofficial liaison to the Dominican Republic students. He quickly found himself fascinated with these newcomers. He liked their spirit and tried to learn as much as possible about their cultural norms and ways.

More recently, in the past two months, a group of families from southern Africa moved to the district. Many of the fathers instantly found construction jobs in the new housing developments of the far western suburbs. Mr. Perez jumped at the chance to expand his cultural liaison role to include welcoming and supporting the new students from Zimbabwe, Namibia, and Botswana.

Mr. Perez's role as unofficial cultural liaison involved handling a wide variety of issues and problems. Just last week Mr. Perez had been called from a classroom to mediate a heated dispute between two second grade boys, immigrants from the Dominican Republic. The three of them sat down in a room to discuss the problem. The two boys rattled off Spanish sentences at such a speed that Mr. Perez's rusty high school Spanish was left far behind. When the teacher tried to talk in slow, clearly enunciated English, puzzled looks came across the confused boys' faces. After fifteen minutes of such effective, cross-cultural communication, Mr. Perez gave up. He handed each boy a dozen jelly beans and sent them back to class. Problem solved.

As the young mother and little girl entered his classroom, Mr. Perez thought to himself that "young" was an understatement. The little girl looked 6 or maybe a small 7 and her so-called mother couldn't have been more than 14 years old. He quickly found out that the little girl was named Nyasha. She wasn't accompanied by her mother. It was her older sister Thenjiwe who had brought her in to sign up for school. Nyasha wore a clean but faded dress that seemed a few sizes too small. Thenjiwe was dressed in blue jeans and bright yellow tee shirt. The two girls were extremely respectful, even submissive, as Mr. Perez questioned them.

"Where is your mother?" Mr. Perez asked Thenjiwe.

"She speaks little English. Not bad, but she thinks it is very bad," explained the teenager. "She is embarrassed." Her English was smooth, precise, and spoken with a slight accent. She turned to her sister Nyasha and gave her a firm direction in an African language. The little girl sat up straight in her chair.

"Do you go school?" Mr. Perez asked Thenjiwe.

"Yes," she replied, "Middle school . . . but I took today free for coming here. Nyasha has been staying home with my mother, but she needs school, too. So we are here."

Mr. Perez opened the packet and began asking the standard enrollment questions about the student's family, background, and prior schools. Thenjiwe answered each question. Mr. Perez found out that Nyasha was 7 years, 10 months old. She had attended one year of school in her homeland and had received limited instruction in English.

Then Mr. Perez turned to Nyasha: "Nyasha? Do you speak English?"

Nyasha smiled and looked away. She seemed shy. Thenjiwe spoke to her sister in their native tongue. Nyasha smiled and shook her head. Then Thenjiwe spoke in English to her sister, "You can speak English for the man. Tell him about your dolls." Nyasha giggled and buried her head in her hands. She was timid. Her older sister encouraged again, "You can do it. In English. Tell about the dolls." Nyasha remained quiet. Thenjiwe cast a look of helplessness at Mr. Perez and shrugged her shoulders.

"Thenjiwe, is that Shona you were speaking to her?" Mr. Perez asked.

Thenjiwe smiled. "Yes, that is our home language. *Old* home language. Father says that now we speak English for our *new* home language."

"And Nyasha speaks English well?"

"Yes," replied Thenjiwe proudly, "She speaks almost as well as I do."

"Can she read English?" asked the teacher.

"No, but she knows the letters A through Z. Do you want her to show you?"

"If you can get her to." Mr. Perez opened a drawer in his desk, fumbled around for a moment, and pulled out a deck of alphabet flash cards. He handed them to Thenjiwe.

"Say the letters out loud," Thenjiwe instructed her younger sister. By that time, Nyasha was kneeling on the floor, playing nervously with her shoelace. Thenjiwe lifted her sister's chin with one finger, drawing her eyes to the card. She held up a letter X.

"Ex," whispered the little girl.

"Yes!" cried Mr. Perez. His outburst startled little Nyasha. Her eyes open wide and white like snow-covered ponds and her eyebrows lifted to the top of her face. She froze in place, as if the teacher's volume held her still. Then she giggled and motioned with her hand for her sister to flash another card. Thenjiwe held up an L.

"El!" shouted the small girl in a voice matching Mr. Perez's shout. Thenjiwe and Mr. Perez nearly fell off their seats. They broke into laughter. Nyasha clapped her hands.

Then suddenly, Mr. Perez paused and leaned his face forward toward Nyasha. He bent over and whispered in her ear. The small girl smiled and nodded.

"Yes," she replied, "I am an English speaker and I know all my alphabet."

"Very good, Nyasha," commended Mr. Perez, "You speak English very well." He reached into his desk and pulled out a second pack of cards. On each was printed a different one syllable word. Mr. Perez ran Nyasha through ten sight words. Nyasha struggled, correctly reading four and demonstrating some phonetic skills in her mispronunciation of the other six. The teacher then asked her to count to ten. She did so in Shona and then in English. In Shona she was able to count to one hundred. In English her counting didn't go beyond ten.

"Academically," Mr. Perez presented his shoestring assessment, "she probably needs to be in kindergarten working on school readiness. Age-wise, she's a second grader. But socially...I don't know. It's a tough call. Even though she's fairly short for her age, she would still be a full head above the tallest student in kindergarten. I'm thinking we either put her in first grade with students a little younger or in second grade with students her age. First grade would allow her to work on her English and not fall behind too much in reading." Mr. Perez knew that was not an uncommon occurrence. In his school, the immigrant students were often placed with younger, smaller classmates to allow them time to learn the English language.

Thenjiwe turned to Nyasha and explained the situation in Shona. Mr. Perez could hardly follow it but he understood that Thenjiwe was asking her sister if she preferred to be with children her own age or with children learning the same things as she. Nyasha replied in English: "I want to start at the start. One."

"You're right. Grade one it is," declared Mr. Perez. He reached out and shook Nyasha's hand. "Welcome to Leigh Elementary School." Nyasha smiled. She turned to her older sister and they shook hands triumphantly.

Mr. Perez spoke as he filled out the registration packet. "Ms. Shapiro's class. Room 6. They've gone on a field trip today, but I'll show you where it is. Also, one more thing. We have an after-school tutoring program for the immigrant children. The kids stay until 4:30. They play a lot, but they learn English, too. And the bus can take Nyasha home afterwards. I think you should enroll her in that, too."

Thenjiwe agreed.

"And we need to talk to your mother or father. I'll sign her up, but we need a parent to make this official."

"OK, I'll talk to my father," Thenjiwe agreed.

"Can I see my classroom?" Nyasha asked with expectant eyes. Mr. Perez smiled and the three walked down the hall to see Nyasha's new classroom.

QUESTIONS

1. If you had a student like Nyasha in your class, a student with limited or developing English language skills, what would you do?
2. How could this elementary school arrange to provide the necessary services and supports for an immigrant student population? What needs would these students have?
3. What instructional approaches would be best for students whose primary language is not English?
4. Given the language and cultural barriers between the African and Haitian children and the local students, what can teachers and schools do to promote social integration and cross-cultural friendships?
5. In the case of Nyasha, Mr. Perez makes a placement decision by weighing her academic and social needs. Do you agree with his decision? Why or why not? What additional information would aid such a decision?
6. *Activity:* In your own local area, identify a group or groups of students who are a cultural minority or recent immigrants. What social, political, economic, historical, and practical obstacles do these families and children face?

 C**A**S E 7. LORETHA

Issues: Instructional Methods/Techniques

When 7-year-old Loretha's mother is sent to prison, Mr. Campbell, her grandfather, steps in to care for her. Mr. Kalk, Loretha's second grade teacher, meets with Mr. Campbell to discuss some academic and emotional concerns. The two are determined to work together to meet Loretha's needs during this difficult time.

"Since her Mama went away, she's been hard. I tell her to clean her room. I tell her to do her homework. But most the time she don't mind." Mr. Campbell's face beamed with hope, but he also looked tired and over-whelmed with the sudden task of raising his 7-year-old granddaughter Loretha.

"How long will her mother be away?" Mr. Kalk, Loretha's second grade teacher, asked. As he said "be away," he self-consciously noted that they were using a euphemism to avoid repeating that Loretha's mother had been sent to prison. The care of this child had fallen to Mr. Campbell.

"Bout ten months, maybe more, could be less, God willin'."

"Loretha won't talk to me or our school counselor about her mother," Mr. Kalk continued, "Is she talking to you about how she feels?"

"No. Every time I mention her Mama, she just turns away. Turns away like there's nothin' to it. I tried to tell her we got a hard situation here, but she won't talk nor listen to none of it." Mr. Campbell wrung his dark hands as he talked. His fingers were calloused and the knuckles were swollen. The grand-son of southern plantation slaves, he had worked for many years as a share-cropper in North Carolina before taking a job as a custodian in a public school. He had sat at his wife's bedside as she died of cancer two years earlier. Now his only daughter had been imprisoned on a drug charge and he had to take care of his granddaughter.

"I'm concerned, Mr. Campbell. When Loretha first came into my class, I knew we had some ground to make up. She behaved well and worked well with her peers, but her reading and writing skills were behind." Mr. Kalk knew the child's family history: possible fetal exposure to drugs and alcohol; a father who works as a lawyer in another state, sending child support checks but never visiting his daughter; a mother caught between devotion to Loretha and addiction to cocaine. Loretha was an independent, even bossy, little girl who had taken on many adult tasks and roles at a tender age. It was not an unusual family story to this veteran teacher.

"She writes her name for me on those pictures she colors." Mr. Campbell added.

"Yes. And now she can read maybe ten sight words, but she hasn't yet caught on to the idea that the letters and words on the page represent things and ideas in the world. I supplemented the children's literature and writing program with a special phonics group for her and four peers who were also struggling to decode words. She's making slow but sure progress. But these last four weeks, since her Mom went away, she's been an emotional wreck. Probably twice each day, I'd say, she just stops everything. She sits down and refuses to go on."

"She does that at home!" Mr. Campbell exclaimed. "She plops down and hums. If I talk to her, she hums even louder."

"Hums? Well, she hasn't hummed here. But she will just freeze up in the middle of a lesson or on our way to the cafeteria. When I direct her to keep going, she digs in her heels all the more. Yesterday we were taking a spelling quiz and she threw down her paper after three words. When I asked her to pick it up and continue, she closed her eyes, pushed her head against the wall, and ignored me."

"She's a strong-willed girl. You can't break her of it once she's set her mind to it. I know. I've tried."

"I think you're right, Mr. Campbell. She's very strong-willed. I also think she's hurting emotionally right now with her Mom away. I think we need to come up with a way to help her feel better and help her participate in class. My principal suggested that I refer her for testing to see if she qualifies for special education services."

The mention of "special education" seemed to jolt Mr. Campbell. His eyebrows raised and he scrunched up his face. "She's not retarded, is she?"

"No, but the testing may diagnose a learning disability. She'd probably be placed in a special class, at least part time."

Mr. Campbell still looked worried. "Is this special education going to help her?"

"Well, it might. But I honestly don't want to go that route yet. I take it personally when one of my students goes on to special education. It's as if I gave up and said I can't teach this child. And I don't give up easily. Besides, I think you and I have a few more tricks up our sleeves."

Mr. Campbell nodded in agreement.

The teacher continued. "I'd like to have the chance to work with Loretha on improving her language skills—reading and writing—and on helping her through this difficult time. I don't think she should change to a new class now, when she most needs stability and security. She has good friends in the class, and she has me."

"She likes you. She don't like all teachers, but she likes you."

"Thank you. Do you think we can work together on figuring this out?"

Mr. Campbell agreed. He and Mr. Kalk began discussing ways of helping Loretha. They set two goals, one of improving Loretha's reading skills and one of helping her express her sadness in less disruptive ways. Their discussion extended into the late afternoon as they wrote out a plan.

QUESTIONS

1. What instructional approach should Mr. Kalk employ to help Loretha improve her reading skills?

2. How can Mr. Kalk encourage Loretha to participate without "freezing up" and help her handle her feelings regarding her mother's absence?

3. It is clear from the discussion between the grandfather and the teacher that the family and classroom systems seem to be working in harmony. What do you think would have happened if Mr. Kalk had told Mr. Campbell that Loretha should be referred for the diagnostic evaluation? Why?

4. If you were giving a spelling test and Loretha threw her paper on the floor and refused to continue, what would you do? Why?

5. Mr. Kalk tells us that he views a referral to special education as giving up on his abilities to teach a certain child. Is this a view that

we special educators wish more general education teachers had or does Mr. Kalk merely have a negative opinion of special education?

6. *Activity:* Interview a classroom teacher, school social worker, or guidance counselor. Ask how they help students experiencing extreme stress or sadness due to divorce or the loss of a parent.

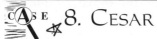

8. CESAR

Issue: Social Diversity

Cesar is a middle school student. His family comes from Mexico and works picking crops in Florida and other states. Mrs. Ellison, a school guidance counselor, is concerned that Cesar has not been coming to school. She encounters an education experience as she travels to the fields to talk to Cesar.

Mrs. Ellison hit the gas but her tires only spun deeper into the muddy rut. The car was going nowhere but down. She stepped out of her car and began to walk the dirt road toward the tomato fields. Hot streams of sweat were rolling down her neck by the time she reached the blue pickup and the Mexican workers carrying baskets on their shoulders.

"Who are you?" A sharp voice startled her. She turned to see a beet-red, sunburned man with full eyebrows and an impatient scowl. "Are you from the government?"

"No. No. I'm a school guidance counselor. I'm here to see Cesar Ramirez."

"Who?" The man didn't know Cesar. Mrs. Ellison wondered if this man was the owner.

"Cesar. He's a middle school student who works for you."

"You don't belong here. Did you bring a camera?" The man began to motion with his hands for her to leave the property.

Mrs. Ellison talked fast. She explained that she had no camera, that she worked for the public schools, and that she only needed to talk to Cesar for a minute. The man finally let her pass through, directing her to the crew leader, a small man who seemed to be in charge of the other workers. The crew leader directed her to row number nine where the Ramirez family was working.

Mrs. Ellison stumbled across the field, climbing over the ridges of dirt and green plastic sheeting. Under the rows of tomato plants and tall grass were crouched bodies and stooped heads. Pieces of rotten and broken tomato were strewn along the small trails that separated the rows. The workers—men, women, small children, all dark-skinned—hovered low over wooden buckets, their hands moving at miracle speed. Mrs. Ellison paused to watch a woman who seemed to be about her age and size. Squatting with her chin to her knees, the woman's piston-hands pumped back and forth, snatching tomatoes from the plant and smoothly slipping them down between her legs to the bucket below. After maybe three minutes of rapid hand action, the bucket suddenly flew up to one shoulder, and the woman stood. A face could be viewed, momentarily, and she hustled down the trail to the waiting truck. There was a real person under there, thought Mrs. Ellison.

Mrs. Ellison watched as the woman neared the pickup truck at the end of the trail and stepped in line behind three other workers. In sequence, each launched the heavy bucket into the air. A man on the truck worked like a juggler, catching bucket after bucket, deftly slipping the tomatoes into the truck bed, slapping a ticket in each, and away they flew back into the air. The woman caught the bucket neatly as it reached her ear and marched quickly back to pick more. She looked up at Mrs. Ellison and smiled slightly. Mrs. Ellison suddenly felt embarrassed at her voyeurism and averted her eyes.

Cesar was two rows over. He looked stunned when he realized that his school counselor was standing at his side. It was the collision of two worlds, the American public school and the migrant worker's hidden drudgery. Cesar hardened his face to a serious squint and motioned for Mrs. Ellison to walk with him toward a garden hose with running water.

"I can't take much time. There isn't a full day's crop left. What do you want?" Cesar asked without looking up, his dirty hands cooling under the stream of water.

"I'm concerned because you haven't been going to school."

"I can't go right now, " Cesar said, finally looking up at Mrs. Ellison. As the boy spoke, Mrs. Ellison thought how he looked much older out here in the fields than he looked in school. Cesar continued, "My father is sick. My family needs me to work. Besides I'm dropping out anyway. We leave for the North in a few weeks. School's not worth it anymore."

The migrant students were constantly moving, changing schools, or often not registering for school. In the six years Mrs. Ellison had been working in central Florida, she had seen dozens of migrant worker children flood into her school in the late fall. They were gone before the school year ended. Another incomplete school year. They would follow the crops, off to Pennsylvania or North Carolina or Michigan. Mrs. Ellison had read that over 600,000 migrant family children live this poor, nomadic life in America. Although she knew that the produce economy was the dictator over this entire situation, Mrs. Ellison tried to encourage her students to stay in school. "I know its hard, Cesar, but it is worth it. You are a good student. You're a little behind, but I want you to keep going so you can finish the year and enter high school in the fall. Your family and your father want you to graduate from high school, don't they?" Mrs. Ellison felt somewhat faint as she talked. The midday heat had become unbearable for her.

"Miz Ellison. I know you mean well. But you just don't understand. Graduating is OK for me, but my family needs me to work. I have my mother, two little brothers, two sisters. We are all working. We need to save the money to drive up north."

Mrs. Ellison didn't want to give up on Cesar. She knew that most of the migrant students had a fierce work ethic that would put to shame the most dedicated student's idea of hard work. She appealed to Cesar's pride. "I know you are very strong. Can you come to school and work in the evening or on the weekends?"

Cesar chuckled. "See? You do not even know. That's what I always do. I work weekends, holidays, vacation days. That's why I fall asleep in class."

The guidance counselor felt foolish at her ignorance. She glanced across the fields at the workers setting down their baskets and breaking for lunch. Cesar began to walk slowly toward the shaded clearing where the families had settled to eat. Mrs. Ellison remembered how excited she had been when her local supermarket remodeled and expanded their produce section. Suddenly she felt terribly out of place, as if she should have stayed home and quietly allowed this student to slip away like so many others.

"Cesar. Will you be back?"

He nodded and switched to Spanish, "Si," and a flurry of words that Mrs. Ellison could not understand. She tried to salvage something. "I will see you when you return. I will come up with an idea, a plan so that you can continue your education. OK?"

"Sure." He smiled softly and walked away.

Mrs. Ellison walked back toward her car, forgetting that it was stuck and that she would need to ask for help. She was too busy thinking about Cesar. She had heard that a local university had a grant-funded program in which migrant students like Cesar lived in the college dormitories during the summer and attended classes to earn a high school equivalency diploma. Perhaps Cesar would qualify. She would check it out. She was just one educator taking on an enormous problem, but she felt an urgent need to do something, anything that might bring change.

QUESTIONS

1. Realistically, given the enormity and complexity of the problem of educating migrant worker children, how much can one teacher do to bring about change?
2. Sometimes students who drop out of school due to nonattendance are viewed as lacking the values necessary for success in this country. How would you describe Cesar's system of values?
3. How does mainstream American society view the education of migrant worker children? Is this a priority in America?
4. What do you think would be the unique educational needs of a migrant worker student? How can a school provide for those needs?
5. What unique experiences and knowledge does a migrant worker student like Cesar bring to school? How can schools work to use this knowledge?
6. *Activity:* If you live in an area where fruit or vegetables are picked by migrant farmworkers, arrange to interview a student like Cesar. Find out what life and schooling are like for one of these children.

C**A**S E 9. JULIAN

Issue: Behavior Management

*Julian is an African American student from an urban area who
participates in a voluntary desegregation program that busses him to
a suburban high school in a middle class, predominantly white suburb.
Academically, Julian has always been successful. Recently, he has
responded in violent ways to what he perceives to be racist insults
from peers.*

Julian rested his back against the trash dumpster and stared at the door to
the gymnasium. He took a long draw off his cigarette and flicked the
glowing butt onto the pavement. No way, he thought. No way I'm gonna put
myself in for that scapegoat game again. He turned in bitterness and walked
away from the school building. His low pant-legs drooped like deflated accor-
dions as he shuffled off toward the railroad tracks that would lead him back
to his home in the city.

Inside the high school, the school principal Dr. Putin waited impatiently
in his office with another student, a slender, pale boy named Todd, and Todd's
mother, Mrs. Phillips.

"Where is that Julian boy?" Mrs. Phillips asked, checking her watch. "He
found the time to beat up my son. The least he can do is find the time to attend
this meeting."

"Please, Mrs. Phillips," Dr. Putin encouraged, "Let's not pronounce judgment until we have all met to ascertain the facts."

"The facts, Dr. Putin, are clear. Members of this community pay for that
boy to be bussed out of the city to our wonderful schools and he repays our
kindness with violence. He's a gang member I tell you, a hoodlum. I've seen
the way he dresses."

"Now, Mrs. Phillips . . ." Dr. Putin tried meekly to soften Mrs. Phillips'
harsh criticisms of Julian. This was the third disciplinary incident involving
Julian, and the principal found his words of defense becoming old and stale.
A strong proponent of the desegregation program that brought the African
American students from the inner city to his suburban, predominantly white
school district, Dr. Putin's progressive views had fallen on hard times. He had
watched the rising statistics, the increasing number of African American students suspended or expelled from his district's schools. Repeatedly he had
defended the bussing program in school board meetings, explaining the many
difficulties of being a minority student attending school in somebody else's
town. He explained how cultural rifts and gaps can play out in misunder-
standings between urban, African American students and suburban, white
teachers. But his words were often countered by protests of some parents of
white students who did not see the benefits of racial integration. Instead, they

wanted to isolate their community from the nearby city to hold off what they perceived to be the creeping onslaught of inner-city violence.

Walking along the rusted train tracks, Julian had plenty of time to reflect on his life. He had grown up with his mother and three older sisters in Old West, the poorest part of the city. He had met his father only once many years ago. He had begged his mother for weeks to take him to see his dad. When she finally gave in, 6-year-old Julian met a small, round man on the front steps of a small house. They drank warm sodas and talked like strangers. After an hour or so, Julian suddenly dropped the empty Coke bottle and sprinted to his mother waiting in the car.

"You were right! You were right! I shoulda never seen him!" Julian cried all the way home and never asked about that man again. Even as a youngster, though, he knew he was lucky to have such a good mother, a woman who worked hard and taught her four children to respect others and themselves. Julian had learned to concentrate in school and do his homework as soon as he got home. Through his first nine years, he had been a strong student, earning As and Bs in the city schools. Now as a tenth grader attending a suburban high school, Julian felt like he had been thrown to the wolves, well-dressed and high-talking wolves, but wolves no less. His grades had stood the test in an academically competitive high school, but his behavior had suddenly become troubling.

This latest incident was the third in the last month. The first two had been instances of racial insults to which Julian responded with angry, threatening words. He had received in-school suspensions for each incident while the white boys whose jeering provoked his anger denied their role in the incidents and received no punishment. It seemed to Julian that the teachers and students had begun to view him with great suspicion. His reputation as an excellent student faded behind his new role as the stereotype of a disruptive, nasty, black male. In the most recent incident, Julian had pushed Todd Phillips against the lockers and pinned him at the neck until teachers arrived to talk him into releasing his grip.

The pattern of racial discord in the high school was unnoticeable to most, yet obvious and persistent to Julian. A group of white boys taunted Julian in subtle ways that allowed them to seem passive and innocent. In contrast, Julian's retaliations were blatant incidents of disorderly behavior. The boys would accidentally bump him in the halls, apologizing with a contrite "Excuse me, boy." They would greet him with jubilant shouts of "Wha' sappenin', dude?" and strike a mock gangsta posture, arms crossed, weight shifted cooly back, eyes dull yet firm. During the nationally televised O. J. Simpson trial, they whispered "O. J.! O. J.!" and asked him repeatedly if he owned a white Bronco.

Sometimes the racist affronts came with such subtlety that even Julian wondered if he wasn't overreacting, reading too much into the looks and gestures of his peers. He questioned his judgment. After all, he had made many white friends at his new school. His teachers treated him well and provided much encouragement. Maybe he was going paranoid. Maybe the insults weren't happening. Julian was losing confidence in his ability to make sense of things. As frightening as his recent violent behavior was to others, it scared him most.

Dr. Putin looked up at Mrs. Phillips. "It's been twenty minutes. It doesn't seem like Julian or his mother will be attending this meeting."

"And they don't have the decency to call and cancel," Mrs. Phillips complained. "I know that you, like me, are a busy person, Dr. Putin. These people should know better than to waste our time like this."

"I appreciate you coming." Dr. Putin escorted the mother and son out of the office. "Would you be willing to come in tomorrow afternoon if another meeting can be arranged?"

Mrs. Phillips agreed, and she and Todd left.

Dr. Putin called Julian's beeper and left a message for Julian to call him at the high school. Julian, walking the tracks in the fading afternoon sunlight, checked the number on his beeper and laughed to himself. He couldn't figure out that Dr. Putin. Sometimes he seemed to be on Julian's side and sometimes he seemed no better than the cruel students who taunted him in the hallways. Julian didn't trust him. Sure, he was a liberal white man who talked about giving everybody a fair chance, but he really didn't understand what it was like to be Julian, to be the black kid trying to make his way in alien, and sometimes hostile, territory.

Julian wondered whether to call Dr. Putin. Here was a top notch high school with great academic programs, the sort of place where Julian could excel and earn his admission to a prestigious university. But it seemed this school had turned the tables on him, transforming him from highly ranked student into hallway thug. It was a tangled mess and Julian couldn't understand how to get out of it.

Stepping off the tracks, Julian walked three blocks to a pay phone outside a 7-Eleven. He dropped in a quarter, hit the buttons, listened to the first ring and wondered what to say.

QUESTIONS

1. Is Julian becoming too sensitive to insignificant remarks or is he being abused because he is black? How might responses to this question vary depending on one's racial perspective?

2. At the end of the case, we are left wondering what Julian will say to Dr. Putin, the school principal. As professional educators, we might wonder what Dr. Putin should say and do at this point. What actions do you suggest to solve this problem? Why?

3. It has been asserted by some writers that racism in America has not so much decreased since the Civil Rights era as it has gone into hiding. Surface language and behavior has changed, but the tension, discomfort, fear, and anger between races continue. Based on this case and your experiences, would you agree or disagree? Explain.

4. This case doesn't tell why Julian's mother does not attend the meeting at the high school. What are the possible reasons why she is not there? If educators decide that Julian's mother's reasons are not legitimate, how will this judgment influence the way they work with her?

5. *Brainstorm:* What can you as a teacher do to help your students become more tolerant and understanding of racial and cultural differences?

6. *Here's a situation to puzzle over:* You are teaching in the high school described in the case, a predominantly white, suburban school with a small influx of African American, urban students. Julian pulls you aside between classes to tell you that two white boys have been pressuring him not to socialize with white girls. You are confused because you have not observed anything like this and the two students Julian names are honor roll students with excellent reputations. What might you do?

7. In the case, we give Julian a certain amount of credence and respect because he has a history of academic achievement. Change the case. Make Julian a student labeled emotionally-behaviorally disordered with a history of disciplinary difficulties. How would this possibly change our perceptions of who Julian is and what is happening?

8. *Activity:* If you live in an area where court-ordered desegregation has occurred, conduct interviews with minority culture students to find out how they experience their education. You might also interview parents or desegregation program administrators.

 C**A**S E 10. KENNY

Issue: Transition

> *As a senior at Weaver High School, Kenny Kim has a powerful level of ambition, a desire to make his family view him with pride. He is a good student who hopes to attend a highly competitive university. Under strong pressures to succeed, he tries to improve his chances for admission through some illegal alterations to his school record.*

A s Kenny entered his calculus class, he couldn't help but notice the two police officers waiting inside the door.

"Kenny Kim?"

Ken ignored the officers and proceeded to his seat. They couldn't be there to talk to him. He wasn't involved in drugs or gangs. He was a serious and talented twelfth grader with prospects of enrolling in an Ivy League college. He had spent the evening before working on his application essay for Yale. Ken felt that success would serve as his alibi.

"Kenny Kim. We'd like to speak to you." The two officers escorted Kenny out of the classroom. He stared at the ground to avoid the inquisitive eyes of his calculus classmates. In the principal's office sat his parents, his mother crying softly and his father looking stern, ever demanding, and maybe heart-broken. The principal motioned to a seat. Kenny sat down between the two police officers.

The principal was abrupt. "We know you did it."

Kenny had been caught. He breathed a deep sigh. He felt shame but he also felt an odd sense of relief. He didn't have to fake it anymore. He didn't have to extend himself, overwhelm himself, oversell himself. He could even fail for once and no one could stop him.

The next day the newspapers told the fascinating tale: an achieving young man whose need for school success pushed him over the edge. Kenny Kim, the only son of Korean immigrant parents, had always been a good student. Entering his senior year at Weaver High School, he had a grade point average of 3.6 and a class rank of 26th out of 340 students. On standardized tests, he had always scored in the average range, yet his incredible perseverance and dedication to academic work had propelled him to the top tenth of his high school class.

But he had gone too far. He had broken into the high school computer system and changed his grades, switching three B's and one C to A's. Kenny had calculated that this change of four grades, an unnoticeable alteration of the official records, would boost his class rank from 26 to 10. He knew that a student who graduates in the top 10 would receive much notoriety and have a greatly improved chance of gaining admission to Yale. And Yale, Kenny well knew, was the key to his success as an American.

When Kenny's father had come to this country three decades before, arriving with a new wife and great dreams for prosperity and happiness, he had worked as a maintenance man in an office building in New Haven, Connecticut. Each morning as he walked to work, he passed the great stone library of Yale University and dreamed of one day sending his son to this prestigious school. To Mr. Kim, making it in America meant being educated, and being educated meant graduating from Yale.

This lesson had been clearly passed on to young Kenny. As an elementary school student, Kenny was required to sit down each evening after dinner to study for two-and-a-half hours. Some nights Kenny would plead with his father to let him watch TV because he had finished his homework in an hour, but Mr. Kim directed the boy to read books and work extra math problems to further develop his skills. He would need those skills and there was no time to waste. Kenny's parents sacrificed greatly over the years, paying for special tutors to teach Kenny in the evening or on weekends, saving away a little from each paycheck for Kenny's college fund.

As the day of mailing his admission application to Yale grew closer, Kenny had become increasingly aware of his less than certain chances. His SAT scores were good, not great. His grades were also good, not great. He had a recurring dream that dominated his sleep. In the dream, he saw himself opening an envelope from Yale and reading the decision aloud to his father.

It was an acceptance! He read the first sentence of the joyful news to his father's beaming smile: "Congratulations! We are proud to inform you that you have been selected . . ."—and suddenly the words on the page began to move. They shifted around from top to bottom, left to right, and finally swirled like a giant toilet bowl of letters. He looked up from the page to see his father's smile melt into a deep, disappointing frown. When he looked back at the page, the letters had stopped moving. They had realigned themselves into sentences. Kenny read quickly: "Congratulations! We are proud to inform you that you have been selected as one of the worst applicants in Yale history. Your application for admission has not only been rejected, but it will be burned in effigy in a special ceremony. You and your family are graciously invited to attend this ceremony. . . ." At this point, Kenny would wake up with a jolt.

Sitting in the principal's office listening to the police officer describe the charges against him, Kenny knew that day of opening up a letter from Yale University would never come. The moment of wondering about acceptance or rejection would not occur. Instead, Kenny had to speak to a lawyer and figure out how to live with his father's scathing silence.

QUESTIONS

1. Educators typically encourage students to work hard and strive to achieve. Yet these are not always positive values. Besides hard work and competitive spirit, what other values might educators encourage students to hold?
2. What attitudes or beliefs might Kenny's family hold that ironically pressured him toward breaking the law?
3. Do persons of all racial and ethnic groups face the same degree and type of social pressures? Or do social pressures vary depending on such factors as one's racial or ethnic group, gender, and social class? Explain.
4. How can teachers encourage students to work toward success while maintaining a balanced lifestyle?
5. What should Kenny do now? What plans should he make for the future?
6. *Activity:* Interview National Honor Society students. Do they feel intense pressure to succeed academically? If so, to what do they attribute that pressure?

CHAPTER 5

Individuals with Learning Disabilities

Definition

According to the Individuals with Disabilities Education Act (IDEA)*, the federal definition of learning disabilities is:

> ". . . children with learning disabilities means those children who have a disorder in one or more of the basic psychological processes involved in understanding or in using language, spoken or written, which the disorder may manifest itself in imperfect ability to listen, think, speak, write, spell, or do mathematical calculations. Such disorders include such conditions as perceptual handicaps, brain injury, minimal brain dysfunction, dyslexia, and developmental aphasia. Such terms do not include children who have learning problems which are a primary result of visual, hearing, or motor handicaps, of mental retardation, of emotional disturbance, or of environmental, cultural, or economic disadvantage."

Key Terms

accommodations An adaptation or adjustment made in the child's environment to assist them. For example, one type of accommodation might be to allow a student with learning disabilities additional time to complete a test.

attention deficit hyperactivity disorder (ADHD) A disorder characterized by inattention, hyperactivity, and impulsivity that may interfere with the child's educational performance.

hyperactivity Overactive behavior that may include fidgeting, squirming, or tapping of feet/hands.

impulsiveness The child's inability to control his inhibitions.

inclusion classroom A classroom that incorporates students with and without disabilities and is typically taught by both the general education and special education teachers. It is characterized by team teaching or collaborative teaching/planning, cooperative grouping, peer tutoring, enhancing techniques (e.g., web or diagram), and learning strategies.

---

* *Individuals with Disabilities Education Act Amendment of 1997*, 105th Cong., 1st Sess. (1997).

learning strategies   Specially designed techniques that teach students to use steps or procedures to complete academic tasks.

prereferral interventions   Interventions incorporated into the regular education classroom in an attempt to remediate the learning or behavior problem and prevent a referral to special education.

psychological evaluation   An evaluation that includes information about the child's performance on educational and psychological assessments.

resource room   A classroom in which children receive special education services for part of their school day.

self-contained classroom   A special education classroom in which students receive most, if not all, of their education.

C A S E 11. DONALD

Issue: Instructional Methods/Techniques

Donald had always struggled through school because of his learning disabilities. One teacher however, tried some new, different techniques with him and found success.

Donald has always had problems in school. His problems were related to poor academic performance. For example, if Donald knew he would be reading aloud in a class, he would skip class and hang out in the gym rather than go to class and attempt to read. While his behavior problems were minor, it was clear that they were in some way related to his learning problems. More specifically, his poor reading ability appeared to be the root of his behavior problems. Many of Donald's teachers knew that he was not "dumb," yet knowing that only made them require more of his performance on academic tasks.

His learning problems were first noticed by his parents during Donald's preschool and kindergarten years. During this time while other children were learning their letter names and numbers, Donald was struggling to remember even a few letter names. It wasn't that Donald was "dumb," because as reflected by intelligence test scores, Donald scored above average. When told information verbally, Donald had no trouble recalling it at a later time; however, if asked to remember letter names or letter sounds, he had much difficulty. As he advanced through first, second, and third grades, Donald continued to struggle in school. One day, his third grade teacher, Mrs. Fernandez, decided to have a conference with Donald's parents, Peggy and Bill, to discuss Donald's lack of progress. It was at this meeting that his teacher first suggested that Donald remain in third grade for another year. Peggy and Bill were mortified upon hearing such news and immediately told his teacher that they would hire a tutor for Donald.

Despite his parents' best attempts to help Donald, he still continued to perform poorly in school and at the end of the school year, school personnel strongly recommended that Donald be retained. The parents agreed with this recommendation. After a few months repeating third grade, Donald still failed to make progress. Prior to midyear, Donald's teacher sent home a note requesting permission to have Donald tested to determine if he had a learning disability. Peggy and Bill agreed to the evaluation and within a few days received a letter from the school asking them to attend a meeting about the assessment results. During that meeting, the school psychologist reviewed the results of Donald's performance from an intelligence test and an achievement test along with some other supporting observations and test scores. As expected, Donald qualified to receive special education services, and it was suggested that he attend a learning disabilities (LD) resource room for half a day each day. Donald began attending the resource room for half a day and spent the other half in the regular education classroom. He was mainstreamed into the regular education classroom for nonacademic subjects such as art, music, and physical education and for the academic subjects of science and social studies, Donald's two favorite subjects. Donald continued to slowly progress through school, but it wasn't until sixth grade that Donald began to make major gains.

It was at the beginning of sixth grade that Donald's teacher, Mr. Swanz, decided to try a teaching technique called "learning strategies" with his class. Using this strategy, Donald would use a mnemonic that contained step-by-step directions for improving his reading comprehension. Mr. Swanz pretested Donald, found his current reading level, and began teaching the strategy to Donald. At first, Donald was skeptical, but in time he began to see that the strategy was helping him to remember the important points of reading passages and textbook chapters.

A few months later after Donald successfully used the strategy with short reading passages at the sixth grade level, Mr. Swanz decided that it was time for Donald to use the strategy with textbook assignments. Shortly after that, Donald found that he did not need much help understanding the content of his textbook chapters and he began studying for tests on his own. With Mr. Swanz's assistance, many of the regular education teachers allowed and encouraged Donald to use the strategy in their classrooms. Within five months after learning the strategy, Donald was not only making above average grades in his classes, but he was also on the honor roll for the first time. Moreover, many of his teachers remarked about how confident Donald was about school.

When Donald moved on to high school, he began to develop effective notetaking and study routines. Many of these routines incorporated learning techniques and strategies. For example, Donald found that it was easier to remember a list of items by using the first letter from each item to form a word or acronym . He also prepared simulated test questions that he would answer in preparation for a test. When taking notes, Donald found it much more useful to relate ideas by drawing lines and arrows to them (i.e., developing a cognitive map or web). He also rewrote some of his notes that weren't clear and developed questions from notes that he did not fully understand. Finally, he also carried around a day planner that contained all of the assignment dates and test dates.

Years later Mr. Swanz heard that Donald was considering going to college. According to Donald's parents, with the help of special admission policies designed for persons with disabilities, Donald had received acceptance letters from three different universities and he was planning to major in education. It seems that Mr. Swanz not only motivated Donald to do well in school, but he also influenced his decision to become a teacher.

QUESTIONS

1. How is it that Donald could have an average IQ, yet perform so poorly in school?
2. Could Donald's disability have been detected earlier? How?

3. Should universities have special policies to admit students with disabilities? If so, what scores or evaluation evidence should be allowed and what should not be allowed?

4. What other intervention or technique could have been used to help Donald improve his reading?

5. To help Donald transition from home to college, what could his parents and teachers do?

6. What could universities do to assist persons with disabilities? What accommodations should college or university professors do or allow to assist college students with learning disabilities?

7. When considering the system "society," there are differences between what society "says" and what it "does." Discuss how society views persons with learning disabilities and how these views translate into actions. (Hint: Consider how teachers treated Donald in his classes before he was classified as LD.)

8. *Activity:* Visit or call a university or college and find out what special services they offer for students with learning disabilities. Compare different responses and decide which college or university environment you would recommend for a college student with LD interested in attending one of these postsecondary schools.

 C A S E 12. TOBY

Issues: Educational Goals/Objectives, Instructional Methods/Techniques

Toby was always a kid in motion. Diagnosed with learning disabilities and attention deficit hyperactivity disorder finally put a label on his problems. He is a smart child, yet his disabilities prevent him from reaching his potential.

Toby was always an active child, overactive to be precise. When he was born, his mother, Luisa, tells the story that she knew from the beginning that he was different. She remembers that while she was still in the hospital recovering from her delivery, she could tell when Toby was being brought from the nursery to her room. She could always distinguish his cry from the other babies because Toby had a high shrieking cry that could be heard throughout the hospital floor. Whenever she heard the cry, she knew Toby was on his way. When nestled in her arms, he was always in constant motion and she could never quite comfort him. From his first days, Luisa and Jose, Toby's father, knew that he was no ordinary child.

Toby's preschool years were turbulent. His teachers recall how he was "always in motion" and caused havoc particularly in group activities. In one incident, when he was 4 years old, he wanted a toy truck from the top of an eight-foot high book stand. After repeatedly being told "no" by his teacher, Toby decided to take matters into his own hands by climbing up the shelves to the top of the book stand. As he neared the top, he reached for the truck. Suddenly the book stand gave way and tumbled him and all of the contents onto the floor. Fortunately he managed to walk away from the incident with only a bruise. At the teacher's request, Toby was quickly removed from her class and never returned. As Toby moved to another preschool class, his impulsivity and hyperactivity became worse and his academic and behavioral problems continued.

Throughout much of his early education, Toby had great difficulty learning even the most basic skills such as identifying the letters in his name and the numbers to ten. His teachers always knew that Toby was intelligent, yet realized that he was not learning at the same rate as the other children. As they watched him complete children's puzzles, they were amazed with his speed and accuracy at correctly matching the pieces. But when it came to learning tasks, particularly reading tasks, he had a lot of difficulty focusing on the task. Many of the learning activities ended with Toby laying his head on the desk because he was too tired and frustrated to finish. Though he was always eager to try new tasks, he would quickly lose interest and become distracted.

It was early in third grade that his teacher, Mrs. McDonald, noticed that Toby's reading problems were serious enough to warrant a closer look. In one incident, she requested that her students work at their desks as they completed a worksheet. This particular worksheet involved having the children find the missing word in the sentences (fill-in-the-blank). As she watched Toby at his desk, she saw that he quickly began to work on his assignment. He worked diligently—head down, eyes on paper, writing responses for each question. Two minutes later she again scanned the room and saw all of the other children working on the worksheet with the exception of Toby. Toby was sitting at his desk spinning his pencil around in circles and chuckling in delight. Sensing that something was wrong, Mrs. McDonald approached his desk to find that Toby had completed the worksheet, but he had answered all of the items incorrectly. As she sat working with Toby, she soon found that he was unable to identify certain dipthongs and blends in some of the words. Over the next few weeks she also noticed that Toby exhibited other reading problems, such as frequent reversals (saw for was, when for then, and b for d), frequent confusion of the vowel sound (i for e), and numerous sight word errors (his for this, the for they, and this for that). Mrs. McDonald also reported that even when Toby sounded out each letter to a word, he would often say a completely different word than the word in front of him. (For b-l-a-c-k, Toby was able to pronounce the letter sounds but then pronounced the word as game.)

During many of his reading tasks, Mrs. McDonald noticed that on some days Toby would do well, yet on others he would do poorly. She knew he took medication to control his inattentiveness; she suspected that his inconsistent performance might have something to do with how often he took his medication. The more she looked back at his grades, the more she saw that his test and quiz scores reflected this inconsistent pattern, one day high and the next day low.

His hyperactive behavior and small size made him an easy target for other students' abuse. They often ridiculed him about black-rimmed glasses ("four eyes"); his small size ("shrimp"); and his overactive, fidgety behavior ("weirdo").

Because Toby was a new student in her class, it took Mrs. McDonald several weeks before she could document these problems and bring them to the attention of the school principal. Before referring the student to the school psychologist, the principal suggested that Mrs. McDonald try several pre-referral interventions with Toby and that she document his progress while she used these techniques. If after one month of using these techniques Toby continued to exhibit learning and behavioral difficulties, then he would be recommended for a full psychological evaluation.

During the next month, Mrs. McDonald tried three different techniques during Toby's reading class. The first technique that she tried was to have him review missed words from the previous day's story before reading a new story. When she tried this technique for one week, she found that Toby still missed many words, at least twenty words in a 500-word reading passage. The next week, prior to him reading a new story, she had Toby practice saying words that he missed from the previous story and she also had Toby practice fifteen new sight words taken from the new story. At the end of the week, she again examined her charts and found that Toby had reduced his number of errors but still had eight errors per story. Finally during the third week, she decided to add a repeated reading procedure to further reduce the number of reading errors. After evaluating Toby's oral reading scores, she found that Toby reduced his error rate to five words per story. Mrs. McDonald was proud of Toby's performance, however, she knew that in his other classes those teachers would not be using these techniques. She also realized that Toby still had numerous other learning problems, particularly in the area of written language. Because of her concerns, she decided to refer Toby to the school psychologist for further evaluation.

The psychologist, Mr. Zambie, found that Toby performed above average on the Wechsler Intelligence Scale for Children—Revised (WISC-R), but performed poorly on the Wide Range Achievement Test (WRAT) subtests of reading and spelling and performed poorly on the Broad Reading and Broad Written Language subtests of the Woodcock-Johnson Psychoeducational Battery (WJPB).

The following table summarizes Toby's scores:

WISC-R Scores

Verbal IQ = 108
Performance IQ = 128
Full scale IQ = 119

WRAT Scores

Reading standard score = 77/grade equivalent score = 1.6
Spelling standard score = 67/grade equivalent score = 1.8
Arithmetic standard score = 90/grade equivalent score = 3.1

WJPB

Broad reading standard score = 94/percentile rank = 34
Broad mathematics standard score = 112/percentile rank = 78
Broad written language standard score = 86/percentile rank = 17
Broad knowledge standard score = 104/percentile rank = 61

To further assess Toby's reading, Mrs. McDonald followed up with the Hudson Education Skills Inventory–Reading (HESI-R). The results from the HESI-R confirmed her suspicions of Toby's deficits by showing Toby's poor performance in the areas of phonic analysis, structural analysis, and comprehension. More specifically, the HESI-R yielded nonmastery in the skill areas of r-controlled sounds (ar, ir, er), dipthongs (oi, oy, ou, ow), word endings (es, ing, ed), and silent consonants (kn, mb, gn, wr, ght, tch). Toby's reading comprehension results from the Silvaroli Classroom Reading Inventory indicated that his independent reading level (reading comprehension) was at the first grade level, his instruction level (reading comprehension) was at the second-grade reading level, and his listening comprehension was at the fourth-grade level.

Upon examining the results from the battery of tests that had been administered to Toby, Mrs. McDonald remarked to the third grade LD teacher, Mrs. Ridge, that she was finally getting rid of him from her classroom and that she should make room in her classroom for the kid. When Mrs. Ridge commented back that she was looking forward to working with Mrs. McDonald and Toby to help resolve many of his reading deficits, Mrs. McDonald remarked that she has done all that she can and she was hoping that Toby would be in Mrs. Ridge's class full time.

QUESTIONS

1. What was the purpose of the prereferral interventions that were used? Did they help Toby?
2. Can you think of any other prereferral interventions that could have been used?
3. In what type of placement do you think Toby should be placed and why?
4. How do you think Mrs. McDonald feels about placing Toby in the LD classroom?
5. If Toby is placed in Mrs. Ridge's classroom, what could she do to create a collaborative environment with Mrs. McDonald or with other regular education teachers?
6. If Toby goes to Mrs. Ridge's class, what could be done to help Toby transition from his regular education class to her class? How should the teacher handle telling the other students about his disability?
7. Using the information from the case, develop one goal and two short-term objectives for Toby.

8.   *Activity:* Using a special education journal, find one technique that could be used to improve reading skills. Describe the technique and how it was used. Next, describe how effective the technique was at improving the reading skills of the subjects in the article.

---

13. GABRIELLE

Issues: *Behavior Management, Instructional Methods/Techniques*

Gabby is a sweet student who happens to have learning disabilities. She has learned to turn on the charm to get herself out of trouble, but soon her teacher begins to understand why Gabby has so many problems.

Gabrielle, or Gabby, is a 7-year-old student in Mrs. Bethel's second grade classroom. Gabby is a friendly student who has quite a few friends, likes school, and enjoys participating in many after-school activities such as Girl Scouts and basketball. Because of her gregarious personality, Gabby has always been well liked by students and has a good reputation with teachers and staff.

Teachers first noticed Gabby's learning problems when she was in preschool. Although minor at the time, her inattention and hyperactive behaviors eventually became more prominent as the academic demands increased and her teachers required her to attend to activities for longer periods. Despite her academic and behavioral problems, Gabby's friendly smile and teacher-pleasing behaviors always seemed to prevent her teachers from giving her poor grades and reporting her minor incidents of misconduct. Her manipulation of her teachers worked to her advantage, because no teacher ever referred her for a special education (psychological) evaluation until she entered second grade.

Mrs. Bethel, Gabby's second grade teacher, has known Gabby for sometime. Mrs. Bethel lives in the same neighborhood as her student, and Gabby frequently plays with her children who are the same age. Having watched her grow up, Mrs. Bethel suspected that Gabby had some learning problems, but assumed that teachers would pick up on them and remediate if they were severe. To her surprise, when Gabby started in her class, Mrs. Bethel was shocked to see how far behind Gabby was from the rest of her second graders. In addition to her academic woes, her teacher also found that Gabby had a short attention span and was extremely active.

Mrs. Bethel discovered that Gabby's numerous learning problems included difficulties with fine motor skills (i.e., tracing, cutting, pasting), difficulties with oral directions, confusing words with similar beginning sounds, and difficulties with gross motor skills (e.g., bumping into walls and furniture, tripping on objects).

Perhaps the most frustrating problem for Mrs. Bethel was that Gabby did not follow directions. This was evident during one art lesson in which students were to complete a project by coloring it according to the step-by-step directions given by the teacher. Throughout the lesson, the teacher frequently corrected Gabby, yet Gabby still continued to complete the project incorrectly. As Mrs. Bethel explained the first step of the directions to the class, she observed Gabby engaging in many off-task behaviors (i.e., walking around to different desks, waving her paper in the air, telling other children the incorrect directions). During the second step when students were supposed to use a red crayon to color in a part of the picture, Gabby chose an orange one. When the teacher told her that it was the wrong color, Gabby continued coloring. As students completed the final steps, Gabby's picture was the only one that was unrecognizable. Throughout the final minutes of the project, Gabby began humming and never completely finished the project. Finally, when the students were told to put their papers in their desk before lining up, Gabby did not comply; instead, she left her paper on her desk and ran to get in line. When Mrs. Bethel asked Gabby why she didn't put her project away, Gabby responded that she did not hear the teacher's directions.

Her difficulty at following directions was also evident in other lessons as well, often with the same disastrous results. A recent writing lesson provides another example. For this lesson, Mrs. Bethel showed students a picture of a Christmas tree with presents beneath it. Next, she instructed students to take a few minutes to explain to their neighbor what they did with their family over their Christmas break. After a short discussion, they were supposed to begin writing three sentences about what might be inside the Christmas presents. Throughout this activity the teacher noticed that Gabby was not working; instead, she sat in her seat spinning her pencil and nodding her head. After a few minutes of observing this, Mrs. Bethel told Gabby to begin working on her paper or she would have to take it home for homework. Gabby moved around in her seat and placed her pencil on her paper as if she was ready to work, but then decided to place her head down on her desk. Again, Mrs. Bethel tried to get Gabby's attention and finally, Gabby began to write a sentence. As soon as Mrs. Bethal went to work with another student, Gabby began going through papers in her desk. Again, her teacher called out to her to get to work. Finally she went over to her desk again and gave explicit step-by-step directions for starting the assignment. Mrs. Bethel began by telling Gabby to work on the next sentence. During the entire time that Mrs. Bethel was explaining these directions, Gabby sat working diligently as she followed the teacher's directions. Once Mrs. Bethel saw that Gabby had started, she began to walk around the room to monitor the other students. Once Gabby saw her leave, again she began to look around the room at the different posters on the walls. When Mrs. Bethel returned to find that Gabby was not working, she prompted her again in an attempt to find out more information about

Gabby's Christmas. Thinking that Gabby's Christmas gifts might help her complete the sentences, Mrs. Bethel began discussing Gabby's Christmas. Gabby mentioned a few gifts that she received, but said that she didn't want to write about them. By now, it was the end of class and Mrs. Bethel began collecting papers. Before the bell rang to signal the end of the school day, the teacher told Gabby to take her writing assignment home and complete it for homework. After all of the students had gone home, Mrs. Bethel opened Gabby's desk only to find Gabby's writing assignment.

The next day Mrs. Bethel saw Mr. Blackburn in the hallway and explained Gabby's learning and behavioral problems to him. Mr. Blackburn immediately called the school psychologist to set up an evaluation and notified Gabby's parents. Within three weeks Gabby was tested and found to be under the classification of learning disabilities (LD). Unfortunately, at the time of testing, there were no more openings in the self-contained LD classroom. However, the LD coordinator worked out a deal with the LD teacher that allowed the teacher to work with Gabby on a part-time basis.

QUESTIONS

1. If you were Gabby's preschool teacher, would you have done anything different when confronted with Gabby's learning problems?
2. Are Gabby's gross motor problems a concern? If so, what would you do? If not, what problems are?
3. What type of behavioral interventions could be used to help Gabby stay on task?
4. Would you recommend to Gabby's parents that they see their family physician about some form of medication therapy (Ritalin, Dexedrine, or Cylert) to help control her attention and impulsive problems? Why or why not?
5. If you were Gabby's teacher, what changes could you make in your teaching style to help her follow directions?
6. During the next writing assignment, what could be done to help Gabby stay on task and finish her writing assignment?
7. What could be done to help ease the transition from Mrs. Bethel's regular education classroom to the self-contained LD classroom?
8. *Activity:* Visit a local school that has classes for students with learning disabilities. Conduct written observations of what the teacher does to deal with the academic learning problems of her students. In other words, what techniques or interventions are used to help students with learning disabilities?

14. JOSE

Issues: Educational Goals/Objectives, Inclusion, Social Diversity

Jose is a preschooler with developmental delay. His learning and behavior problems not only create havoc in his life, but also in the life of his teacher.

Jose Manez is a 5-year-old student in a preschool program at Pestolie Elementary School. Jose is considered developmentally delayed with suspected learning disabilities (LD). Because any intelligence test will probably vary from month-to-month due to growth spurts, it is premature for his teacher to identify him as LD. His current preschool teacher, Mr. Keiz, suspects learning disabilities because he has observed Jose's short attention span and hyperactivity. He also noticed that Jose does not share toys with other children and he cannot remember his letters or numbers from one day to the next. Mr. Keiz is also concerned because he knows Jose comes from a home environment in which Spanish is the only language spoken.

In a recent conversation with Jose's mother (Felicia Manez), Mr. Keiz asked Mrs. Manez about Jose's medical history. Mrs. Manez told Mr. Keiz that everything was fine with Jose when he was born. Other than being under some pressure from opening a new business while pregnant with Jose, Mrs. Manez felt that her pregnancy was normal. She did report that Jose had meningitis when he was two, but felt that there were no negative effects from his illness. In addition, Mrs. Manez told Mr. Keiz that Jose seemed normal as a baby and toddler (e.g., sitting up, crawling, walking) when compared to her other children.

At about the age of 3, Jose's mother first suspected that Jose was different. She frequently tells people that Jose was always "getting into things." Whether he was knocking over household items (e.g., lamps, ash trays, bottles, etc.) or dumping cereal and other foods onto the floor, he was always into something, but she was sure that he would outgrow it. As Jose grew older (about the age of 4), his mother began to notice his impulsiveness and inability to stick to an activity for more than a few minutes. As she watched him playing with his toys around the house, he would move from one toy to the next leaving a trail of toys in his path. At about this age, she also noticed his inability to make and keep friends. When she would invite neighborhood children over to play, the result was often the neighbor child running out of the house in tears because Jose had hit, punched, or bit them. While this may seem normal for most children, it turns out that this could be a problem for Jose later in life.

Now at the age of 5, Jose was recently diagnosed as developmentally delayed with suspected learning disabilities. Mrs. Manez feels that all of the pieces to the puzzle are beginning to fit. She was relieved to learn that Jose qualified to receive special help (special services) earlier this year. Although she still does not agree with the label of developmentally disabled, she is happy to see him finally get some help. He is in a regular preschool classroom; his special education teacher, Mrs. Serenti, visits him daily in his class to work on preacademic skills (prereading and premath). Mr. Keiz spends extra time with him before and after school providing him with extra drills on basic skills.

For the most part, Jose is a pleasant child to work with. His teacher reports that he does not have any difficulty getting Jose to do his work; however, as the day progresses Jose becomes more easily distracted and frustrated. There are occasional days when Jose refuses to work because he is too tired or too distracted by events around him (e.g., Christmas, birthdays, snowy days, etc.).

Despite their apparent success at remediating his academic difficulties, Jose still has numerous behavioral problems. On one occasion, Mrs. Manez had to leave work early to come to the school to take Jose home because he bit another child. According to Mr. Keiz, Jose and Suzanne were playing together using the same kiddie kitchen kit. When Suzanne asked Jose for a tea cup and he refused to give it to her, she yelled into his ear. He then threw the cup at her and called her a name. After Mr. Keiz heard this, he stopped the two children and had them sit down to talk about what had happened. After talking it over with the two children (with Mr. Keiz doing most of the talking), he had both children shake hands and play in different areas of the room. As both students made the transition from playtime to storytime, they were still angry at one another. During storytime, Jose and Suzanne sat next to each other and soon began to elbow each other. As this occurred, Mr. Keiz ignored the behavior thinking it would go away. Finally when Suzanne elbowed Jose's ribs he turned and bit her in the arm. Mr. Keiz felt that the best remedy for this situation was to have Mrs. Manez pick up Jose and take him home. He requested that Jose apologize to Suzanne.

Two weeks later when Jose and Johnson were in the playhouse together, Jose attacked him. According to Mr. Keiz, Jose started the incident by throwing Johnson's toy car out of the house. Upon hearing the crash of the car, Mr. Keiz went over to the boys to investigate. When he asked Johnson what happened, the boy replied that Jose got mad at him because he would not share his car. Knowing Jose's past history, Mr. Keiz grabbed Jose and placed him in the corner for the rest of the day despite Jose's sobbing and cries of apologies. At the end of the day Mr. Keiz remarked to Jose that "he hoped that he had learned his lesson."

One day later, when Mr. Keiz had Jose try to match similar letters, he again had a tantrum that resulted in a phone call to his mother. During this incident, Mr. Keiz gave all of the children a worksheet of letters to trace. Despite that it was too difficult for many of the students, it kept them busy while he wrote their progress reports. Mr. Keiz knew something was unusual when he saw Jose in his desk breaking all of his crayons, but thought that at least he was busy doing something.

After a few minutes, his teacher approached Jose to find him ripping up paper in his desk. When Mr. Keiz asked him what he was doing, Jose responded that he hated reading and was going to quit school. As the other children laughed, Mr. Keiz, who became enraged, gave Jose a new worksheet and demanded that he "do it right." When Jose refused, Mr. Keiz placed his hand on top of Jose's hand (hand-over-hand) and began to force Jose to complete the worksheet. When Jose went to bite his hand, Mr. Keiz grabbed Jose by the back of his neck and carried him off to a chair in the corner.

When Mr. Keiz turned around to go to the front of the room, Jose jumped from his chair and flipped over his desk, spewing all of its contents onto the floor. As the other children laughed and applauded, Mr. Keiz reached down, lifted Jose up in the air, and carried him to Mr. Rake's (the principal) office. Once there, Mr. Keiz demanded that Jose be expelled from his class. As he left Mr. Rake's office, he was heard grumbling that "Jose never should have been in his class in the first place." When Mr. Rakes asked him what he said, Mr. Keiz remarked that, "this is no way to run an inclusion program." Mr. Keiz never fully accepted the concept of inclusion. To him, things were running fine before inclusion was invented.

QUESTIONS

1. Why is it so difficult to identify a preschool child with LD? Is the use of generic labels, such as developmentally disabled, helpful at identifying students with LD?
2. You are the person responsible for conducting evaluations of students suspected of having learning disabilities. Prior to your evaluation, you find out from the teacher that the student's home language is Spanish. What adjustments should be made prior to and during the student's evaluation?
3. What are some factors that may cause LD in children?
4. Is there a positive relationship between Mrs. Manez and Mr. Keiz? What can be done to help establish more positive interactions between the parent and school?
5. What could be done by Mrs. Manez to increase Jose's positive relationships with other children at home?
6. A true inclusion classroom first establishes new beliefs about the way children (both disabled and nondisabled) learn and grow. Is Mr. Keiz the best teacher for an inclusion classroom? What support could be provided by the school, other teachers, and the principal to assist this teacher of an inclusion classroom?
7. At school, what could Mr. Keiz do to help Jose establish positive relationships with other students?
8. Name one goal and two objectives that could be written for Jose's individualized education program (IEP).
9. *Activity:* Visit a local day care or preschool program that consists of students with and students without disabilities. Describe the modifications or accommodations that are made to include students with disabilities into their activities.

CASE 15. BILL AND LISA

Issue: Transition

*As high school sweethearts, Bill and Lisa dreamed of the perfect life.
When they were married they thought they would live happily ever
after, but soon came to understand that learning disabilities continue
long after graduation.*

Bill and Lisa are a married couple living in the town of Rockburg. In high
school they were sweethearts, and one year after exiting high school they
married. Both have GEDs (Graduate Equivalent Diplomas) and both have
learning disabilities (LD). Bill was first identified with LD when he was in
fourth grade and Lisa identified in second grade. They have spent most of
their educational careers in special education—self-contained LD classrooms.
Now they work at Martinwood Retirement Center, the local nursing home, as
nurses' aides earning minimum wage.

Taking nursing classes at Wassen Community College, both Bill and Lisa
were able to earn nursing aide degrees. At Martinwood, they assist elderly
persons in their daily care and daily living skills. Some of their job duties
include assisting them with feeding, dressing, hygiene, and medication. They
are also responsible for preparing meals, doing custodial work, and taking the
residents on walks and outings. Even though their employer pays for health
insurance, the couple rarely uses it. They say that they don't believe in doctors.
Both were excited to work at the same place and enjoy the independence of
working and living away from home.

Although they are still dependent upon their parents in a few areas, they
have become independent in many other areas of life. Bill and Lisa have one
car, a dog, and rent a house. They manage their money fairly well, but occasionally need short-term loans from their parents to help float them through
until the next payday. Because of her difficulties in math, Lisa often relies on
a calculator when she goes grocery shopping. Her mother often helps her cut
out coupons and write a grocery list for the weekly trip. Though they own a
car, Bill relies on his father to help him with car repairs. Because Bill has difficulty reading the car repair manual and instructions that come with the parts,
his father's assistance is often needed. Typically, Bill relies on the illustration
or pictures, thereby avoiding reading. His father also helps him with home
repairs and advice on money. Bill and Lisa once owned a credit card, however,
after the couple overspent on several large items, they found that they could
no longer keep it. Because of their limited cooking skills and lack of knowledge about diet and nutrition, both sets of parents frequently have the couple
over for dinner. If they are not at one parent's house for dinner, they often cook
burgers or pork chops, accompanied by chips or pretzels and cake.

Because of their disabilities, the couple still has difficulties in the workplace, especially on tasks that require reading (or in some cases, memory). For
instance, as part of her job, Lisa has to write down the names of the medicines,

the times that they were administered, special drug reactions, and the patient's name receiving the medication. After she failed to do this on one occasion and a patient had to be hospitalized, a job coach was called in to assist her. To help her with this task, her job coach taught her the mnemonic strategy DRUG to help her remember to record the proper information for each patient. Each letter of the acronym DRUG specifies a step that Lisa should do with each patient. For example, D—Determine what time it is and write it down; R—Are there Reactions to other drugs?; U—Use the patient's name; and G—Write the dose down in Grams.

Similar to Lisa, Bill's poor reading skills often interfere with this ability to complete his job. To compensate for his poor reading skills, his boss often explains what to do, rather than giving him directions. Bill covers up his reading disability by making excuses or faking it when patients ask him to read information (e.g., birthday cards, letters from their children, etc.). Thus far, Bill has managed to conceal his disability from the patients. In addition, Bill carries a newspaper to give the appearance of knowing how to read. When asked about news stories, Bill often looks at pictures or keywords in the headline to "fake" his explanations. Both have much difficulty with written language, particularly spelling; in an attempt to cover for this disability area they will not write down information in front of people. Although their employer knows about their disability, some people at Martinwood think that they just don't listen well, particularly when they fail to follow through on written directions.

Related to their financial difficulties, they are renting a house that has not been upgraded and repaired in some time. Whenever they call the landlord about a repair or problem, he usually says that he is going to come out immediately to make the repair, but he often arrives days later or fails to show up. On one occasion, Lisa called the landlord to tell him that some squirrels had gotten into the attic and were chewing their way through her ceiling. Upon hearing this, the landlord told her to call the town's animal control. In turn, animal control told her that only the owner of the property could request their services. When Lisa called the landlord back to report this to him, he responded that he would call animal control. Months later the squirrels are still living in the attic and chewing on beams and wires. On a number of other occasions, their landlord has raised the rent without notice. For example, when Bill and Lisa were first married, the landlord asked if Bill was going to move in with Lisa. When she told the landlord that Bill would be moving in, he immediately raised their monthly rent by $25. They stay in the house because it is the only place they can afford. The other choice would be to move in with one set of parents.

Not only does the couple have landlord problems, but they also have problems with their neighbors. During the past year, their relationship with their neighbors has slowly deteriorated since the police were called in to quiet a loud party. It began about a year ago when the couple was forced to report their neighbors to the police for a loud party they were having. At first, they nicely asked their neighbors to turn down the music because it was midnight and they were unable to sleep. When the neighbors refused, the couple called the police. Within minutes the police arrived and requested that the neighbors turn their music down to a reasonable level, and when they refused, they were fined. Since this incident, the neighbors have been harassing Bill and Lisa by placing nails under their tires, calling them names ("retard"), and destroying their shrubs. Lisa and Bill are terrified of their neighbors and try to avoid them. They hope to move, but until they can find a place for the same or less rent, they will have to remain in the house.

A month ago, Lisa found out that she is pregnant. Their current health insurance only pays for hospital emergencies and other minimal costs. It does not however, pay for regular doctor's visits, so the couple goes to the local clinic (no cost). Even though the doctor has warned Lisa about her poor nutrition and smoking, she continues to eat snacks and candy for her meals and smokes a half-pack of cigarettes a day. She is also concerned about putting on weight during her pregnancy, so she refuses to eat regularly. Bill does not help Lisa; instead, he continually makes comments about how much he likes thin women. Both are excited about the arrival of their baby, yet they feel bad that they do not have better jobs. Bill often complains to Lisa about what a failure he has been. Bill has two older brothers who are successful (doctor and lawyer). He constantly compares his life to his siblings' lives and often remarks how unfair life has been to give him "no brains." These personal problems have created some marital problems for the couple as is evident in their numerous domestic disputes.

QUESTIONS

1. How has society placed a value on "intelligence"? How have Lisa and Bill been affected by society's stigma of "stupidity"? How should society view people with disabilities?

2. How much support and what kinds of support should Bill and Lisa's parents be giving them?

3. What should the couple do about the problems they are having with their landlord? What skills are needed for dealing with this problem? Whose responsibility is it to teach these skills to students? At what point in a student's education should teachers teach these skills?

4. How should the couple deal with their neighbors? What skills are needed for dealing with them? Who is responsible for teaching these skills to students with LD?

5. Describe some characteristics of this couple and compare them with teenage students with LD? How are these characteristics the same? How are they different?

6. As educators, we know the importance of proper nutrition and fetal development. What should Lisa be doing to better care for her unborn child? Should she receive education or training in this? Who should teach her these skills?

7. *Activity:* Read a book or journal article about adults with learning disabilities. Discuss the issues/problems they face as they try to get jobs, get married, and start a family. Also, discuss how their problems differ from adults without disabilities.

CHAPTER 6

INDIVIDUALS WITH MILD OR MODERATE MENTAL RETARDATION

DEFINITION

The federal (IDEA)* definition of mental retardation is:

> a child with "significantly subaverage general intellectual functioning existing concurrently with deficits in adaptive behavior and manifested during the developmental period that adversely affects a child's education performance."

In addition, the following classification system has been used to further delineate levels of mental retardation:

mild retardation: an individual whose intelligence quotient test score is between approximately 55 and 69;

moderate retardation: an individual whose intelligence quotient test score is between approximately 40 and 54;

severe retardation: an individual whose intelligence quotient test score is between approximately 25 and 39;

profound retardation: an individual whose intelligence quotient test score is below approximately 25.

For educational purposes, students with mental retardation are often classified as educable, trainable, and severe/profound. In accordance with this classification system, students having educable mental retardation typically fall within the mild retardation range, students having trainable mental retardation typically fall within the moderate retardation range, and students classified as having severe/profound mental retardation typically fall within the severe and profound retardation range.

The American Association on Mental Retardation (AAMR) has defined MR slightly differently. They expand on the adaptive skill areas and focus on the supports needed for success in school, work, leisure, or community

---

* *Individuals with Disabilities Education Act Amendment of 1997*, 105th Cong., 1st Sess. (1997).

environments. In their definition mental retardation is characterized as an individual who has:

" . . . substantial limitations in present functioning . . . characterized by: significantly subaverage intellectual functioning, existing concurrently with; related limitations in two or more of the following areas: communication, self-care, home living, social skills, community use, self-direction, health and safety, functional academics, leisure, and work."

KEY TERMS

adaptive behavior   Nonacademics skills that include the areas of communication, self-care, home living, social skills, community use, self-direction, health and safety, functional academics, leisure, and work.

attention deficit hyperactivity disorder   A disorder characterized by inattention, hyperactivity, and impulsivity, which may interfere with the child's educational performance.

Collaboration   A system whereby the general education and special education teacher work, plan, and teach together. It may also include a number of teachers or other specialists working together to solve problems and plan the education of students with or without (e.g., at-risk) disabilities.

Cylert   A medication used to improve the performance of students with attention problems.

developmental delay   Students who exhibit behavioral or academic delays prior to entering school.

Down's syndrome   A chromosomal abnormality that results in the person being born with characteristics that may include: mental retardation, small skull, slanting eyes, flat-bridged nose, short stature, or stubby hands.

grand mal seizures   Seizures characterized by involuntary violent shaking or jerking of the muscles. It is often accompanied by loss of consciousness.

inclusion classroom   A classroom that incorporates students with and without disabilities and is typically taught by both the general education and special education teachers. It is characterized by team teaching or collaborative teaching/planning, cooperative grouping, peer-tutoring, enhancing techniques (e.g., web or diagram), and learning strategies. For students with more moderate to severe disabilities, other characteristics such as disability awareness programs and "circle of friends" components may also be incorporated.

job coach   A person who works with a student on-the-job in a workplace.

Mebaral   A drug from the barbiturate group used as an anticonvulsant to prevent epileptic seizures.

response cost system   Used in conjunction with a token economy whereby students lose tokens as a result of inappropriate actions.

Ritalin   A medication used to improve the performance of students with attention problems.

time-out   A procedure whereby a student is removed from a reinforcing environment as a consequence of an inappropriate action.

token system   A behavior management system used with students whereby students are reinforced with tokens that can later be exchanged for a reinforcer that is valuable to the student.

C͟A͟s E 16. Simon

Issues: Collaboration/consultation, inclusion

Simon is a student with mild mental retardation. From birth it was obvious that Simon was different, yet his hard working attitude often compensated for his poor performance.

Simon is a 13-year-old boy with mild mental retardation. Sometimes called a "slow learner," Simon attends an inclusive classroom at Elkenton Junior High School in central Pennsylvania. He needs limited to extensive support in the areas of functional academics, work, community use, and communication. His strengths (areas in which he needs little, if any, support) include: social skills and home living. His individualized education program (IEP) goals and objectives focus around functional academics, vocational, and communication skills.

During Simon's preschool and primary school grades, he functioned much like the other children and displayed no telltale signs of Down's syndrome or any other "mental retardation" syndrome that carries with it distinct facial or physical characteristics. Born into a family of four boys, Simon did his best to emulate his brotherly role models. As they did their chores, so did Simon. It was only over time as Simon reached school age that his parents, Hildegard and Gunter, began to notice subtle differences between him and his brothers.

Being born directly from German immigrants, Simon was raised with a work ethic that valued hard work and pride in one's work. Because of his work ethic, even as a preschooler Simon worked hard and strove for perfection with his learning activities in school and his chores at home. Unfortunately for Simon, perfection was often in the eye of the beholder. For example, on one recent evening Simon presented to his parents a paper with scribbling on it (that was supposed to be his name). As they praised him for his diligence, in the next breath they asked him to describe what was in front of them. Throughout Simon's early years, Hildegard and Gunter suspected that something might be wrong with Simon's learning skills; yet, they felt that many of his problems were due to his poor language skills, a combination of English and German. Despite suspecting problems, it came as a surprise to his parents when they received a call from the preschool to discuss Simon's slow progress.

Mrs. Wilson, Simon's preschool teacher, had delayed calling his parents because she had seen other children in her class make tremendous education gains over the first few months of preschool because this was their first year of academic (preacademic) schooling. However, what bothered her was not only Simon's lack of progress, despite his tremendous effort at learning information, but his frustration at not being able to complete the task correctly. When Mrs. Wilson showed Hildegard and Gunter Simon's work and the work of the other students, it became obvious that indeed something was seriously wrong. When Mrs. Wilson suggested that Simon repeat preschool, his parents agreed. At first, repeating preschool seemed to help Simon, however, over time Simon began to have difficulty learning at the same rate as the other children.

As Simon progressed to grade school, he managed to maintain average grades, but only with the help from tutors hired by his parents. During these intense learning sessions, the tutor would drill Simon on basic reading and math skills. These were tough times for Simon, as evidenced by his sleepless nights and anxiety attacks.

Once Simon reached second grade, his teacher, Mr. Mettson recommended that he be assessed for special education. Following this evaluation, a multidisciplinary meeting was set to discuss the results and to make recommendations about Simon's placement in special education. During this meeting Dr. Wasaw described the results of the psychological examination to the parents, teacher, and director of special education. In his description of Simon's performance, Dr. Wasaw told the group that Simon had scored low on the intelligence quotient and achievement tests. He also reported that on an adaptive behavior scale used to assess his social and communication skills, Simon performed below average. Dr. Wasaw then explained to the parents that Simon learned information at a slower rate than the average child and he would need special instruction, instruction that could not occur in the regular education classroom. As Simon's parents listened intently, the director of special education explained that the results of Simon's assessment indicated that he should be placed in a classroom for students with educable mental retardation. Simon's parents were reluctant at first but later agreed to the placement after visiting it and meeting the teacher.

Simon remained in an educable mentally retarded (EMR) classroom for the remainder of second grade and until fifth grade when a new classroom opened in his school, called an inclusion classroom. In this classroom, the students are integrated using a one-third, two-thirds ratio. One-third of the students in the classroom are students with mild disabilities (learning disabilities, behavior disorders, and educable mentally retarded) and two-thirds of the students are from regular education classrooms, including gifted students. Because Simon was a good student and diligent worker, he was immediately deemed eligible as a participant for this inclusion classroom. Simon receives almost all of his special education services in this classroom, except for reading, which he receives in the resource room. Simon's teacher is Mr. Versane, the fifth grade teacher. Only during the more challenging activities, history and science, does Simon's special education teacher, Mrs. Ramsome, provide additional in-class instruction for the special education students.

Being new to this type of classroom, Mr. Versane and Mrs. Ramsome have had some minor problems. For instance, during one science lesson, as Mr. Versane was teaching, Mrs. Ramsome continually interrupted him to correct some minor errors that he was making on cell structure. For three days, Mr. Versane did not talk to Mrs. Ramsome. It was only after the principal intervened that they began to talk again. In another planning session,

Mrs. Ramsome demanded that Mr. Versane slow down his presentation of information because "her special education students" could not keep up. Mr. Versane was upset by her comments about "her" special education students and about her persistence at slowing down his presentation. He constantly remarked to her that he had to "cover" at least fifteen of the eighteen chapters in the science textbook, otherwise the students would not be ready for sixth grade science. Up to this point, he had always felt like a team with Mrs. Ramsome and he deeply cared for all of the students in his class, even the students with disabilities. After many verbal battles, the two teachers requested another site the following year. It was only at their principal's urging that the two remained in the inclusion program and continued for many years.

QUESTIONS

1.   Why do schools segregate students with disabilities from students in regular education? What are the advantages and disadvantages?

2.   What role should tutors play in educating Simon (e.g., help him with coursework or remediate skill deficits)? Did it hurt Simon in the long run by having his tutors assist him at maintaining minimal grades, thereby preventing him from being eligible to receive special education services early on? Explain.

3.   In an inclusion classroom like the one described in this case, what role should the special education teacher play at educating special education students in the classroom?

4.   As the regular education teacher in an inclusion classroom, how would you strike a balance between needing to cover the entire science textbook (so that students would be ready for sixth grade science) and having to slow down to help students understand science concepts?

5.   If you were Mr. Versane, how would you want Mrs. Ramsome to tell you about mistakes made during your lectures? For example, would you want her to interrupt class to tell you about the mistakes in front of the students? Are there other ways that you could resolve this issue?

6.   What communication skills are important for successful teacher collaboration?

7.   What are some anticipated problems that you might expect when an inclusion program begins?

8.   *Activity:* Check with your special education department and find the location of inclusion programs in local schools. Set up an appointment to visit an inclusion program and note the differences between it and a special education program. Discuss with your fellow students the key components of inclusion programs.

CASE 17. ISAAC

Issues: Behavior management, transition

Isaac is a student with mild mental retardation, but if you just met him you may have to ask twice abut his label. Isaac's "street smarts" keep him alive in a tough neighborhood and dispel the myth that students with mental retardation behave in a stereotypic manner.

Isaac is an 11-year-old boy with moderate mental retardation (sometimes referred to as trainable mental retardation—TMR) who needs limited to extensive support in the adaptive areas of work, functional academics, and social skills. In other adaptive behavior areas such as community use, home living, and communication, Isaac needs little, if any, support. Isaac currently attends a self-contained mentally retarded (MR) classroom at Marshall Elementary School in southeastern Pennsylvania.

Despite Isaac being born with mental retardation, in many ways he is more like his peers than different from them. Whether it is because Isaac is street smart or because he lacks the visible signs of a disability, he functions much like other children his age. He has excellent communication skills and can move within his community (via public transportation) quite well; however, from an academic standpoint he performs poorly.

Born in the projects of Dissburg, Pennsylvania, Isaac grew up on the mean streets of Dissburg and became independent at an early age. In the evenings when Isaac goes out to play, he promptly returns home at dusk. Isaac's mother, Jesse, reported that Isaac was born when she was only 15 years old. As a single mother, she worked two jobs to support herself and Isaac. In turn, due to his mother's frequent absences, he has learned to depend upon himself in many different areas such as cooking, buying groceries, and completing chores around the apartment.

His mother refers to Isaac as street smart. In a recent meeting with Isaac's teacher, Mr. Peterman, Jesse related some street smart stories to him about his unusual yet appropriate street smart behavior. For instance, every morning Isaac goes to the bus stop to get the special education bus to his school. At the same bus stop, students from regular education ride a different bus (a regular school bus) to the same school. After watching the other children ridicule the students that ride the special education bus, Isaac came to learn that he does not want to ride that bus. So every morning when the special education bus comes to pick up the students with disabilities, Isaac purposefully misses that bus (he hides) and then rides the regular education bus. In another example, Jesse describes how she has observed him paying for snacks (soda and candy) at the corner grocery store. First, Isaac will ask the clerk how much the item costs. After the clerk's response, Isaac hands the clerk only a few coins and waits for the clerk to ask for more. By paying for the item in this manner, Isaac is fairly certain that he will never pay more than the item is worth.

Academically and intellectually, Mr. Peterman reports that Isaac has a full-scale IQ of 49, with his verbal score being the highest score. Isaac works hard on all of the academic tasks, yet he is easily distracted and impulsive. Isaac is taking the medication Ritalin, or at least his mother reports that she gives it to Isaac before he goes to school. Because of Isaac's impulsive and inattentive behaviors, Mr. Peterman believes that Isaac may not be getting his medication daily; he suspects that Jesse may be selling it on the street. (Ritalin increases the arousal or alertness of the central nervous system in "normal" functioning children/adults. Because of its stimulating characteristics, it has been commonly sold on the "black market" on college campuses, particularly during "finals week.")

On numerous occasions Isaac has not been able to control his behavior. In one incident, Isaac was sent to the principal's office for fighting with a student who called him a "retard." The fight occurred while Isaac was riding on the regular education bus and the driver sent him directly to the principal's office. Once there, the principal, Mrs. Griffin, wanted Isaac to stay after school for two weeks to clean the lunchroom. Isaac snapped back that he did not have to listen to her because she was not his boss. Mrs. Griffin immediately responded that he was suspended for five days for talking back to her. By the time his teacher, Mr. Peterman, arrived in the office, the principal and Isaac were yelling at each other. Mr. Peterman explained that he would handle the incident, but Mrs. Griffin responded that it was too late and that Isaac would have to "serve his sentence."

Back in the classroom, because Isaac was on a token system, Mr. Peterman took five tokens from him (five tokens are equivalent to a half of a day's worth of work) due to his fight. When the teacher retrieved the five tokens from Isaac's desk, Isaac turned around and threw all of his tokens from the previous three days at the teacher. Mr. Peterman, not knowing how to respond, took *all* of Isaac's tokens away from him. For the remainder of the week, Isaac refused to work and was at times disruptive. In an attempt to get Isaac to work, Mr. Peterman called Jesse and asked her to talk to Isaac about his behavior. Unfortunately her talk was not helpful.

With only two months to go until the end of the school year, Isaac's behavior continued to deteriorate. In addition to being suspended five days for fighting, Isaac was suspended for four days for other incidents such as cursing in school, breaking a window, and stuffing towels down the toilets so they would overflow. After each incident, Mr. Peterman placed Isaac in time-out for an hour.

Because Mr. Peterman knew that Isaac would be leaving his class at the end of the school year, Mr. Peterman decided that time-out combined with suspension was the best method for curing Isaac's inappropriate behavior. Little did his teacher know that when Isaac was suspended, he would have fun causing havoc in his neighborhood. On one occasion, the police were called because someone was breaking the taillights of each car on Isaac's block. When the police caught him in the act of breaking another taillight they placed him under arrest and charged him with vandalism.

When Mr. Peterman heard of the incident, he felt guilty about suspending Isaac; however, he did not know what else he could do to deal with Isaac's behavior. To add to his frustration (or relief), Mr. Peterman knew that Isaac would be attending a new school and he would have a new teacher. Mr. Peterman also felt guilty that Isaac was leaving on such a negative note and felt sorry for Isaac because his new junior high school TMR teacher, Mrs. Cassle, did not use a reinforcement system.

QUESTIONS

1. If you were Isaac's teacher, how would you handle an incident in which a regular education student called one of your students a "retard"? What would you tell your student to do if this name calling were to occur in the future?
2. Do you feel that using stimulant medication, such as Ritalin, is appropriate for Isaac? How long should he continue to take this medication?
3. Because Isaac is transitioning to a new class that has a different class structure, what would you do to help Isaac's transition to this new class?
4. Besides time-out and a token system, what other behavioral modification techniques could be used to deal with Isaac's inappropriate behavior?
5. Knowing that Isaac has a history of behavioral problems, what should Mrs. Cassle do to prepare for Isaac's arrival in her classroom?
6. If you suspected that Isaac was not getting his daily medication (Ritalin), what would you do?
7. Do you feel that it is appropriate for Isaac to be riding the regular education bus? If so, why? If not, what would you do?
8. *Activity:* Visit a classroom for students identified as trainable mentally retarded. What are some of the academic activities that students work on? What behavioral management techniques does the teacher use? How is this classroom different from a regular education classroom?

 **CASE 18. KIMIKA**

Issues: Behavior management, educational goals/objectives

In addition to her mild mental retardation, her seizure disorder often compound her learning problems. While her medication helps, it makes her fatigue easily and often cuts short her learning. Her teacher, Mr. Bubski tries to deal with her learning and behavior problems, but often loses it.

K imika Kanzia is a 9-year-old girl with moderate mental retardation. She needs extensive support in the areas of communication, social skills, and self-direction. When given amenable tasks, Kimika will work hard to complete them. Kimika currently attends a self-contained classroom at Edgemont Elementary School in northern Virginia. In addition to her mental retardation, Kimika walks with a limp due to a gross motor impairment, suffers from grand mal seizures, and is difficult to understand at times due to a speech impairment. To help control her grand mal seizures, Kimika takes Mebaral, a barbiturate, three times a day.

Because of her pronounced educational deficits and obvious gross motor impairment, Kimika has been in special education since preschool. It began when the family physician recommended to Mrs. Kanzia that she have her daughter tested for a cognitive delay. The local school district tested Kimika and found significant language, academic, and motor delays. At the multidisciplinary meeting (MDT), school officials suggested that Kimika might benefit from their early childhood special education program.

In the preschool program, Kimika made slow but steady progress. Over the next few years, Kimika was moved to a classroom for students with trainable mental retardation (TMR), ages 6 to 8. While enrolled in this program, her teacher, Mrs. Askov, instituted a variety of behavioral management plans to help Kimika control her violent outbursts and to motivate her to complete tasks. During these early years, Kimika earned "stars," which could later be exchanged for recreational privileges. For the most part this technique worked well, however on a few days each month her behavior was deemed "unmanageable" by Mrs. Askov.

As Kimika grew older her violent outbursts and apathetic work behavior increased. At the age of 9, she was transferred to Mr. Bubski's classroom (for older TMR students). In Mr. Bubski's classroom, Kimika was reevaluated. The following table highlights the results.

Developmental Test of Visual Motor Integration = 4 yrs., 1 mo. M.A.

Wide Range Achievement Test—Revised
   a. Reading = .03 percentile
   b. Arithmetic = .04 percentile

Draw-A-Man-Test = Not scorable

Vineland Adaptive Behavior Scale
   Communication Domain = 40
   Daily Living Skills = 50
   Socialization = 68
   Motor Skills = 52
   Adaptive Behavior Composite Score = 48

Stanford-Binet Intelligence Test
   Full Scale Score = 40

As evidenced by her intelligence score, Kimika's IQ score of 40 fell within the range for persons with moderate mental retardation. Furthermore her adaptive behavior score indicated that she was functioning within the moderate range of mental retardation.

Academically on the Brigance Inventory of Basic Skills, Kimika performed below grade level on measures of reading, math, and written language. In reading she recognized only five words on the preprimer level (it, to, come, for, red), and only knew seven initial letter sounds (M, B, S, K, P, R, F). In math she could rote count to 12, recognized numbers to 15, and wrote numbers to 8. Her other present level math skills included knowing addition facts to 5+, the value of three coins (penny, nickel, dime), and telling time to the hour. In written language, Kimika could write a number of her letters (M, K, S, P, F, B, A, C, D, I). In the area of functional language, Kimika recognized several functional words (Exit, Danger, Go, Police, Poison, Walk, Keep Out, In, Ladies, Women, Out) and some directional words (name, address, telephone, date). There were several other areas in which Kimika performed significantly below average, such as spelling, directional skills (listening comprehension), and oral language skills.

In Mr. Bubski's class, Kimika spent time each day working on the basic reading, math, and written language skills. On two mornings of each week she worked on vocationally related tasks, such as assembling, packaging, and sorting items. It was while performing these vocational tasks that Kimika had the most difficulty maintaining her attention to task and completing the tasks at high levels. Despite being on a reinforcement system of earning pennies for correctly completed work and behaving appropriately, Kimika still had numerous incidents of inappropriate and disruptive behavior.

For instance, during one morning while working on vocational tasks, Kimika exhibited three separate violent episodes. In the first episode, Kimika had completed a task, was rewarded with a penny, and was given the next task. When Mr. Bubski placed the new task (packaging) at Kimika's work station, she immediately threw it across the room and complained that she was "worked out." Having only worked for fifteen minutes, Mr. Bubski recognized that Kimika was trying to get out of work. Mr. Bubski placed Kimika in time-out for thirty minutes and removed all of the pennies that she had earned for the morning and prior day. After this cooling-off period, Mr. Bubski asked Kimika to return to her work station and begin working on a new task (stamping objects). He decided to use a new task rather than fight with her over the packaging assignment.

Everything went smoothly for Kimika until lunchtime. At lunch Kimika did not like the beans that were being served with her school lunch. After she received her lunch tray, she went to her assigned table and began spooning the beans onto the floor, complaining that they were "nasty." When Mr. Bubski discovered what she was doing, he grabbed her by the arm, took her back to the classroom, and placed her in time-out for thirty minutes. After her time expired, he made her get the remaining pennies from her desk (she had earned five prior to lunch) and made her forfeit these for her inappropriate behavior.

After lunch, the class began their review of functional/emergency words. As Mr. Bubski began his review of these words, he noticed that Kimika was at her desk sleeping. He immediately became flush with anger. He stomped back to her desk, yelled "get up," grabbed her by the arm, and placed her in time-out for one hour. While in time-out, Kimika kicked the walls, yelled obscenities at him, and spit over the wall onto other students. After repeatedly warning her to stop, he finally announced to her that she would be losing any pennies that she earned for the next two days. Ironically, Kimika was conspicuously absent over the next two days. Upon her return, Mr. Bubski felt sorry for her and decided that she would not have to lose any pennies.

These incidents were repeated throughout the school year until Mr. Bubski requested that Kimika be placed in another classroom. Because his special education supervisor was sympathetic of Mr. Bubski's problems, he agreed to place Kimika in a new, more restrictive, setting.

QUESTIONS

1. In certain cases students with disabilities may be placed in more restrictive settings because the teacher lacks adequate skills or support to deal with behavioral problems. Is this fair for the student? Teacher? Other students in the class?

2. Should teachers use a response cost system whereby students lose tokens that they have already earned? What are some advantages/disadvantages of using a response cost system with students? What are some other behavior interventions that could be used to help Mr. Bubski deal with Kimika's behavior?

3. Did Mr. Bubski appropriately use time-out with Kimika? Why or why not? If a student is having trouble completing a task, should the teacher have the student work on a different task? Why or why not?

4. In emotionally charged situations, what should Mr. Bubski do before deciding upon the consequences for Kimika's behavior? How could emotions interfere with decision making?

5. Write two short-term objectives and one goal for this student in any academic area.

6. For students with disabilities, how early in a student's education should the teacher begin teaching functional life skills, as opposed to academic skills? Would it make a difference if the student had a mild disability (learning disability or behavioral disorder)?

7. Is early intervention, such as early childhood special education, effective? Name three different skills that should be taught during this time.

8. Would this student be a good candidate for an inclusion program? Why or why not? If this student did not have behavioral problems, would this student be a good candidate for an inclusion program?

9. *Activity:* Speak to a school psychologist about the types of tests used to determine moderate mental retardation. Ask the psychologist to describe the components of the different tests.

CASE 19. ADAM

Issues: Collaboration/consultation, transition

Adam loves his work study program, but his short fuse often results in his termination from most jobs. His parents' "loose" management style often conflicts with that of his teacher.

Adam is a 17-year-old boy with moderate mental retardation. In addition to his label of trainable mentally retarded (TMR), Adam has been diagnosed as having attention deficit hyperactivity disorder (ADHD). To help control his inattention and hyperactivity, he is taking the drug Cylert, a stimulant medication believed to increase the arousal or alertness of the central nervous system.

Adam attends a self-contained classroom at Williamson High School in southern California. Adam has been receiving special services in self-contained special education classrooms since he began school. His placement is a half-day work study program at Williamson. He needs limited to extensive support across many of the adaptive skill areas such as social skills, self-direction, work, leisure, and health/safety. Every morning Adam attends classes in functional reading, math, and written language. In the afternoons Adam works at Fuzulies restaurant bussing tables and preparing food.

Adam is often a pleasant child, but if confronted with a task that he does not want to complete he can be stubborn. He often smiles and laughs with other students in his class and at his worksite. Adam can be a diligent worker, provided he is working on a task that he enjoys. During leisure time activities, Adam often sits and does nothing. If left alone, Adam will sit for hours watching other students play. Typically, an adult has to direct Adam to a "low energy" activity and the adult must constantly provide encouragement to get him to continue the activity. On a number of occasions, Adam was caught harassing other students, particularly younger students.

Academically, Adam has made slow, steady progress toward achieving his educational objectives. However, on certain days Adam becomes highly agitated and hyper. It is on these days that his teacher, Mr. Fout, has noticed that not only does Adam have academic difficulties, but he also has behavioral difficulties. For instance, one morning when students were filling out simulated applications as part of their vocational training, Mr. Fout noticed Adam becoming frustrated trying to fill in the correct information. After a short while, the frustration became too much as Adam let out a yell and ripped his application to pieces. When this occurred, Mr. Fout sent Adam out into the hall to calm down. Once calm, Adam returned and began to fill out the form but did not complete it. This wasn't the first time that Mr. Fout noticed Adam's "short fuse."

Later that day while Adam was at Fuzulies restaurant bussing tables, a customer accidentally spilled coffee on a table that Adam had just cleaned.

Adam's immediate reaction was to call the embarrassed customer a "butthole." The customer, an elderly man, was shocked to be called such a name and promptly informed the manager of Adam's behavior. Mr. French, the manager, grabbed Adam by the arm, yelled at him, and told him to take the rest of the day off without pay. Later when the work-study supervisor, Mr. Bell, found out what had happened, he pleaded with Mr. French to let Adam return. Mr. French refused saying that he had tried to work with Adam, but there were too many problems.

Fortunately for Adam, another worksite was recently established with the Williamsonian Post Office. Mr. Bell, eager to place Adam at another worksite, decided that the post office was the perfect place for him because he would have minimum contact with customers. At the post office, Adam's job would require him to take large packages and bar code them according to their zip code. Mr. Bell had prearranged the jobsite with easy to follow instructions and modified labels. Despite his efforts and because of the complexity of the zip code system, Adam had much difficulty learning this job; he had several explosive episodes in which he threw packages against the wall because he was so frustrated. After the first incident, his job coach, Mrs. Casey, sent him home from work.

While at home, Adam managed to set fire to his mother's curtains after watching another child do the same thing on a television show. When Adam wasn't getting in trouble at home, he was usually sitting around the house watching television and munching on snack food. His parents, June and Warren, worked and frequently left Adam alone. To assist Adam's parents, their neighbor, Mrs. Steward, checked up on Adam two or three times a day. Because Mrs. Steward was retired, she had a lot of free time to help neighbors. Despite their neighbor's watchful eye, Adam's parents often received calls at work about his inappropriate behavior, such as harassing the neighbor's cat and dog, pulling out prize-winning rose bushes from his neighbor's garden, and yelling obscenities to passing motorists. Many of these behaviors had become progressively worse over the years, yet there were few consequences for Adam. June and Ward often blamed Adam's inappropriate behavior on his ADHD and dismissed the suggestion that he needed behavior therapy to control his behavior.

When Adam returned to work the next afternoon, he found that Mrs. Casey had called Mr. Bell to speak to Adam. After a long conversation, Mr. Bell informed Adam that this would be his last chance, and if he blew it here, there would be no other work programs for Adam to participate in. Adam, realizing that he might get in trouble with his parents, agreed to work hard and behave. Over the next few weeks, Adam's behavior was much improved. Even Adam's work coach was surprised at Adam's change in behavior. Despite his efforts, Adam still lacked the most fundamental social skills to help communicate to his boss and coworkers. For instance, during breaks and lunch, Adam would quietly sit in the corner and eat his lunch. In these social situations while the other workers were discussing sports or their favorite TV shows, Adam would sit quietly, almost eerily, and say nothing. While this behavior could be tolerated while Adam was on breaks and lunch, it caused some problems for Adam during the workday. In many instances, he would not ask his boss for more supplies when he ran out of them; instead, Adam would sit back and wait until his boss came around.

Finally, the different behavioral management styles between Adam's parents and school officials caused friction. At one parent-teacher conference, June and Warren recommended that school officials back off of Adam because they were putting too much pressure on him. Mr. Fout immediately became infuriated, stood up, and exclaimed that he was fed up with their pandering of him. He then told the parents that what Adam needed was more discipline and less hugs. Adam's parents were shocked to hear Mr. Fout make such a statement and stormed out of the room. Later, the principal called to apologize to June and Warren.

QUESTIONS

1. Because of Adam's short fuse, was he a good candidate for working in a job in which he was constantly in contact with customers? What are the attributes that a good candidate for this position should have?
2. Knowing that Adam is a special education student, does he deserve a second chance working at Fuzulies restaurant?
3. If you were the work-study supervisor, what are some things that you would do to insure that your students are successful at their worksites?
4. Besides watching TV, what else could Adam be doing with his free time? Who is responsible for teaching Adam what to do in his spare time?
5. If after several attempts Adam is still unable to hold and maintain a job, what should school officials do?
6. What social skills or behavioral management techniques could be taught to Adam to help him control his anger? To communicate with coworkers? Who is responsible for teaching him these skills?
7. If Adam's parent told you to back off during the parent-teacher conference, how should you respond? Does the difference in behavioral philosophies send a mixed message to Adam? Why?
8. *Activity:* Visit a worksite that trains students with disabilities as part of their organization. What people are involved in the student training and what are their roles?

 CASE 20. RANDIE

Issues: Instructional methods/techniques

Randie is a Hispanic student with mild mental retardation that interferes in her learning. Sometimes children who speak a language other than English, like Randie, experience difficulties.

R andie is a 5-year-old, Hispanic girl with mild mental retardation. Randie attends a special education kindergarten class at Orange City Elementary School. Randie was diagnosed at birth as having Down's syndrome, a syndrome whose characteristics include distinctive facial characteristics (slanting eyes, small head and ears), short physique, poor muscle tone, and mental retardation. In Randie's case, she is small for her age, lacks muscle tone and strength, has poor communication skills (slow speech and too immature), and cognitively lacks many of the necessary school skills when compared to her peers (poor short-term memory, vocabulary skills, and fine motor skills).

In the area of reading readiness, Randie has poor listening comprehension skills. She can remember facts about a story only if given frequent prompts to recall information (i.e., every few minutes the teacher has to ask her a question about what she just read) or if shown pictures from the story. If asked to sequence events from the story, she has difficulty. In addition, Randie does not know many letter names and knows even fewer letter sounds. She does however recognize her name.

In a recent reading readiness lesson, Randie made numerous errors typical of someone with mild mental retardation. The lesson began by Mrs. Funsom asking students to form a circle around her seat as she prepared to read to them. All of the students except Randie grabbed a carpet square and went to the reading area. Randie sat at her seat coloring the picture that was given to her fifteen minutes before. When Mrs. Funsom counted heads and noticed Randie's absence, she asked her to join the group. When Randie arrived, she appeared to be thinking about something else as she gazed out the window and giggled to herself. As the teacher read the story, she asked many questions Randie was unable to answer. For example, immediately after reading a sentence about a boy dumping water on his sister, Randie was asked what happened. She gave a blank look and responded "nothing." Later the teacher read a funny part of the story about the boy getting his hand caught in a cookie jar. The students laughed. Mrs. Funsom asked Randie what happened to the boy and again Randie replied that she did not know.

In the area of preacademic math, Randie exhibits many deficits. She is unable to identify her numbers from 1 to 10, unable to rote count to 10, and unable to count objects to 5. She cannot group objects by size, color, or shape. During a recent math lesson, Mrs. Funsom had Randie name numbers 1 to 5. She decided to present the numbers multiple times in an attempt to get Randie to remember them. Over and over she presented flashcards of the numbers 1 to 5, but Randie could not remember any of the numbers. Mrs. Funsom repeated this training over the week with the same results on each day.

Handwriting is another area in which Randie made little or no progress. On numerous informal assessments, Randie performed poorly when it came to writing the letters to her name, numbers 1 to 5, or drawing shapes. She performed poorly on measures of far and near point copying. For instance in one handwriting session, Mrs. Funsom wanted Randie to correctly write her name. In this particular lesson, Mrs. Funsom would place Randie's name on the board and then have Randie write the letters to her name on a piece of paper. Each day Mrs. Funsom would start Randie on this lesson and then walk around to assist the other students. Upon her return, Mrs. Funsom would usually find that Randie was walking around the room and talking to other students. Because Mrs. Funsom had other students, she was concerned at the amount of time that she spent working with Randie.

In the area of learning behaviors, one of Randie's biggest problems is remaining in her seat for more than three or four minutes. Mrs. Funsom is aware that much of the class work completed in first grade (next year) will be done while students are sitting in their desks. To prepare her students for first grade, Mrs. Funsom has her students complete kindergarten activities at their desks. Mrs. Funsom has been using a variety of techniques to help Randie remain seated during preacademic activities. During one week Mrs. Funsom tried the following techniques: on day one, verbal reinforcement (telling her "you are doing a good job sitting and working"); on day two, time-out whenever Randie was out of her seat; on day three, providing verbal prompts whenever she was out of her seat; on day four, ignoring her out of seat behavior; and on day five, reprimanding her. At the end of each day, Mrs. Funsom examined her data of Randie to determine if the technique was effective. If she deemed that the technique was not effective, she would use another technique. At the end of the week, Mrs. Funsom decided to read her education textbooks to help her. After reading a child development textbook, Mrs. Funsom decided that Randie was not developmentally ready (she was too immature) to sit and complete seat work. Therefore, Mrs. Funsom decided that she would not force Randie to sit and work until she felt that Randie was ready (i.e., developmentally mature).

In addition to her learning problems, Randie does not speak English very well. Instead, she uses a mix of broken English and Spanish, which has resulted in her poor performance on most language measures. At first Mrs. Funsom was not certain how to teach students with Spanish as their primary language, but finally Mrs. Funsom decided that the best method was total immersion, whereby Randie would receive all of her instruction in English. Despite that Randie knew most concepts and skills in Spanish, Mrs. Funsom refused to use Spanish in her classroom.

QUESTIONS

1. What other techniques or activities could the teacher use to help Randie remember important story points?
2. What other techniques or activities could be used with Randie in math?
3. What other techniques or activities could be used with Randie in handwriting?
4. Should teachers, such as Mrs. Funsom, force Spanish-speaking students to receive all of their instruction in English? Why or why not?
5. What could Mrs. Funsom do to increase Randie's in-seat behavior?

6. What was wrong with Mrs. Funsom changing techniques daily in an attempt to increase Randie's in-seat behavior?
7. Mrs. Funsom remarked that Randie was not developmentally ready to sit in her seat. What role should behavior modification play for children who may not be developmentally ready to sit and listen in class? Is Mrs. Funsom's reason an excuse to avoid dealing with the problem?
8. *Activity:* Visit an early childhood center or kindergarten. Take note of the skills that students are working on and the behavioral techniques used.

CHAPTER 7

INDIVIDUALS WITH COMMUNICATION DISORDERS*

DEFINITION

Students with communication disorders are considered under the federal (IDEA)** definition of "speech and language impairments." This is defined as:

> "a communication disorder such as stuttering, impaired articulation, a language impairment, or a voice impairment that adversely affects the child's educational performance."

KEY TERMS

accommodations Modifications or adaptations provided that allow the individual to better function in their environment (e.g., allowing a student with a learning disability in written language more time to complete a history test).

articulation The production of sounds (phonemes).

artificial larynx A device placed over the voicebox (larynx) that produces speech from vibrations.

augmentative or alternate communication (ACC) A system that serves as an alternative method of communication such as a communication board.

communicative technology The use of computers or other technology to enhance a person's ability to communicate.

dysfluency The flow of words being pronounced (e.g., stuttering or cluttering).

emphysema A progressive respiratory disease characterized by coughing, shortness of breath, and wheezing.

etiology The origin or source of a disability.

expressive language The ability to express thoughts into words, either written or verbal.

fistula A cavity that forms in the soft palate.

---

* We are grateful to Debra Hoge for her contributions to this chapter.

** *Individuals with Disabilities Education Act Amendment of 1997*, 105th Cong., 1st Sess. (1997).

FM Trainer A device comprised of two parts: a microphone used by the teacher and an FM receiver worn by the student that amplifies the teacher's voice and/or reduces background noise.

hypernasality Speech that is "nasally".

otitis media Commonly known as "middle ear infection".

prosthodontist A dentist who specializes in creating and inserting dental structures such as dentures, tooth implants, crowns, or bridges.

receptive language Comprehension of language (e.g., the ability to follow verbal directions).

CASE 21. TELSA

Issues: Instructional methods/techniques

Telsa is a college student who has a voice disorder. Despite her attempts to make and keep friends, she often fails. At times, college doesn't seem like it fits her style.

Telsa is a 23-year-old college student with a speech disorder, more specifically a voice disorder. She suffers from emphysema, which she contracted through smoking cigarettes and breathing polluted air. She lives in a poor section of Westlouis. Her house is located down the street from a paint factory, which for years has dumped toxic levels of arsenic, mercury, and lead into the air through its smelters. Mornings and afternoons are the worst times to be outside because of the thick smog that covers the small town.

Born in Westlouis, she has lived there all of her life. She is an only child and experienced some rough times as she grew up. When she was 10-years-old, her mother and father divorced. After their divorce, she never again saw her father. When she was 18, her mother died of cancer. It was at this time that she inherited some money and property left to her by her mother. Her mother left her the house and thirty thousand dollars. Growing up poor, Telsa was never certain where she would get the money, but she knew that she wanted to go to college.

Smoking since she was 11-years-old, she began to experience serious medical problems when she was 19. First, she would develop bad coughing spells that could only be relieved by lighting a cigarette. At about this same time, she noticed that she was always sick. Whenever she contracted a cold or the flu, she would remain sick longer that most people and the symptoms were often severe. Then came the bad news that she had emphysema.

Her doctors believe that the emphysema was brought on by Telsa's habitual smoking and the air pollution from her town. Although the disease does improve when the person stops smoking, Telsa has repeatedly tried but failed to quit smoking. Emphysema has caused her to have shortness of breath as a result of her damaged lungs being unable to take in much air. As she talks, she has difficulty regulating her air intake and output causing her to speak in short, rushed phrases. Because of this, she not only has breathing difficulties, but also speaking difficulties, hence her disorder. To complicate her disorder, her many years of smoking have damaged her vocal cords to such an extent that she recently underwent surgery to have one vocal cord removed (commonly referred to as a partial laryngectomy or hemilaryngectomy). Her receptive language is appropriate for her age; however, her expressive language is reduced to three to four word phrases mostly due to breath control and partial use of her vocal cords. Because of acute expressive language difficulties, Telsa can only be understood through the use of an electronically powered artificial larynx. Although different types of artificial larynges exist, Telsa uses a hand-held, neck-type artificial larynx. When placed firmly against her, the device works by transmitting sound from her diaphragm into the device, which in turn transmits the sounds. Although she uses the electronic larynx frequently as her disease worsens, she has become more reluctant to use it because of its side effects (squawking sounds). The device frequently gives off irritating squawking sounds when she does not hold the device tightly against her neck. She claims that this squawking sound is annoying and embarrassing.

Telsa, a special education major at Southwestern State University, would like to be a teacher for children with communication disorders. Because of her disability, she has gained access to additional communicative technology through the disabled student services program on campus. For example, she uses a word processor to complete many of her assignments. As her speech has become progressively worse, she has begun using an augmentative or alternative communication (ACC) device to produce speech for her. The device is programmed so that each key can be a word or phrase. With this hand-held device, the machine produces audible, but brief, sentences or phrases.

In her classes, certain professors have made more accommodations than others. For instance, though many of her professors have agreed that she does not have to make oral presentations, Telsa makes them anyway to "fit in" with the rest of the students. Because her mode of communication is often time-consuming and tedious, many of her classmates would prefer that she does not present information through oral presentations. When she speaks in class, most instructors feel uneasy, particularly when she discusses lecture points that are often tangential to the discussion. Also, she frequently makes inappropriate sounds (e.g., grunts) when she disagrees with statements made by other students. These noises are embarrassing to the students sitting next to her. When she does speak, most students roll their eyes and make comments to each other knowing that she is taking up too much class time with her discussion of unrelated ideas. Her inappropriate behavior continues in most classes because professors are not certain how to address this issue.

Through her classes, Telsa has made a few friends. Telsa's hostile personality frequently interferes with her ability to make and maintain friendships. In addition to her anger, she lacks many social skills, which interferes with making more friends. For example, recently she went to a movie with her friend Jill. After the movie was over, the two women went out for drinks at a local cafe. As they were discussing the plot of the movie, Jill mentioned how she could understand why the villain felt the need to hurt other people. With this statement, Telsa grew angry and immediately shot back that people should not hurt each other. She then threw down her drink and ran out of the cafe. Jill sat in her seat dumbfounded by the exchange and embarrassed by the incident. The next day, Jill called Telsa to discuss the incident, but Telsa refused to talk to her.

These social problems are also prominent in her interactions with others. One of her biggest problems involves not knowing when a conversation has ended. Even when nonverbal cues are made, such as looking at your watch, looking up at the clock, or making statements to end the conversation (e.g., "I really have to get going"), Telsa continues the conversation. Most students and professors continue talking with her because they are unable to get her to leave. Often, the person has to make an explicit statement that they can no longer talk to her. Upon doing this, Telsa responds with comments like, "Why didn't you say something earlier?"

QUESTIONS

1. What are some problems that you foresee by having Telsa teach students with communication disorders? What are the advantages and possible disadvantages of having a student with disabilities become a teacher?
2. While Telsa's initiative to "fit in" to her classes is admirable, is it appropriate?
3. Who is responsible for teaching social skills to Telsa?
4. Social norms play a major role in determining what behavior and the frequency of it are considered "appropriate." List five social skills used during a conversation that are appropriate and five that are not. Of the social skills on your list, specifically what determines whether the skill is appropriate?
5. What would you do to encourage less hostile behavior from Telsa?
6. What could you do to assist Telsa at making and keeping friends?
7. *Activity:* Check with your university to find out what services they offer to college students with disabilities. Discuss with your classmates the key components of each program.

 C A S E   22. ANGIE

Issues: Instructional methods/techniques, transition

Angie is an elementary school student with a communication disorder. She does well in school, but often has obvious social problems that her parents fail to recognize or choose to deny.

Angie is a 6-year-old girl with a speech impairment. She currently attends a first grade classroom at Maryville Elementary School in western Kentucky. At school, she receives all of her education in the regular classroom, except for three hours per week of speech-language services that she receives in the speech and language pathologist's room. There, Mrs. Romerez works with Angie providing her with a series of articulation drills meant to remediate Angie's production of certain phonemes.

Born to McKenzie and Elizabeth Wilson, Angie had obvious lip and palate deformities at birth. Within days, Angie received her first of six operations to repair the hole (or fistula) in her palate and fissure in her lip. Angie's split lip was visible, and this split caused her nose to be malformed. All of these facial deformities only compounded her communication disorder. During this time, hospital personnel began to assemble a team to help Angie and her family deal with the disability. The team included a pediatrician, a plastic surgeon, a speech-language pathologist, an audiologist, a feeding specialist, an orthodontist, and a prosthodontist. This team approach is common for infants born with disabilities as part of early intervention services in an attempt to circumvent any future learning or behavioral problems.

Angie's disability came as a surprise to the Wilson family. Being one of five children, Angie was the only child with any type of disability. Even today the parents are puzzled as to the etiology of her disability. Nowhere in their family history has any member displayed any type of disability or abnormality. From what they have learned about Angie's disability, they know that there usually are both genetic and environmental factors involved with this type of disability. However, to them the disability remains a puzzle that they must deal with on a day-to-day basis. For instance, they know that Angie will probably need additional operations as she grows older because the fistula will also continue to grow despite the success of earlier operations.

Despite that Angie is still receiving speech and language services, her academic functioning is well within the normal range. In some children, communication disorders often interfere with academic development; in Angie's case, her disability has only played a minor role. Perhaps it was the early intervention services that have circumvented her academic difficulties. Or perhaps her intense language sessions that she continues to take have prevented these difficulties.

At Maryville Elementary School, Angie receives intense speech-language services three times a week. The speech-language pathologist uses drills that focus on Angie's most difficult articulation sounds of *t, d, p,* and *b* and her hypernasality. Many of these drills involve her placing her finger or a mirror under her nose (so she either feels or sees her breath) in an attempt to get Angie to speak (blow air) through her mouth, not her nose. Her speech services are seen as an ongoing process because each operation causes her muscles to be pulled together, interfering in articulation of certain sounds. As stressed by her speech and language pathologist, Angie must retrain these muscles or she will continue to experience difficulties with her speech.

Despite the wonderful services being provided by the school, in the classroom Angie does experience some behavioral (i.e., aggressive behaviors and lying) and social difficulties (i.e., shyness and withdrawal), which some blame on her facial deformities. On one occasion, the teacher, Mr. Pithe, caught two boys making faces at Angie. It seems the two were making fun of her deformities. Upon seeing this behavior, Mr. Pithe sent the two boys to the principal's office. Mr. Winer, the school principal, yelled at the boys and told them to go back to class to apologize to Angie. She graciously accepted their apology, but she vowed to get even with them. Later that day after recess when the boys returned to the classroom, they found their worksheets for the day had been torn to shreds. Without proof, Mr. Pithe did not accuse Angie but he suspected that she was the culprit.

On another occasion as Angie was playing outside, Bobby Nerson, a neighbor child, rode his bike past Angie and made gestures imitating a pig. Angie called him a name, but it was too late, Bobby had ridden out of earshot. The next day when Bobby went to ride his bike, he found that he had two flat tires. Immediately, Mr. Nerson went to the Wilsons and demanded that Angie confess to the crime. Mr. Nerson stated that he saw her running from his back porch last night. When Angie's parents asked her if she did it, she responded that she would never do something so terrible. Despite Angie's statement, Mr. Nerson still insisted that Angie did it. Angie added that she was over at the Nerson's but she was there looking for Bengi, their dog, who had run off.

At school, Mr. Pithe has noticed on numerous occasions how Angie avoids playing with other children and how angry she becomes in certain social situations. When asked about her shy and withdrawn behavior, Angie often responds that she doesn't feel like playing with anyone else. Even when Mr. Pithe has arranged a recess game that has Angie paired up with other students, she often drops out and eventually plays by herself in a corner of the playground. Mr. Pithe feels that Angie does not know how to interact with other students, yet he is not able to teach these skills because they would take too much of his time and social skills are not part of the curriculum. Angie's parents have also been aware of her shy behavior, but do not consider it a problem because they are shy.

Academically, Angie does well. She exerts a tremendous amount of effort to earn good grades and do well in her academic areas, particularly math. Although she has some difficulty pronouncing phonemes while reading, she is a quick learner and comprehends well. She gravitates to math because she often works independently and does not have to speak. Angie is often one of the first to finish her math worksheets and Mr. Pithe rewards her with free time on the computer (another independent activity). When working on the computer, Angie uses "Math Smashers," computer software that develops fluency of math facts. As she works on the computer, Mr. Pithe observes how happy she is to find success in this nonsocial activity.

At her recent individualized education program (IEP) conference, Mr. Pithe suggested to Angie's parents that they seek counseling for her because of her shy and angry behaviors and possible problems dealing with the disability. Upon hearing these comments, the Wilson's became angry. They said that they were insulted by his comments and that Angie is no different from other children her age. The Wilson's knew, but never admitted to anyone, that Angie was different from the rest of their children. They felt that her behavior was due to their overprotectiveness and their fear that she would not be able to handle the cruel comments about her disability. Mr. Pithe then suggested that they try to teach her some social skills that would enable her to play with other children. Mr. and Mrs. Wilson responded defensively that there was nothing wrong with being an independent individual, someone who relies on no one.

Later that week, Mr. and Mrs. Wilson spoke to their best friends, their only friends, the Frackverns. During their discussion of Angie, the Frackverns mentioned that they thought Angie seemed a bit withdrawn on her many visits to their house. Whenever company comes over to the Wilson's house, Angie quickly hides in her room until the company is gone. In addition, the Frackverns went on to say that they thought Angie was only 4 years old, not six, because of her immature behavior. These comments made the Wilsons think about whether Angie's shyness was a problem or part of her personality.

QUESTIONS

1. With obvious facial deformities, how do you think people reacted to Angie upon first seeing her? How should her parents handle these awkward situations in which people respond differently upon first meeting Angie?
2. What types of activities could the teacher do in the classroom to assist Angie with her language development and speech production? What role could her strengths play in her language development?
3. When does shyness become a problem? Define what you feel shyness is and provide examples of shy behavior. Recently, psychiatrists have suggested administering antidepressant drugs (such as sertraline— Zoloft) to children that are shy. What do you think should be done to help these students become more outgoing?
4. A physical abnormality, such as a facial deformity, could cause a child to become withdrawn. What should be done to help a child with a deformity interact better with other children? What skills should the child learn? What skills should the other children in the class learn?
5. If Angie were to have plastic surgery to repair her nose and facial deformities, do you think that the surgery would be enough to remediate her social and emotional problems? Why or why not?
6. How does society treat people with speech impairments (or communication disorders)?
7. What are the advantages of early intervention occurring in the hospital?
8. *Activity:* Conduct an Educational Resources Information Center (ERIC) search and find an early childhood intervention that has been used and proven effective at remediating some aspect of a communication disorder. Report on the intervention, its effectiveness, and the area remediated.

CASE 23. MARVIN

Issues: Instructional methods/techniques, transition

Marvin is a middle-aged man who has found a job and lifestyle that he loves. He has developed compensatory strategies to compensate for his problem with stuttering, but there are times when they fail.

Marvin is a 35-year-old African American man who has a speech disorder, or fluency disorder. More commonly known as stuttering, Marvin has been dysfluent since an early age. Marvin lives by himself, with his dog Mel, in a one-bedroom apartment and seldom ventures out. Marvin works for Joffenburg Water Company as a water monitor (or meter reader). Marvin has worked for this company since he graduated from high school. He says that he likes working as a water monitor because it gives him the chance to work outdoors and he rarely has to interact with other people.

Marvin exhibits dysfluency through three common patterns: repetition, prolongation, and blocking. When nervous or anxious, Marvin usually repeats or blocks his speech. Marvin's dysfluency with repetition occurs as he repeats words three or four times (e.g., "that that that") before speaking the next word. For Marvin, blocking is perhaps the most frustrating aspect of his dysfluency, frustrating for him and anyone he is speaking to. Blocking occurs when Marvin is unable to speak the word that he wants to say. Often when Marvin blocks, the listener says the blocked word in an attempt to help Marvin. When this occurs, Marvin usually responds with "yes, yes." The last aspect of Marvin's dysfluency is his prolongation of words. Prolongation, originally taught to him as an alternative technique to repetition and blocking, occurs when he relaxes and tries to speak slowly (e.g., "forrrrevvvvvver"). To Marvin, these patterns of dysfluency have made his interactions with others a painful experience.

Marvin displays a "social pattern" common to persons with dysfluency. They usually have a job that allows for little, if any, contact with other people. Moreover, Marvin avoids contact with other people in most social situations. For example, because he finds that talking to his boss is one of the most difficult aspects of his job, he has to prepare his speech (dialog) ahead of time. He does this by sitting alone in his truck and verbalizing what he wants to say to him. He also silently repeats phrases or sentences that he is going to say prior to saying them. Another difficult task for Marvin is talking on the telephone. Because the person he is talking to cannot see Marvin's face (i.e., receive nonverbal feedback), often long moments of silence occur during phone conversations as Marvin tries to verbalize his words.

Some activities that Marvin does enjoy include being around children and pets and singing in his church choir. Marvin enjoys being with his nieces and nephews because there is little pressure during his conversations with them. He also enjoys being around his dog and other animals for the same reason. Finally, Marvin enjoys singing in the church choir. As with other stutterers, singing is an effortless activity (e.g., Mel Tillis) because Marvin is accessing a different part of the brain.

Initially, teachers at his elementary school believed that Marvin might have a learning disability, however, test results did not concur with their suspicions. At that time, his third grade teacher mistook his dysfluency for a learning problem. He was never found to have a learning disability, but easily qualified to receive speech-language services. Although he received these school-based services from third grade on, there has been little if any change in his dysfluency. During junior high school, because Marvin did not see any progress in his speech, he stopped attending speech sessions and skipped school.

Despite his eligibility, Marvin never received further speech-language services until he was 25 years old. It was at this time that he saw another stutterer on a news program, called "Newstime USA," football star Leonard Spavis. For Leonard, his was a story of success. In the news piece, Leonard spoke about how much difficulty he once had with stuttering, particularly during sports interviews. Leonard spoke about a new and highly successful therapy called "precision fluency shaping." Using this program, the participant retrains his or her motor abilities to become more fluent. According to Leonard, for three thousand dollars anyone could be trained in three weeks to overcome their dysfluency. The only stipulation of this program is that the participant must practice regularly on their own or risk becoming dysfluent again.

Marvin decided to inquire about the training and found that it was offered through the local university, Johnsville University. Having to use money from his retirement, Marvin enrolled in the program and in only one week found a tremendous difference in his fluency. By the end of the training, Marvin found that his speech was fluent, however, he did not want to practice. As a result of his lack of practice, Marvin, then 26 years old, saw his dysfluency problems slowly resurface. Moreover, his dismal failure in the training caused him to become clinically depressed. After his yearlong bout with depression, Marvin again began a search for other promising training programs.

Now at the age of 35, Marvin has come to learn that nothing lasts forever, friendships included. Marvin has made most of his friends from his church choir. These three friends are cognizant of his disability and never make jokes about it in front of him; however, when they do talk to Marvin, he frequently becomes angry with their lack of patience. During their conversations with him, if he blocks and prolongates words, they often unintentionally supply the blocked word(s). Marvin finds this demeaning. It irritates him to such an extent that lately he has ceased his conversations with them. Rather than deal with the problem, Marvin has found it easier to avoid conversation with certain friends. Because of his behavior, many of the previously established friendships are fading and he often finds himself alone during evenings and on weekends.

Until a few months ago, Marvin enjoyed going to the supermarket. Going to the market meant that he could be social without socializing. Marvin would smile and nod his head to people he knew, and because he rarely had to hold a conversation with most folks, he found his monthly trips refreshing. However, three months ago Marvin had a devastating experience. As he pushed his cart along in the seafood department, he noticed that they had his favorite food, salmon, in stock (behind the counter). Unfortunately for Marvin, this meant that he had to ask for salmon. When the clerk asked him what he wanted, he began to prolong the word salmon, but blocked only to produce a stream of "ssssss." The clerk thought he saw Marvin point to the shrimp and he assumed he was saying "shrimp." As the clerk placed more and more shrimp on the scale, Marvin got more and more anxious and when he began to speak, he blocked again. While the clerk was waiting on Marvin, a number of other customers arrived at the counter. As the clerk wrapped the shrimp, Marvin tried again to speak but instead he blocked. As the clerk handed him the wrapped shrimp, Marvin finally blurted out that he wanted salmon not shrimp. When the clerk heard this, he became angry and said to Marvin, "Why didn't you tell me that in the first place?" Immediately, Marvin became embarrassed and quickly ran out of the store. Since that incident, Marvin has not returned to that store. Now he buys his groceries at a small food mart near his house. Although he does not have a wide variety of food items to choose from, he feels that he does not have to risk being embarrassed by the food clerk.

QUESTIONS

1. What could Marvin do to improve his social skills?
2. What should Marvin say to his friends to explain his stuttering?
3. Did Marvin react appropriately when the clerk at the grocery store yelled at him? How would you handle this situation?
4. What could Marvin do to improve his telephone conversations or to ease his use of the phone?
5. Should Marvin continue to search for programs that will improve his speech? Why or why not?
6. How does society view someone who is dysfluent?
7. In television sitcoms, how does the audience usually react when a comedian stutters? Why?
8. *Activity:* Speak to a speech-language pathologist and ask them what techniques are used to improve stuttering. Bring these ideas to class and discuss them.

 CASE 24. RITA

Issues: Educational goals/objectives, instructional methods/techniques

Rita is an elementary school student who developed language delays at a young age. Her records indicate that she does well in school with the exception of one area: written language.

R ita is a 10-year-old girl with a speech and language disorder. In addition to her communication disorder, she has a moderate hearing loss and must wear two hearing aids. Rita was born to a Hispanic mother, but shortly thereafter she was presented to the local adoption agency because her mother felt that she could not care for her. Rita was soon adopted by a young couple from Littleton, Arizona. Rita has been raised by this couple all of her life and attends a regular fourth grade at Oscur Elementary School.

Rita's language delays began at an early age. First, she did not speak understandable words until she was 3 years old. Even as she grew older, she continued to experience language delays such as using improper pronoun and verb tense. Finally, in first grade Rita's teacher noticed that Rita had moderate speech and language delays when compared to other children her age. These language delays were believed to be associated with delays in her reading and written language skills. At that time, informal measures indicated that Rita did have some difficulties with reading and written language. Despite having average intelligence, Rita usually earns grades of Cs and Ds in her classes. It was not until a recent evaluation that teachers knew she did not have a significant deficit in reading, but did have deficits in oral and written language.

From this battery of tests, it was found that Rita had significant difficulties with vocabulary and written language. From this battery, Rita's scores were as follows:

Wechsler Intelligence Scale for Children—Revised (WISC-R)

Subtest	
Verbal IQ	101
Performance IQ	95
Full Scale IQ	98

Peabody Individual Achievement Test —Revised (PIAT-R)

Subtest	Standard Score	Percentile Rank
General Information	104	61
Reading Recognition	86	18
Reading Comprehension	117	87
Total Reading	102	55
Mathematics	138	99
Spelling	91	27
Test Total	108	70
Written Expression	4	<1
Written Language Composite	80	9

Test of Language Development—I:3 (TOLD-I:3)

Subtest	Standard Score	Percentile Rank
Sentence Combining	1	<1
Picture Vocabulary	5	5
Word Ordering	10	50
Generals	11	63
Grammar Comprehension	6	9
Malapropisms	8	25
Composite Quotients	**Sum of Standard Scores**	**Quotient**
Spoken Language	41	78
Listening	19	76
Speaking	22	83
Semantics	24	87
Syntax	17	55

Test of Written Language 3 (TOWL-3)

Subtest	Standard Score	Percentile Rank
Vocabulary	5	5
Spelling	7	16
Style	6	9
Logical Sentences	5	5
Sentence Combining	6	9
Contextual Conventions	5	5
Contextual Language	4	2
Story Construction	3	1
Composite Quotients	**Sum of Standard Scores**	**Quotient**
Contrived Writing	31	74
Spontaneous Writing	18	56
Overall Written Language	49	64

The results from the PIAT-R indicate that Rita scored within the average range for general information, spelling, and total reading subtests. She scored below average on the written language composite and scored within the high average range on the mathematics subtest. On the TOLD-I:3, Rita scored within the average range on the subtests of word ordering, generals, and malapropisms. She scored below average to very poor on the subtests of grammar comprehension, vocabulary, and sentence combining. Moreover, Rita performed very poorly on all of the composite scores. On overall written language, Rita performed within the very poor range as indicated by her score from the TOWL-3.

To further assess language skills, an error analysis of writing and spelling skills was conducted to determine specific skill deficits. From this analysis, Rita exhibited written composition deficits using adjectives and adverbs; she also had problems with subject-verb agreement. In addition, Rita exhibited difficulties in using correct punctuation and correct capitalization.

Rita's strengths seem to be in reading comprehension, general information, mathematics, and spoken language. Rita's weaknesses seem to be in vocabulary, spelling, and overall written expression. Specific analyses revealed deficits with use of descriptions (e.g., adjectives and adverbs), punctuation, and capitalization.

Other classroom data indicates that Rita does use a frequency modulated (FM) trainer to amplify the teacher's voice. Her teacher indicated that she gives a lot of verbal information to her students. When Rita was observed in the classroom, the school psychologist noted that Rita was seated four desks from the front and in front of a tall student. She was observed talking to classmates Billy Johnson (a student diagnosed as ADHD) and Judy Warsaw throughout most of the observation period. Furthermore, from recorded on-task measures, Rita was found to be on-task 58 percent of the time during social studies and only 40 percent of the time during English.

According to the teacher, Mrs. Classen, Judy is Rita's peer tutor. In an attempt to assist Rita, Mrs. Classen decided that pairing her with Judy would allow her to have someone to ask questions concerning assignments or classwork. Mrs. Classen mentioned how wonderful this arrangement was working because the number of questions directed at her had significantly decreased since she paired up the two students. Mrs. Classen also mentioned that Judy knew Rita so well that she was often able to anticipate Rita's needs.

QUESTIONS

1. Develop one goal and two supporting objectives for Rita in the communication area.
2. Is it appropriate to pair up another student with Rita? What are the advantages and disadvantages of this pairing?
3. Mrs. Classen refers to the pairing as peer tutoring. Is she correct? What is peer tutoring?
4. Despite that Rita does not lip read, she does use verbal cues. What are some accommodations that Mrs. Classen could make for Rita in the classroom to assist her use of verbal cues?
5. Should Rita's parents do anything special to assist her at learning more about her Hispanic background? If so, what?
6. What are some techniques or interventions that Mrs. Classen could use to improve Rita's written language skills?
7. *Activity:* Find out more about the FM trainer described in this case. What is it? How does it work? How does it help students? Should it be used all of the time?

CASE 25. ANITA

Issues: Collaboration/consultation, instructional methods/techniques

Anita is a preschooler who has mild communication problems. She attends an inclusion classroom at the local university, but trouble soon erupts between the classroom teacher and speech pathologist.

Anita Gifford is a 3-year-old girl with a mild communication disorder. Anita currently attends an inclusion prekindergarten classroom at Leewood University's Child Study Center. Children from the surrounding community attend the center. Because the university offers free admission to the children of faculty and staff members and the school is located on campus, many faculty and staff have chosen to send their children to the Child Study Center, instead of using local day care. Other children, many from poor sections of town, also attend the center. The center offers individualized and group activities and groups children by ages, regardless of ability level. This heterogeneous population provides for a conducive environment for inclusion education.

Anita's speech disorder involves her inability to articulate the ending sounds of words. Although Anita's parents, David and Renee, can understand her speech and communicate effectively with her, others find her speech difficult to understand. Her parents blame her speech difficulties on the numerous ear infections that Anita had during the past two years. Her problems with otitis media (middle ear infections) finally improved after she received "tubes in her ear." Through an operation, the doctor placed myringotomy tubes into her eardrum to relieve fluid build up in the middle ear. To date she has had no hearing loss. To compound her problems with articulation, Anita's older sister, Sasha, usually speaks for her at home, limiting Anita's opportunities to practice and develop speech at home. With only a year difference between the sisters' ages, Anita relies heavily on Sasha for her communication.

After this operation, her pediatrician found that Anita still had language delays and recommended that she be tested by the local district to assess any possible learning problems. The screening found that Anita had potential problems with language. The results from the DIAL-R were as follows:

Developmental Indicators for the Assessment of Learning—Revised (DIAL-R)

Subtest	Standard Score	Decision
Motor	10	OK
Concepts	10	OK
Language	7	Potential Problem
DIAL-R Total	27	Potential Problem

Further testing found that she had difficulties on the expressive portion of the Preschool Language Scale-3 (PLS-3). The following scores document her performance on the PLS-3:

Preschool Language Scale—3 (PLS-3)

Subtest	Standard Score	Age Equivalent
Auditory Comprehension	112	4 years–2 months
Expressive Communication	82	2 years–3 months
Total Language Score	98	3 years–1 month

Further informal testing by the speech-language pathologist, Mrs. Kavale, revealed that Anita had difficulties with final consonants (e.g., says "ca" for "cat") and stridency (e.g., says "du" for "zoo") of the phonemes s, z, f, and v. Based upon this assessment and the recommendations of some family friends, Mrs. Gifford, Anita's mother, enrolled Anita in the Child Study Center.

Anita is one of four students in her classroom with some type of developmental delay; the remaining eight children consist of a mix of average- to high-achieving students. Those students with disabilities in need of special services usually receive services in the classroom. In the case of speech services, Mrs. Kavale comes to the classroom daily and presents short lessons to the entire class. In this way, she feels that those students with disabilities can use their peers as role models. Mrs. Kavale also collaborates with the classroom teacher, Mr. Noonan, on other language-based classroom activities. On occasion, she has suggested that they team teach a lesson, but Mr. Noonan is often reluctant.

Mr. Noonan, who has a degree in early childhood education, has taught for two years. While he is patient with the children, he finds it difficult to work with some of the children, particularly those with developmental delays. At times he feels frustrated because he has to repeatedly explain directions or content to some of these children, while at the same time keeping the high-achieving students motivated and challenged. Furthermore, he does not feel comfortable teaching language activities to children because he never took a course on speech-language development.

Mrs. Kavale has also noticed some problems with the way Mr. Noonan interacts with some of the students, particularly Anita. On numerous occasions when Anita would say something to Mr. Noonan, he would respond by saying "OK" and turn away, without knowing what she said. On other occasions, when Anita would ask a question or make a statement, Mr. Noonan would have her repeat the mispronounced word after he would say it. For example, one day, Anita was telling Mr. Noonan that she gave her dog a bath. When Anita said "ba" instead of "bath," Mr. Noonan shot back, "No, say bath." Upon observing this interchange, Mrs. Kavale told Mr. Noonan that he was not responding appropriately to Anita. Miffed, Mr. Noonan replied that he did the correct thing.

Unfortunately this is not the first time that Mr. Noonan and Mrs. Kavale have disagreed on different aspects of instruction. For example, Mr. Noonan feels that Anita needs more intense instruction and he cannot understand why Anita is not pulled out of his classroom for some intense speech-language therapy. Although he agreed to allow Mrs. Kavale to instruct students in a group in his class, he feels that Anita has not made much progress. He feels that it is time to provide intense one-on-one instruction to Anita and other students in the class who have communication disorders. Mrs. Kavale, on the other hand, disagrees with him and feels that speech instruction should occur in a naturalistic context and should be play-based. Due to her extensive background in the speech-language field, she is well aware of the research that supports her approach to teaching speech-language to children with disabilities.

When Mr. Noonan approached Mrs. Kavale about his concern, she defended her teaching and said her methods are supported by research. Mr. Noonan, who has only seen children receive speech services through "pull-out" programs, vehemently disagreed with her. In the best interest of the children, Mr. Noonan voiced his concern to the parents of his students at a recent school open house.

QUESTIONS

1. Is it possible that Anita's ear infections, early in life, could have caused her communication disorder? Why or why not?
2. Is Anita's older sister, Sasha, a help or a hindrance to Anita's development? Why?
3. How does Mr. Noonan address Anita's communication problems in the classroom? What else could he do to facilitate Anita's language development?
4. How would you react if you were visiting Anita's house and found her speech unintelligible? What would you do or say? How does society treat young children who have unintelligible speech?
5. What are some of the concerns or questions that you anticipate from parents who have their children enrolled in an inclusion classroom of the Child Study Center?
6. What should Mr. Noonan and Mrs. Kavale do to resolve their differences in teaching (one-on-one versus whole class instruction)?
7. If you were the teacher, would you have mentioned "one-on-one versus whole class instruction" issue to parents? Why or why not?
8. *Activity:* Speak to a speech-language pathologist about how teaching methods have changed over the past twenty years. Ask him or her to describe older methods and how these older methods have fallen into disuse as newer techniques became available.

CHAPTER 8

INDIVIDUALS WITH VISUAL IMPAIRMENTS*

DEFINITION

"Visual impairment" describes disabilities of sight ranging from students with partial sight to students who are legally blind. A student is described as partially sighted if that student's visual acuity (ability to accurately see objects at distances) in the better eye with correction measures between 20/70 and 20/200. Normal visual acuity is defined as 20/20. A student is considered legally blind if the student's visual acuity in the better eye with correction measures 20/200 or greater or if the student's visual field is less than an angle of 20 degrees. The latter criterion refers to tunnel vision, a severe loss of the ability to see in peripheral areas, leaving only a small, central area of sight.

KEY TERMS

bilateral optic atrophy   A dysfunction of the optic nerves in both eyes, causing loss of vision.

Braille   A written language composed of symbols that may be read through tactile (fingers) means instead of visual means.

Braillewriter   Machine or device that produces Braille symbols on a page.

glaucoma   A group of eye diseases that have certain common features, including an eye pressure too high for the health of the eye, damage to the optic nerve, and visual field (sight) loss.

myopic and astigmatic refractive error   Nonspherical shape of eye causing symptoms such as nearsightedness and blurring.

nystagmus   An involuntary eye movement that usually results in some degree of visual loss. The degree and direction of eye movement, amount of visual loss and resulting impairment varies greatly from person to person.

optic nerve   A cable of nerve fibers that carry electrical impulses from the retina to the brain. The retina converts light into electrical impulses, transmitted to the visual centers of the brain. It is there that the electrical impulses are interpreted into sight.

---

* We are grateful to Buddy Coard for his contributions to this chapter.

orientation and mobility   The variety of skills that a person with a visual impairment has or needs to effectively negotiate her or his way around in the physical environments of the indoor and outdoor world.

Retinopathy of Prematurity (ROP)   A medical condition (typically among infants born prematurely) whereby the growth of abnormal blood vessels accompanied by scar tissue in the retina rapidly progresses to possibly cause blindness over a period of weeks.

screen reader   A computer software that reads aloud text on the computer screen.

visual field   The complete span of area from far peripheral right to far peripheral left that is effectively seen by eyes.

vocational rehabilitation   A government service that helps persons with disabilities develop the skills necessary for employment and find employment.

26. BERTHA

Issue: Inclusion

Bertha is a kindergarten student with a severe vision impairment caused by a condition called Retinopathy of Prematurity (ROP). Her disability has a profound and varied impact on her parents and grandparents. Her mother and her teachers work to devise a suitable educational program in a typical kindergarten class.

Cecilia and Julio Arruda had a great desire to have a child. After years of unsuccessful attempts, they went to a fertility specialist who placed Cecilia on a medication designed to increase her chances of pregnancy. Soon she was pregnant with not one fetus but twins. Unfortunately, after only 28 weeks of gestation, the pregnancy was in danger and Cecilia underwent a cesarean section birth. The premature twin girls were dramatically underweight. The first child weighed only one and a half pounds and died within hours of birth. The second child, Bertha, weighing a mere two pounds, was placed in an intensive neonatal unit where she struggled to survive. She did live, gradually gaining strength over a 3-month hospital stay.

One result of Bertha's premature birth is called Retinopathy of Prematurity (ROP), a condition causing severe vision loss in infants born premature and of low birthweight. During her first two months, Bertha was given high quantities of oxygen to help her survive and develop. This helpful oxygen also caused damage to her eyes, overwhelming her underdeveloped retinal blood vessels. The result in Bertha's case was Stage V ROP with a complete detachment of the retina. She underwent a number of surgical procedures to reattach the retina, but she remained completely blind.

Early intervention services began in the hospital. A case manager from the local county health department and an early intervention specialist from the school district completed an assessment of Bertha and her family's needs at the hospital. During her preschool years, in-home instruction focused on preparing Bertha for later Braille instruction through a variety of tactile experiences and teaching her mobility through the use of a cane. Formal Braille instruction began at age $3^1/2$. Cecilia was extremely diligent in teaching Bertha at home. She founded an incredible support group on the Internet, the Cyber-Network of Parents of Blind Children, a group of parents of children with visual impairments around the world that share advice and information. With the encouragement of other parents who had been through similar situations, Cecilia taught herself Braille as she simultaneously drilled her daughter on the dot cells, the little bumps of meaning on the page. By the time Bertha entered kindergarten, she was able to read the Braille alphabet. She could also use her cane to get around her house and preschool hallways with ease.

Sometimes, Bertha's disability has seemed like a wall between her parents. As her mother has accepted the disability and reached out to others for support, her father Julio has gone the opposite direction. He still does not accept that Bertha is completely blind and will not regain her vision. He maintains a constant search for new medical breakthroughs that offer hope for his daughter to regain sight. Sometimes he notices subtle signs that she can see. He watches her run quickly through the family living room to the stairs and up to her room. She sweeps through with comfort, speed, and grace, grabbing the staircase railing with all the timing and accuracy of any sighted child. In this and other details of Bertha's life, Julio finds reasons to believe that his daughter is gaining sight. He believes that this small bit of vision will be surgically improved at some future date and his cherished daughter will be able to see her father's face and know who he is from across a room.

Bertha's mother, Cecilia, views her daughter in a different light, accepting the visual impairment as a reality that demands a supreme mothering performance at all times. Cecilia has always been diligent in taking her to therapeutic sessions. She has spent hours working with the early intervention specialists, learning every medical and educational detail about Bertha's vision and the needed services. Perhaps as a way of coping with the painful loss of one daughter and the loss of the sight of another, Cecilia has thrown herself into her daughter's care, thereby neglecting other aspects of her life. She has cut herself off from friends. The large social network that she and Julio enjoyed prior to Bertha's birth has been lost as Cecilia has focused exclusively on Bertha's needs.

Bertha's paternal grandparents have withdrawn from their relationship with the family. They have very limited contact with their son and daughter-in-law's family since Bertha's birth even though they live in the same city. They feel uncomfortable with Bertha's disability. They don't know how to play with a blind youngster without feeling intense sadness. Also, their discomfort is exacerbated by their son's fantastic claims about Bertha's ability to see and new medical treatments for vision loss being developed in South American research centers.

Fortunately Cecilia's parents remain close and supportive. They often take Bertha on weekend adventures to the zoo or to a local fishing lake. Bertha, Cecilia, and Julio draw great strength from this support. Additionally, the weekend stays allow Cecilia and Julio to occasionally set aside their preoccupation with their daughter's needs to attend to their own relationship. Recently Julio surprised Cecilia by flying her away for a weekend in a luxurious lakefront hotel in downtown Chicago. They enjoyed two days of restaurants, shopping, and museums. At one point, as they walked along the shore of Lake Michigan with the late afternoon sun shining and a light September breeze blowing, Cecilia turned to Julio and admitted that she had been thinking of Bertha all day. She felt guilty going away from her daughter to have fun and relax. Julio encouraged her to ease up and enjoy the big city, but Cecilia struggled with guilt and anxiety throughout the weekend.

Bertha has recently started attending a half-day kindergarten program that runs until noon each day. She is the only blind youngster in her class. Her unique educational needs are addressed in many ways. She participates fully in the typical activities that any kindergarten student enjoys. Mrs. Rhodes, a teacher specializing in the instruction of students with visual impairments, works in Bertha's class during half of each school day. She works directly with Bertha on skill development and adaptation to the learning environment. She also provides consultation and assistance to Mr. King, the kindergarten teacher, as he learns how to meet Bertha's needs within the activities and routines of his classroom.

Mrs. Rhodes and Mr. King arranged for Bertha to have a sight guide to help her get around the hallways of the school building. They worked with Phyllis, another student in the kindergarten class, and Bertha to teach them how to walk as a team. Bertha walks one half step behind her classmate guide, grasping Phyllis' arm just above the elbow. Phyllis learned to give Bertha verbal cues about upcoming obstacles and turns in their path. For example, a small flight of stairs must be navigated to walk to the wing housing the school gymnasium and auditorium. Phyllis tells Bertha of the upcoming stairway, the direction of the stairway (down), and the number of steps required. She also initiates a pause at the top of the steps so that they can synchronize their motion before beginning to go down the steps.

In the classroom, Bertha is learning to do her academic tasks in Braille. She writes on a Braillewriter, a six-key typewriter that produces Braille print. Mrs. Rhodes brings a variety of early reading materials in which favorite children's stories are printed in Braille. Due to the cumbersome nature of the Braillewriter, Mrs. Rhodes is working to arrange for Bertha to use a computer and printer that will allow her to read and write in Braille. When Bertha types into the computer, a special software and printer convert her keystrokes into Braille. For counting and early math activities, Bertha uses an abacus specifically designed for blind students.

Additionally, Mrs. Rhodes is excited about a new device called a Virtual Reality Mouse (VRM). The VRM is a computer mouse that allows persons with visual impairments to use the World Wide Web or any software that uses windows and dialog boxes. The VRM does three tasks that make this possible for the blind computer user. First, it jumps to new windows and dialog boxes that come up on the screen, dragging the cursor and mouse toward the new opportunity. Then, it tells the user where the cursor is on the computer screen by tactile feedback, by pushing against the user's hand. Third, it contains a software system, called a screen reader, that reads the contents of the screen aloud so that the user knows what a given box of window says. Mrs. Rhodes bought the VRM with a grant from her school district, and she is learning how to use it to teach it to her students.

Bertha's classmates are gradually beginning to accept her and enjoy her as their friend. A small group of girls has made a point of watching out for Bertha, sitting with her at lunch and playing with her on the playground. Mrs. Rhodes says that young children are uniquely open and flexible in their views of normality. By Christmas they'll all but forget Bertha is blind. They see her as their classmate Bertha.

QUESTIONS

1. What are the advantages and disadvantages of placing Bertha in a mainstream kindergarten program?
2. Use the Internet or other resources to search for the many new technological tools for persons with visual impairments. What do you find?
3. Should professionals encourage Cecilia in her devotion to Bertha's needs? Or should she be encouraged to back off and allow others to accept larger roles in her daughter's care?
4. In this case, Bertha's classmate Phyllis is trained to be her sight guide. Is it fair to ask other students to provide care and services to a peer who has a disability? If not, why? If so, what possible benefits are there for the helping student?
5. Why do you think Bertha is introduced to Braille print at age 3$^1/_2$?
6. *Activity:* Research further on ROP. Learn in greater depth how this condition damages the retina and the five stages of severity.

C A S E 27. KIM

Issues: Educational goals/objectives

Kim is a 9-year-old girl with a vision impairment. This functional vision evaluation provides a picture of her abilities in the areas of vision, orientation and mobility, and academics.

FUNCTIONAL VISION EVALUATION REPORT

Tests Administered

Classroom Observation
Lighthouse Near Vision Test
Learning Media Assessment
Ophthalmological Report
Diagnostic Assessment Procedure (DAP)
Feinbloom Distance Test for the Partially Sighted
Woodcock Reading Mastery-Revised
Pseudo-Isochromatic Plates

Interpretation

Vision History

Kim is a 9.4-year-old female. She had a recent opthamological examination in which Dr. Mejia noted distance acuities of 20/200 in the right eye and 20/200 in the left eye. He reported near vision with a right head turn. Dr. Mejia also noted that Kim has a vertical and horizontal nystagmus (a rhythmic, involuntary movement of the eyes), bilateral optic atrophy (degeneration of optic nerve fibers), and a myopic and astigmatic refractive error (nearsightedness and blurring due to nonspherical shape of eye). Glasses were prescribed.

Parent, Teacher, and Student Interview

Kim's parents are concerned about the impact of her legal blindness on her educational performance. The parents have two specific concerns: 1) Kim's close-viewing distance, and 2) the best print size. Dr. Mejia recommended large print materials for her to read.

Mrs. Smith, Kim's teacher, specified three areas of concern in regard to Kim's educational performance: 1) duration of reading assignments, and 2) working in small detail (e.g. studying maps), and (3) the possible use of software to help her use the computer.

Kim voiced no specific concerns. She stated that she is able to complete her work at the same time or earlier than other students in her class. In addition, she stated that she is able to see the blackboard.

Classroom Observation

Kim was observed for twenty minutes each in Mrs. Smith's and Mr. John's classrooms. In both settings, she was provided preferential, front-row seating. Her desk surface was of a low-glare material and no glare was present. During the observation in Mr. John's class, Kim was asked to solve math problems in her textbook. Her working distance was three to eight inches away and she used a No. 2 pencil. She had no difficulties reading back her work when requested by the teacher. Mr. John reported that the observation was typical of Kim's performance everyday.

Functional Distance Acuities and Fields

Kim was assessed within her school environment to determine her distance visual acuities. Right eye acuity was 20/60. Left eye was 20/120. No head turn or tilting of her head for eccentric viewing was noted. In her left eye, there appeared to be a decreased response to objects presented in the temporal visual field; however, this was inconsistent. The right eye visual field appeared to be full.

Color Vision

Using the Pseudo-Isochromatic Plates, it was determined that Kim may have difficulty in the area of red-green vision.

Diagnostic Assessment Procedure (DAP)

Portions of the DAP were administered to assess Kim's use of vision in a variety of tasks. The assessment room was illuminated by the overhead fluorescent lighting. Kim worked on the desk surface and her viewing distance was approximately three to ten inches for near tasks. Kim identified a No. 2 pencil as that which she uses for pencil and paper tasks at school. She demonstrated a mature grasp as she wrote using her right hand.

Discrimination and Identification of Objects, People, and Action

Kim matched one-inch objects by shape (circle, square, triangle) and color (blue, red, yellow) when presented on backgrounds of high and low contrast. She discriminated big from little and short from long when blocks and sticks were presented in a scattered fashion.

Kim identified five pictures (football, kite, tree, television, ball) and matched each to its corresponding outline (oval, diamond, triangle, square, circle). When asked what picture might go with the crescent outline shape, Kim correctly suggested "moon."

Memory for Detail, Part-Whole Relationship, and Figure-Ground Discrimination

Kim located a single picture (calf) within a scene (farm yard) and identified a partially hidden element (boy) within a picture (person behind door). She was able to accurately identify the action in each of four simple action pictures and she was able to place the cards in a logical sequence to make a story.

Kim was presented with four pieces from simple puzzles of a dog and a house. She quickly and correctly assembled the pieces to make each puzzle. She also correctly anticipated what each completed picture would be before assembling the puzzle pieces. She correctly identified the colors of the brown dog and green house. She correctly stated the number of windows on the house.

Discrimination, Identification, Reproduction of Abstract Figures and Symbols

In an activity requiring Kim to match letter and number symbols to those embedded in a patterned background, she correctly matched all eight symbols.

Reading Behaviors and Print Size

The Woodcock Reading Mastery Test—Revised (WRMT-R) form G was administered to Kim to help in the selection of a timed reading section. The results of the WRMT-R were:

	Standard Score	Percentile Rank
Word identification	108	71
Word attack	95	37
Word comprehension	108	70
Passage comprehension	108	70
Basic skills cluster	103	59
Reading comprehension	108	70
Total reading cluster	107	67

From the WRMT-R, it was determined that her classroom reading book could be used. A story was selected that was close to the point of the last story Kim had read. Kim was asked to read regular print orally for twenty minutes and a large print edition of the same text for eight minutes. She read on a table with overhead fluorescent lighting. Kim was given the opportunity to spell any words unfamiliar to her and she did so. The following behaviors were observed during the reading sample using regular print:

Working distance	2.5–3 inches
Total number of words read	917
Reading rate	Mean of 46 per minute
Omissions	2
Insertion of word(s)	0
Skipping word(s)	1
Graphic similarity	2

The reading sample was also examined to determine if duration of oral reading was of concern and the following was found:

Reading Rate

Time	Number of Words Per Minute	Number of Errors
0–4 minutes	39	3
4–8 minutes	42	1
8–12 minutes	45	2
12–16 minutes	53	1
16–20	50	1

The following results were obtained using a 129 percent enlargement of her reading book:

Working distance	4–5 inches
Total number of words read	440
Reading rate	Mean of 55 per minute
Omissions	1
Insertion of word(s)	0
Skipping word(s)	0
Graphic similarity	1

The large print reading sample was also examined to determine if duration of oral reading was of concern and the following was found:

Reading Rate

Time	Number of Words Per Minute	Number of Errors
0–4 minutes	40	3
4–8 minutes	60	1

Analysis of performance on the two reading samples (regular and large print) indicated that there was not a significant difference in performance between the two samples.

Lighthouse Near Vision Test
Kim was also asked to read near vision cards and the following results were obtained:

Print Size	M Size	Viewing Distance
Newspaper subheadlines	4 M 20/200	14 inches
High school text	1 M 20/50	4 inches
Magazine	.8 M 20/40	3 inches

The Lighthouse Continuous Reading Cards revealed that Kim was able to read 1 M print, which is equal to newspaper or a high school textbook at four inches. This test asks Kim to read for a short time to examine her reading behaviors without respect to duration.

Orientation and Mobility Assessment
Interpretation
An informal conceptual development assessment was conducted. The results indicate that Kim does not have any problems with laterality, directionality, or understanding concepts within her environment.

Kim was interviewed and observed traveling within a familiar building. No difficulties were observed. Kim did report some difficulties with stairs, especially in areas of decreased illumination. When asked to travel the railroad tie stairs, she was awkward and not sure of her footings due to the unevenness of the stairs. When asked to travel standard stairs in the building, she had no difficulty. Kim reported consistently using the railing as a visual cue to detect the presence of steps and to negotiate them.

Summary
Kim is a 9-year-old student with a diagnosis of nystagmus, bilateral optic atrophy, and a myopic and astigmatic refractive error. Observation of her within her classroom and school indicates no significant problems with most

tasks. However, she does have problems related to very small detail work that is less than one-fourth inch in size and with duration of reading. As a result of this finding and Dr. Mejia's ophthalmological report, Kim meets the State Department of Education criteria for a student who is blind.

QUESTIONS

1. Give three to five recommendations to Kim's teacher to help Kim handle the typical tasks of moving around a school building and completing her work.
2. Keeping in mind that individualized education programs (IEPs) should involve input from students, parents, and family members, write one IEP annual goal and three short-term objectives that might be appropriate in the area of reading based on the information provided.
3. This assessment of functional vision has specific purposes. Based on your reading, what are the purposes of doing this evaluation?
4. What aspects of the school and classroom ecology are pertinent to Kim's learning that might not matter so much to fully sighted students?
5. Due to the purposes of this evaluation, we are left wondering about issues concerning Kim's emotional adjustment and social support at home and school. What additional information would help you as a teacher work with Kim and her family?
6. *Activity:* Go to the library or interview a knowledgeable practitioner to learn about the current types of technology that can be used with a student with low vision.

 CASE **28. JUAN**✭

Issues: Instructional methods/techniques

After suffering a head injury in an accident involving a rifle, Juan goes through an intense period of hospitalization and rehabilitation. Gradually, his physical and emotional health are restored. He returns to Jerry Kramer Middle School with a visual impairment that requires modified forms of instruction for his success.

Mr. Sanchez slammed his foot on the gas pedal and the pick-up truck lurched into motion. It fishtailed off the dirt road and jumped up onto the pavement.

"Oh God. Oh God." Mr. Sanchez repeated, his eyes shifting anxiously between the road ahead and his wounded son slumped at his side. Fifteen-year-old Victor's jeans were soaking with blood as he held his younger brother

Juan in his lap. Mr. Sanchez had told his sons a thousand times to be careful with a loaded rifle. But there Juan lay, unconscious and bleeding profusely from a gunshot wound to the head.

Doctors and nurses at the nearby hospital were able to save Juan's life. He spent three months in the hospital and rehabilitation unit. The bullet wound to the head caused two serious disabilities for this sixth grader at Jerry Kramer Middle School. The brain injury impaired his vision and his mobility. His visual impairment consists of a complete, bilateral loss of the left visual field. This means that Juan lost the ability in both eyes to see the left half of what most people see. His vision consists of half pictures, as if a shade had fallen to create a blank area to the left. Additionally, the injury produced a physical disability, a near-total paralysis of the right side of his body.

Juan underwent an extensive rehabilitation process. Specialists worked with Juan to prepare him to build the visual and physical skills required to live at home and go to school. The rehabilitation unit staff aided Juan as he grieved the loss of important parts of himself. At first, he refused to talk or participate in the various therapies. A talented psychologist named Dr. Morse ate lunch with Juan every day, talking and reading the newspaper sports page to him even when the depressed boy refused to talk.

One day, after weeks of one-sided lunch conversations that made Dr. Morse look a bit foolish, Juan finally talked. In fact, he screamed and moaned and screeched at Dr. Morse for ninety minutes, demanding that the psychologist somehow heal his sight and mobility. That was the angry beginning of a close and pivotal relationship in Juan's life. In Dr. Morse, he found a caring figure to lead him through an intensely difficult period, a person to inspire him to learn how to operate his wheelchair and to learn how to plan for a worthwhile future. He also found a mentor, someone to stir his interest in a future in the field of psychology. Juan is resolved to go to college to become a psychologist.

When Juan returned to Kramer Middle School, he was quickly declared eligible to receive special education services due to his visual and physical impairments. Juan gets one period per day in a resource class, providing extra time in completing class assignments. Juan is learning to write with his left hand. He is also learning to read with only half of a visual field. This means working to acquire skills necessary to be aware of and use the visual information presented on the left side of the body. Juan practices scanning for objects on the left so that he will develop a habit of looking beyond his limited field of vision.

Additionally, Juan is receiving remedial instruction in mathematics. The loss of the left side of his visual field has made the completion of math problems difficult. Juan often does not see important information on the left side of the page. Moreover, he doesn't realize that he is missing anything. Sometimes he doesn't see the entire problem. Sometimes he fails to see and compute the digits holding far left place value positions.

Juan's teacher has taught him a strategy to ensure that he sees all the numbers to be used in a given computation. Before beginning each problem,

Juan visually locates the number of the problem at the left margin of the page. From this starting point, Juan then allows his vision to shift right to read the mathematical information to be used in the computation. When he remembers to use this strategy, Juan doesn't miss out on any aspect of the problem.

In Juan's regular classes, he studies science and social studies and content area subjects like any other student. A teacher for students with visual impairments provides consultation services to support the efforts of Juan's various subject area teachers, helping them adapt their instructional methods and materials to meet Juan's needs. For example, many of Juan's teachers rely heavily on lectures as the primary means of instruction. Juan benefits from having a peer take notes for him so that he doesn't miss any of the material. Also, when using charts, maps, writing on the chalkboard, or other visual aids, Juan's teachers cue Juan to the far left edge of the visual presentation. This assures that Juan does not overlook necessary information. A third adaptation Juan's teachers have made is avoiding lecturing or presenting visual information from near the window. Juan has difficulty with the glare of the window light.

The accidental shooting with a hunting rifle that caused Juan tremendous pain ironically brought about a hopeful turn of events in his family. At the time of the accident, Juan's parents had been divorced for over five years. He lived with his mother. His brother Victor lived thirty miles away with their father. Juan spent every other weekend with his father and brother, often hunting and fishing in the rural area where his father lived. The accident seemed to unite Juan's parents in a new way as they rallied to his cause. While he was in the rehabilitation unit, Juan noticed that his parents, who had barely spoken a civil word to each other for years, were visiting him together. They seemed to be growing close.

After Juan returned home to his mother's house, his parents continued to mend their past differences and build the beginnings of a renewed relationship. Juan has become hopeful that his parents will remarry and his family will be back together under one roof. Perhaps that is why the accident happened, Juan reasons to himself. Maybe this loss will serve some positive purpose.

QUESTIONS

1. What other instructional modifications can you think of that might help Juan in his regular classes?
2. Can you recall a helping professional like Dr. Morse, perhaps even a teacher, whose assistance and care inspired you?
3. Understandably, Juan went through a serious depression soon after his injury. How can the teachers at Kramer Middle School help him to continue to cope with the emotional pain of losing significant visual and physical abilities?
4. Juan's classmates have known him for years. Suddenly he returns in a different form. What can teachers do to help Juan's peers feel comfortable with their changed friend?

5. Do you think that Juan's hopes that his parents will remarry are realistic?

6. *Activity:* Visit a children's hospital rehabilitation unit to learn about the types of serious injuries that children sustain and how the rehabilitation program works to prepare these young patients to return to home and school.

 CASE 29. SAMMY

Issues: *Consultation/collaboration*

Sammy is a high school student with glaucoma, an illness gradually decreasing his field of vision. His greatest asset is a roaring sense of humor. Mrs. Kopriva, the specialist in educating students with visual impairments, and Mrs. Lansing, Sammy's new teacher, discuss Sammy and plan for his education.

Mrs. Kopriva, the itinerant teacher for students with visual impairments, and Mrs. Lansing, the high school teacher for students with mild and moderate developmental disabilities, met after school to prepare for the arrival of a unique new student.

"The greatest thing about this kid is his sense of humor. When I first met him, we spent twenty minutes together and my cheeks were aching from laughing so hard!" Mrs. Kopriva exclaimed. "He reminds me of how Robin Williams is when you see him on a TV talk show."

"You mean kinda frantic?" Mrs. Lansing asked.

"Yeah, that's it, just incredibly on and wired and racing all about. His mind runs a mile a minute."

"That's great. I have to admit that I'm pretty nervous about teaching a blind student, so I could use the levity to break up my nerves." admitted Mrs. Lansing. "I mean . . . you know . . . he is *completely* blind?" Mrs. Lansing blurted out immediately. In her twelve years experience in a self-contained special education classroom, she had never taught a student with a visual impairment. A mixture of overwhelming excitement and a hint of fear were evident in her boisterous manner.

"No. He has a fair amount of useful vision. He has glaucoma. His primary visual problem is the limitation of his visual field." explained Mrs. Kopriva, an experienced educator of blind and low-vision students. "It's like the way race horses wear blinders that cut off their peripheral vision. Gradually, Sammy's peripheral vision is deteriorating. The central avenue that he can see is growing smaller as the blind spots on the sides grow larger."

"Oh! That must be terribly frightening for him," Mrs. Lansing exclaimed, "Why is that happening?"

"With glaucoma, the pressure inside the eye is elevated by a build up of fluid. The pressure against the optic nerve at the back of the eye causes the visual problems."

"And the tunnel vision keeps getting worse?" asked Mrs. Lansing.

"Yes," replied Mrs. Kopriva, "The tunnel typically becomes progressively smaller with time. Right now Sammy has a visual field of about 40 degrees. Eventually he will lose all sight. One of our jobs is to prepare him academically for that day when he can no longer see at all."

"What do you mean by 40 degrees?"

"Well," Mrs. Kopriva paused to consider how to explain this aspect of Sammy's disability, "If you look straight ahead, you can see all that's in front of you and the areas in the periphery, to your left and right. That would be a visual field of about 180 degrees. Your visual field is probably a bit less than that since you really can't see all the way over to the sides of your head. Sammy's visual field has narrowed down to about one fourth of that, just a 40 degree band directly in front of him. Additionally, he also has a nystagmus. That's like a shaking of the eye, an involuntary, rhythmic motion that sometimes occurs."

Mrs. Lansing looked worried. "Is that shaking painful?"

"No," Mrs. Kopriva smiled, "but it can further limit Sammy's ability to focus."

"Don't his eyes hurt from all that pressure?" Mrs. Lansing continued to be concerned about her new student experiencing pain during the school day.

"He's taking medication to reduce the pressure. He occasionally rubs his eyes, and he has had headaches in the past. Recently, the medication has been doing a good job on the pressure and he hasn't had headaches."

Mrs. Lansing breathed a sigh of relief. She was both enthusiastic and frightened about the challenge of educating Sammy in her classroom. She was pleased to have Mrs. Kopriva providing special services for portions of four days per week. She knew it would be good to have a knowledgeable person nearby to talk to as problems came up.

The two educators shifted their discussion from the physiology of Sammy's condition to the educational strategies necessary to effectively teach him. Mrs. Kopriva explained that Sammy would need instruction in printed language and Braille. Sammy was able to read at about a third grade level. But his visual abilities had been gradually decreasing over the years. In anticipation of his further loss of sight, Mrs. Kopriva and his prior teachers had worked with him on learning to read and write in Braille. Mrs. Kopriva recommended that Sammy continue in functional literacy instruction with standard print and Braille.

"I also want to forewarn you of one odd behavior that Sammy does. In fact, quite a few blind students do this. I call it 'flicking.'" Mrs. Kopriva explained as she demonstrated with her hand. "Sometimes he'll flick his hand back and forth above his eyes. It changes the flow of light into the eye from light to dark, light to dark, a quick alternation."

"Why does he do that?" asked an intrigued Mrs. Lansing.

"No one can be sure, but many think it provides a form of visual stimulation. You can redirect him to his task. Don't make a big deal out of it. Just don't be surprised if you see it."

"OK, I got it."

To Mrs. Lansing, the area of greatest concern was social. She moved on to ask about this. "I'm wondering about how Sammy will fit in and make friends with the other students. Should I tell all the students about his visual impairment on the first day? Or maybe I should avoid drawing attention to him. It would be embarrassing to have your teacher tell everyone about your disability. And how will he get around the classroom and the school?"

"Don't worry," Mrs. Kopriva comforted her anxious colleague, "he'll have no trouble getting around. As for the first day of school, I think you and I can pull Sammy aside and ask him how he wants to handle things. I've worked with all sorts of kids. Some want to tell the world about their disability, and some want to hide it and try to remain unnoticed. I generally encourage students to be honest with themselves and their peers without making too big a deal out of it. What we want for Sammy's peers is an understanding that he is just a kid like everyone else, no better, no worse. We can teach them about his disability in order that they can understand it and get over it, move past the novelty of it. Then they can play with and care about Sammy as a person."

"I think you're right," agreed Mrs. Lansing. "My students are usually curious about new and different things. One year I had a student with no hair. She had cancer and she was undergoing chemotherapy treatments. At first, the kids were dazzled by the bald head and the whole idea of cancer. We talked quite a bit about cancer and the treatments. Pretty quickly, though, cancer was boring and games of kickball were the priority. They just went on with life as usual. The strangeness wore off and being friends took over."

"Exactly!" declared Mrs. Kopriva. "We educate the peers about the condition so that being friends can take over. And don't worry, with this kid's comedy routine, friendship will certainly take over."

QUESTIONS

1. Mrs. Kopriva seemed to say that if Sammy wants to try to hide his visual disability, he should be supported in doing so. What do you think? Should the efforts of a student with a visual impairment conceal the disability be assisted by teachers? Explain.

2. Is it likely that the other students will become accustomed to Sammy's disability as easily as these teachers claim? Why or why not?

3. Should a student like Sammy who has both a visual impairment and a mental handicap be educated in a special class for the visually impaired, the mentally handicapped, or the regular education classroom? What are the possible benefits and risks of each placement?

4. In this vignette, Mrs. Lansing, although anxious, is supportive of Sammy's placement in her class. What could Mrs. Kopriva do in working with a teacher who is not fully supportive of the placement of a visually impaired student in her room?

5. What concerns and fears would you have in teaching a student with a visual impairment?

6. *Activity:* Research further on the various types of glaucoma and how they effect the education of a student who has glaucoma.

 ## 30. WINSTON

Issue: Transition

> *Winston is a recent high school graduate who spends his time hanging around his mother's house and surfing the Internet. Due to his vision impairment, he may receive assistance in finding or preparing for employment from a vocational rehabilitation (VR) counselor. He has continuously put off going to see the counselor. Finally, his old classmates and special education teacher show up at his house to encourage him to go to VR.*

The telephone rang. Winston stirred for a moment, rolling over beneath the bundle of covers. Finally, the answering machine picked up. The sleepy teen poked his head out of bed to catch the message broadcast after the beep.

"Winston! It's after eleven." It was his mother, calling to check up on him. "I hope this means you're not home, that you went to see that VR counselor like I want you to. I'll see you when I get home from work."

"Ugh!" groaned Winston as he sat on the edge of his bed and held his head. He felt guilty. He had agreed to take the bus downtown to see Mr. Harris, a vocational rehabilitation counselor who supposedly specialized in helping blind teenagers get training for employment.

Winston had been putting off going to Mr. Harris for months, since his high school graduation in June. Now that he thought about it, he had avoided going for a vocational rehabilitation assessment for at least a year before that, putting off the teacher of students with visual impairments (VI) at his high school, cajoling her with stories about not being ready yet, not having enough confidence yet. That Mrs. Askew was nice, maybe too nice. She never wanted to push Winston. Here he was, out of school, mid-November, unemployed with no prospects, living at home with his mother and 9-year-old sister without out a cent in his pocket. All he did was sleep, eat, and surf the Internet.

But he was learning much on the Internet. In the past three months, since he received a new computer for his eighteenth birthday, Winston had become a self-made expert on finding Internet sites that are accessible to blind computer users. Recently, he made a new cyberfriend, a blind man living in Nova Scotia, who started teaching Winston how to design webpages accessible to persons with vision impairments and other disabilities. Feeling insecure about his ability to learn how to do something so technical, Winston had not told anyone about his webpage interests.

Winston reached a hand under his mattress and pulled out a large, folded piece of paper, faded and worn around the edges of the folds. He spread the paper out across his bed. Running his fingers along the paper, he read the Braille map of the city bus system. With his fingers, he traced out the route from his house across the bridge, changing buses at Madison and Lake, then traveling west to the Fifth Street Station.

"Disembark there," he said to himself. He liked the sound of the word "disembark." He heard his mother use the word every time she explained to him how to take the bus downtown. He looked forward to that evening when he knew his mother would explain the route one more time and plead for him to go down to see Mr. Harris. He didn't feel so lonely when his mother was explaining the route to him.

From the Fifth Street Station, Winston knew it was only six blocks walking to the east. Off the bus, turn left, six busy city blocks. Winston knew there was lots of pedestrian traffic in the business district. He pictured himself making the entire trip. Roscoe, his seeing eye dog, would sit at his side on the bus. When they boarded the bus, Winston would even crack a joke to the driver, ask him if he had to pay two fares. Ha ha ha ha.

Roscoe would earn his keep once they disembarked and took to the streets. Although Roscoe hadn't been out of the house much lately, Winston still pictured his faithful yellow dog leading the way through the bustling traffic.

In the center of the sixth block, between 10th and 11th Streets, was a set of flags, an American and a state flag. Winston's mother said you could hear them fluttering on any day with wind. The flags stood next to the stone steps that lead into the government building. Once inside, Mr. Harris's office was on the twenty-eighth floor. Winston imagined himself and Roscoe stepping off the elevator, walking down the hall, and entering the vocational rehabilitation office.

"What time is it?" Winston would ask the receptionist.

"Ten minutes of ten," she would reply in a kind voice.

Hmmm. I'm early, Winston would think as he'd sit down to await his ten o'clock appointment.

At least, that's how Winston imagined it would go.

Hopping out of bed, Winston wandered into the kitchen in his underwear. He popped two pieces of bread into the toaster and turned on the television for company. As he leaned against the kitchen counter and scratched Roscoe behind the ears, the doorbell rang.

"Who is it?" Winston shouted through the front door of the small house.

"It's Mrs. Askew. And I brought some friends."

"Just a minute!" Winston called as he scrambled up the stairs to find a pair of pants. That's all he needed was for his old VI teacher to see him in his underwear. Besides, wondered Winston as he reached under his bed for his blue jeans, what's Mrs. Askew doing here? And what friends?

Freshly clad in yesterday's dingy jeans and tee shirt, Winston opened the door. In walked Mrs. Askew and a series of adolescent voices that Winston knew all too well. The whole gang was there—Little Phil, Sarah, Billy Jessup, and even "Brainiac" Suarez. Winston greeted his old friends from the high school VI class with a mixture of joy and embarrassment.

After greetings, Mrs. Askew wasted no time. "We're taking you away with us, Winston. You have an 11:30 A.M. appointment at voc rehab." Mrs. Askew stated in a matter-of-fact tone. "So put on a shirt that doesn't smell."

"How'd you all get out of school?" Winston asked, changing the subject. "Isn't there school today?"

"Yeah, we got school. We're on a field trip," explained Billy Jessup in a strangely adult voice, "Today our class project is you, getting you off your butt and down to VR to get a job."

"I'm going to VR," Winston claimed defensively. "You don't have to take me. I already went down. It's just . . . they put me on a waiting list, you know, and all that red tape. It's just not for me. You know?" Winston backed up against the refrigerator.

Next, Winston heard Sarah's voice. He had always liked and respected her. She was kind and smart.

"Winston, your mom called the school. She's upset. She says she can't get you to go to VR and you're just sitting around the house."

"So?" Winston crossed his arms and shook his head sadly.

"So, we're gonna help you. Just 'cause you graduated from old Jefferson High doesn't mean we've forgotten you." Sarah reached out her hand and touched Winston's shoulder. He felt like stepping back, moving away, but he froze. Being a failure after graduation had been bad enough, but now everyone knew. And here they were in his kitchen. But they were not just there to bring shame but also help and encouragement. A part of Winston sensed that as he allowed Sarah's hand to remain on his shoulder.

"You want to bring Roscoe downtown?" Mrs. Askew asked.

"Yeah," Winston replied softly, "He's been reading that map with me for months. He'd die if I didn't take him."

"OK!" Mrs. Askew called out enthusiastically. "Everyone back in the van! And Winston. A clean shirt. Please."

"Yeah, all right, Mrs. Askew. Can I ask one thing though?"

"Sure, Winston. Today is your day." Mrs. Askew put her arm around her exstudent's shoulder.

"I've been thinking about this trip and planning it for a long time. And . . . I sorta have a way I want to do it." Winston spoke hesitantly.

"Your way is our way," encouraged the teacher.

"I want to take the city bus."

Questions

1. Looking at Winston as an individual and his family system, what do you think is going on with Winston? What is his problem and why is he having it?

2. What could Mrs. Askew have done while Winston was a student to avoid this problem?

3. What are the possible risks and benefits of the intervention that Mrs. Askew and her students performed when they visited Winston's house?

4. Transition typically involves a shift from school-based services for students with disabilities to a maze of adult services located in the community. What possible problems does this case demonstrate in the transition between the two groups of services?

5. What do you think would happen to Winston if not for the rather extraordinary effort of his former teacher?

6. *Activity:* Go online and seek Internet sites that explain how persons with visual impairments or other disabilities access the Internet.

CHAPTER 9

INDIVIDUALS WITH
HEARING IMPAIRMENTS*

DEFINITION

"Hearing impairment" includes auditory disabilities of two broad degrees of severity: deaf and hard of hearing. The Individuals with Disabilities Education Act (IDEA)** defined deaf as a severe hearing impairment such that the child is unable to process speech through hearing, with or without amplification. Hard of hearing describes a mild to moderate hearing impairment, whether permanent or fluctuating, which adversely affects a child's educational performance but is not included under the definitions of deaf.

KEY TERMS

American Sign Language   A complete, free-standing (not attached to a spoken language), rule-governed communication system consisting of handshapes and hand movements.

aural rehabilitation specialist   Professional who helps persons with hearing impairments develop communication skills.

behind-the-ear hearing aid   A sound amplification/clarification device that fits behind and in the ear.

cochlear implant   A small, surgically placed, electronic device that provides a sense of sound to children and adults who have severe to profound hearing loss and who cannot hear and/or understand speech with hearing aids.

conductive hearing loss   A form of hearing loss caused by a dysfunction or malformation of parts of the outer and middle, including the ear canal, ear drum, three middle ear bones (ossicles), and the eustachian tube.

deaf culture   A way of life consisting of (sign) language, values, meanings, and social practices shared by deaf persons primarily in isolation from the numerous hearing cultures.

FM system   A radio communication device consisting of a microphone on the teacher's end and a receiver/amplifier/speaker system on the student's end.

---

* We are grateful to Buddy Coard for his contributions to this chapter.
** *Individuals with Disabilities Education Act Amendment of 1997*, 105th Cong., 1st Sess. (1997).

instructional modifications   Changes in typical or habitual classroom instructional forms and routines that are made to allow students with disabilities or other learning variations full access to knowledge and learning opportunities.

oral communication   The use of language forms spoken aloud.

psychoeducational assessment   A compilation of data collected through tests, observations, and interviews used by teachers and other school professionals to understand a student's strengths, weaknesses, and needs.

sensorineural hearing loss   A typically permanent form of hearing impairment caused by a dysfunction within the nerve cells of the inner ear.

Signed English   A system of handshapes and hand movements that represents the words, phrases, and sentences of spoken English.

total communication   A multiple approach to communication that combines manual (signing), oral, auditory, and written forms, depending on the particular needs of the child.

CASE 31. LADONNA

Issues: Instructional methods/techniques

At first glance, it seems like a cochlear implant is the ideal way for the Davis's to give the ability to hear to their 2½-year-old daughter Ladonna. Ladonna has a profound hearing impairment. The surgical implant, a small device, would facilitate the passage of some forms of auditory data to the brain, acting as a substitute for typical hearing processes. The Davis's must confront the possible problems of the cochlear implant as they consider this enormous decision.

The drive home from the doctor's office for Ladonna Davis, her parents, and her three older sisters seemed to take forever. As the youngest in the family, 2½-year-old Ladonna sat in a car seat next to her sisters in the backseat.

"Can't you speed up, Daddy?" Ladonna's sister Brenda called out in exasperation. "This is taking all day."

"Your father's thinking," defended Mrs. Davis. "Just leave him alone and we'll be home soon enough."

Mr. Davis was deep in thought. The surgeon at the university medical center had explained the procedure completely. At face value, a cochlear implant appeared to be the perfect remedy for Ladonna's profound hearing impairment. Through modern technology, the deaf child could be made to hear. Or so it seemed.

Ladonna was born profoundly deaf. She had sensorineural hearing loss, meaning that the neurological system that translates sound vibrations into electrical impulses and then sends those electrical impulses from the ear to the brain did not function correctly.

Ladonna's physician—an ear, nose, and throat specialist—recommended a surgical procedure called a cochlear implant. A small device could be placed in the brain to facilitate the passage of some forms of auditory data to the brain. A small wire would run from a tiny buttonhole in the back of the skull to a small processing unit about half the size of a Walkman. This processor could be affixed to the back of the child's belt.

The physician emphasized that the cochlear implant would not completely restore the child's ability to hear. Instead, it could only provide the child access to a limited range of auditory frequencies. What the child hears by way of the implant would sound odd to the average hearing person. The child who receives a cochlear implant must go through intensive, lengthy training to learn how to interpret the signals that the implant translates. Without proper training, the child gains no benefit from the implant.

The family sedan finally pulled into the garage. The girls in the backseat grumbled, "Took long enough!" and jumped out of the car. The entire family exited the car and entered the house. Except Mr. Davis. He sat in the front seat, unaware that he was alone in the garage, his mind running over everything he had ever heard about cochlear implants. This was not an easy decision.

Mr. Davis thought about a recent newspaper article that had been critical of the use of cochlear implants with children who have a low probability of fully using the device. The article claimed that many young children who receive cochlear implants are not good candidates for the apparatus. Much of the problem surrounds not the surgery but the extensive follow-up treatments necessary for the child to use the device. The article stated that some children lack the intellectual capacity or the motivation required to learn to interpret the implant's signals. Also, the families of some children do not provide enough support for the years of necessary speech and language therapy, typically two or more days per week. The therapy is expensive, involving payments for a speech and language pathologist, an audiologist, and the additional technology required for instruction. Many families cannot afford to pay for the speech and language therapy over an extended time.

The special education director of the local school district had reported that a number of children were entering public school with cochlear implants but little or no ability to hear and speak. For one reason or another, these children had either never received the necessary speech and language training or they received the training but did not master the use of the cochlear implant. As they entered school, many of their parents insisted that their children receive oral instruction to make use of the cochlear implant. Much to the parents' dismay, the school district judged that it was best to place these students in total communication programs where they could learn to use sign language, essentially giving up on the youngsters' chances of communicating in standard English. This disagreement in approach between parents and school personnel was ongoing and often heated.

Thanks in part to an excellent health insurance plan, Mr. Davis felt reasonably comfortable about his family's ability to handle the cost of surgery and treatment. But what if Ladonna was one of those children who goes through the surgery but never learns to interpret the signals? He was afraid of spending the next two to three years working with Ladonna only to find that she could not benefit from the implant. If they were to forego the implant, Ladonna could start to learn signing and speech immediately. She could be an able user of sign language by the time she entered first grade.

On the other hand, if the implant was effective, Ladonna would hear! She would be able to talk and play normally with her parents and sisters. It might even be as if she had never been deaf. And there was no time to waste. The doctor had said that immediate surgery would provide Ladonna with greater long-term benefits than if the surgery were delayed six months or a year.

Mr. Davis had seen a television report about a little boy in Texas who had the cochlear implant surgery at age 2. The boy was profoundly deaf, like Ladonna. By age 4, the little boy was speaking in full sentences. The speech and language specialist interviewed on the television said that the boy's oral language development was delayed, but that he was learning new words and phrases at such a rate that he might attain the same level of language use as his hearing peers by the time he entered first grade. Imagine that, Mr. Davis thought to himself, up to par by first grade.

A tug on his sleeve snapped Mr. Davis out of his ponderous trance. He turned to his left to see little Ladonna pulling on the elbow of his shirt, pleading for him to come inside the house with her. From her grinning mouth came a strange jumble of gurgles and noises. Out of that mouth, he conjectured, may come words, all sorts of wonderful words and brilliant ideas. He placed an index finger on his daughter's lower lip. She laughed and nibbled at the giant finger with her tiny front teeth.

"Honey!" Mrs. Davis called from inside the house. "Are you coming in to help me make dinner?"

"Yeah. OK," he replied from the front seat of the car, his eyes fixed on his daughter's mouth as she bit down on his index finger. He then looked up through the windshield at the wall of the garage with his lawn tools and gasoline powered appliances hanging neatly in a row. Ladonna snapped down hard on his finger.

"Ow!" Mr. Davis wailed as he snatched his wounded finger back from the crunching jaws. Ladonna roared with laughter. If only she could hear her own laughter, Mr. Davis thought. Maybe, he concluded as he scooped up his screeching daughter, that implant would do the trick.

QUESTIONS

1. What seem to be the possible risks and benefits of Ladonna receiving the cochlear implant?
2. How might the decision to receive or not receive the cochlear implant impact the types of speech and language instruction Ladonna will receive?
3. How might the decision to receive or not receive the cochlear implant impact the degree to which Ladonna is integrated into hearing society in the future?
4. Some persons in the deaf community have criticized cochlear implants as an unnecessary treatment for a nonexistent disease. Why would someone hold this opinion?
5. Why do you think the doctor said that Ladonna would receive greater benefit from the implant if it were installed sooner rather than later?
6. *Activity:* In your library, research the controversy within the deaf community and the broader society over cochlear implants. Some deaf persons support the use of implants. Some vehemently oppose implants. Learn more about this interesting conflict.

CASE 32. TIFFANY

Issues: Educational goals/objectives

Tiffany is an 11-year-old girl with a severe hearing impairment. This psychoeducational assessment report contains information from a number of intellectual, functional, and academic tests.

The following is a complete psychoeducational assessment report.

COMPLETE PSYCHOEDUCATIONAL ASSESSMENT REPORT

Background Information

Tiffany is an energetic and curious 11-year, 9-month-old girl with a profound hearing impairment. Her developmental history is nonremarkable until the age of 15 months when she contracted meningitis. At that time it was discovered that she lost most of her hearing. Her last audiological examination was conducted three months ago. Tiffany has a 90 dB loss in her left ear and a 115 dB loss in her right ear. This was not a change from previous evaluations. She currently uses bilateral behind-the-ear hearing aids. When talking with her, she told me that her hearing aids only help give her environmental information.

Since learning of her loss, the parents have enrolled Tiffany in educational programs for the deaf. After visiting many programs they decided that the sign language approach would benefit their daughter most. Both parents attend sign language classes weekly. The family has been signing to their daughter since she was 19 months old. Her grandparents do not sign, but have shown an interest in learning.

At present, Tiffany is in a self-contained program for students who are deaf with mainstreaming in math, social studies, and science at the fourth grade level. The teacher of the deaf reports that her reading is below grade level, but improving. All instruction in the mainstream is provided through an interpreter.

Explanation of Tests Used

During the evaluation American Sign Language was used by the examiner and Tiffany as the communication method. She willingly came with the examiner to the testing room. Once in the testing room Tiffany was curious about what was in the examiner's bag and on the table. She asked questions about what I had in the bag and what the things on the table were for. Rapport between Tiffany and the examiner was maintained throughout the session.

The Nonverbal Scale of the Kaufman Assessment Battery for Children (K-ABC, 1983) was administered. This is an individualized intelligence test developed for children $2^1/2$ to $12^1/2$ years of age. Since the Nonverbal Scale was designed to assess the mental processing of children with communication difficulties such as Tiffany, only the age appropriate subtests of this scale were administered. The tasks required for the five subtests on the Nonverbal Scale provide measures of Tiffany's ability to precisely copy hand-tapping sequences and repeat them to the examiner, to assemble identical colored triangles in accordance with an abstract design, to make visual analogies, to recall the locations of randomly arranged pictures, and to order a randomly placed set of photographs in their proper time sequence of events.

The Meadow/Kendall Social Emotional Assessment Inventory was administered to assess Tiffany's social adjustment, self-image, and emotional adjustment to her hearing loss. This test was normed on individuals who were hearing impaired and administered as a rating scale completed by two people who know the student well.

In addition to the two previously mentioned assessment tools, the spelling and mathematic sections of the Kaufman Test of Educational Achievement: Brief Form (K-TEA) were administered. These test sections measure spelling of words from a dictated list and mathematical computation skills. The spelling test was administered by signing the word and asking Tiffany to write the spelling of the signed word.

Testing Results—K-ABC

Some confusion occurred with the hand movement subtest in that Tiffany did not understand the appropriate way to respond to the test. Nevertheless, after the examiner taught the first two items to Tiffany, she seemed well-focused and motivated for the task. Tiffany worked on the Triangle subtest with great attention to detail, often adding just one triangle at a time and then comparing the product with the picture. In addition, on all items Tiffany started on the left-hand side and preceded from the bottom up. She had no problem with the other test items.

When the seven chips of the matrix analogies were introduced, Tiffany had a problem in understanding that the chip needed to be placed in the correct orientation. The test protocol states that the examiner may only teach the correct orientation once. Since Tiffany had problems with orientation, the subtest was discontinued. Tiffany offered many answers that were the reverse of the correct answer on the spatial memory subtest.

Overall, Tiffany's performance on the nonverbal subtest using the 90 percent confidence level illustrated below intellectual capabilities compared to children her age. She scored within the average range on the following subtests: triangles, spatial memory, and photo series, but below average on hand movement and matrix analogies.

Subtest	Scaled Score
Hand movements	6
Triangles	10
Matrix analogies	4
Spatial memory	8
Photo series	7

Testing Results—Meadow/Kendall

The Meadow/Kendall Social Emotional Inventory indicates that Tiffany is functioning within the average range in the areas of social adjustment, self-image, and emotional scale.

Testing Results—K-TEA

Tiffany had a standard score of 84 on the mathematics section. Her main problems occurred in the questions that required her to add fractions and make equivalent fractions and those problems that required more than simple division and multiplication. In the spelling section, she had a standard score of 71. All words were signed to Tiffany and she would write the words on the answer sheet. Some of the words she was able to spell were: across, Saturday, circle.

Testing Results—Other

No formal reading measure was given. Her teacher of the deaf shared that Tiffany receives instruction in a small group and that she uses a whole language and language experience approach. The teacher estimates that the material used is at the mid-second grade level. The teacher is transitioning Tiffany from picture books to chapter books. Tiffany is able to read well, but has difficulties with comprehension and answering "what kind" and "how" questions.

Summary

Tiffany is an 11-year, 9-month-old student who is profoundly deaf and receiving education in American Sign Language in both a self-contained and fourth grade mainstream classrooms. Her overall cognitive functioning was in the below-average range; however this should be viewed as a minimal estimation of her cognitive functioning due to her hearing impairment. Her academic functioning in the areas of spelling and reading average around the middle of second grade. Her math skills are low fourth grade. Tiffany's social/emotional functioning is average in the areas of self-image, social adjustment, and emotional adjustment.

QUESTIONS

1. Much of the assessment battery used in this evaluation is standard for any child, hearing or nonhearing. What adaptations did the examiner make in the testing protocol? Why? How could this influence the results of the tests?
2. This text emphasizes the importance of the various ecological systems that surround and interact with a child. What information about the ecological systems in Tiffany's life is/is not included in this report? Discuss.

3. Tiffany's teacher reportedly uses a whole language approach to literacy instruction. How can this be done with a profoundly deaf student like Tiffany?

4. Do you think that Tiffany would benefit from a phonetic approach to reading instruction? Why or why not?

5. Keeping in mind that individualized education programs (IEPs) should involve input from students, parents, and family members, write one IEP annual goal that might be appropriate in the area of either reading/literacy skills or mathematic skills. Write three short-term objectives that might be appropriate to that annual goal.

6. *Activity:* In the assessment report, Tiffany is described as having below-average intellectual functioning and academic skills. The examiner also hints that the limitations of the instruments may underestimate her abilities. Research the following question in the library or by interviewing knowledgeable practitioners: Do students with profound deafness typically score average on standardized tests of intellectual functioning and academic skills? If not, what role do the limitations of the tests play in their scores?

 C A S E 33. EMILY

Issue: Social diversity

Emily is a sixth grader with a hearing impairment who is educated in a general education class. When the battery on her hearing aide expires, Mr. Christian, an aural rehabilitation specialist, tries to find Emily's parents to arrange for a new battery. Emily's parents both struggle with drug addiction and frequently move from one address to another.

One! Two! Three!
With three rhythmic hand claps, Ms. Juarez brought her sixth grade class to order. The thirty-two children sat silently, their papers, books, and pencils set down for the moment, their eyes fixed on their teacher in anticipation of her words.

One of the students, Emily Stuart, did not stop her activities. Humming lightly under her breath, Emily stood in the Book Corner, a small area at the rear of the room consisting of three full bookshelves, a large throw rug, and a series of beanbag chairs. Her back turned to the rest of the class, Emily continued to pick through the shelves in search of an appealing storybook for her independent reading.

"Emily. Emily." Ms. Juarez called the youngster's name into a microphone that hung by a cord around the teacher's neck. Emily also wore a cord bearing a small amplification/reception unit on her chest. Wires ran from the amplification unit up to the small earphones that fit neatly into her ears. When functioning correctly, this FM radio system allowed Emily to directly hear her teacher's words.

Emily had been born with a moderate to severe hearing impairment of unknown origin, a mixed loss of sensorineural and conductive hearing. This means that she had significant deficits in her ability to conduct sounds within the ear and her ability to then translate those vibrations into neurological signals for comprehension by the brain.

Emily and Ms. Juarez relied on the FM system to help Emily weed out the troublesome background noise of the busy regular education classroom. Emily could specifically attend to her teacher's directions and instructions. Unfortunately, on this morning, as the entire class interrupted their activities to listen to Ms. Juarez, Emily did not hear the call to order.

Ms. Juarez quickly delivered instructions for the children to begin to cleanup their materials in preparation for lunch. As the group began the cleanup, the teacher walked back to Emily, moving around to within the child's view.

"Emily. Did you hear me give the instructions for the class to begin cleanup?" Ms. Juarez asked. Emily noticed that her teacher's lips moved but no words came through her earphones. She pulled the earphones out, jiggled them about, and replaced them in her ears.

"Can you hear me, Emily?" the teacher tried again.

Emily shook her head and mumbled a soft "no." Although her speech skills were coming along well, at times of frustration and anxiety, she tended to either not speak or to speak softly.

"Watch my lips, Emily," Ms. Juarez instructed. Emily focused on her teacher's lips as she spoke. "Your FM unit isn't working correctly. Have you been having trouble with it?"

Emily nodded shyly.

"How long has it been broken?"

Emily's eyes were cast to the floor as if in shame over the dysfunctioning assistive device. "Two days," she admitted in a whisper.

"Two days? The whole weekend? " the teacher asked in surprise.

The student again nodded.

Ms. Juarez opened up the rear of the amplifier/receiver unit that hung around Emily's neck. About the size of a small transistor radio, it was fastened to her chest with straps. When Ms. Juarez opened the battery compartment, she found that the unit had no battery. No wonder it didn't work.

"Emily. It's not broken. There's no battery in it. Do your parents know the battery's missing?"

As her teacher spoke, Emily stopped lipreading and began to sway her head back and forth. She seemed to be either terribly bored or uncomfortable with the subject raised by her teacher.

"OK," Ms. Juarez concluded quickly, noticing that the rest of the class was ready to go to lunch. "You pair up with Sally. She'll assist you through lunch while I try to get a battery." Ms. Juarez walked Emily over to Sally's side and explained to Sally that she would need to help Emily in the lunchroom because the FM unit was not working. Sally and Emily were best friends. The pair smiled and seemed to relish the idea of being lunch buddies.

Ms. Juarez knew that Emily would probably need no assistance in the cafeteria, but she felt more comfortable with Sally as an insurance policy. The incredible noise level in the crowded cafeteria effectively nullified any attempts to augment Emily's hearing. The sixth grader had gotten used to navigating the lunch line without being able to understand much of what was being said to her.

As the children walked to the cafeteria, Ms. Juarez slipped into the teacher's lounge to call Mr. Christian, the aural rehabilitation specialist who had worked with Emily and her family since Emily first began receiving services at age $3^1/_2$. Mr. Christian has provided the original in-home speech and language services to Emily and her family. As Emily grew and moved through the grades, Mr. Christian remained the case manager, organizing services and consulting with educators on issues related to Emily's placement in the mainstream classroom.

Mr. Christian and Ms. Juarez quickly agreed that he would contact Emily's parents to solve the battery problem. In the meantime, Emily could wear her old behind-the-ear hearing aids. They were not as effective as the FM system, but they were probably better than nothing.

Mr. Christian had his work cut out for him. The family did not have a telephone, and their address often changed every few weeks. Having worked closely with the family for four years, he knew that finding Emily's family could take days.

Emily lived with her mother, Gloria, her stepfather, Brent, and the couple's 4-month-old infant, Tricia. The parents had struggled with problems of poverty and drug addiction for years. The family bounced back and forth between apartments, homeless shelters, and living with various relatives.

Mr. Christian found that during periods when one of the two parents was clean of drugs, then the family became somewhat stable. They would remain at one address for months. Emily would attend school daily, her clothing clean and her mood relatively calm. However, during periods of increased drug and alcohol activity by both parents, chaos reigned. Rent money became drug money. The family moved from residence to residence quickly, and Emily missed many days of school.

The most reliable figure in this was Emily's grandmother, Gloria's mother Gabby, a sickly but spirited woman who lived in a low-income housing project. Gabby had a lung condition that required her to keep a large tube of oxygen at her side. She was a religious woman with an uplifting smile. Her hunched posture was the primary lasting benefit of many years of scrubbing floors in a downtown office building.

Mr. Christian knew that his search for Emily's parents would begin with a drive to Gabby's apartment. He and Gabby would sit at the kitchen table drinking iced tea and dabbing the sweat from their foreheads with dampened paper towels stored in the freezer. All the windows and doors in the cinder block flat would be wide open, fans would be spinning, but the two would bake in the May heat like stuffed turkeys on Thanksgiving. In the midst of all the discomfort, Mr. Christian would be talking to a woman who cared deeply about her daughter and her granddaughter. He knew that Gabby would help him find Emily's parents.

QUESTIONS

1. How can the stability or instability of a family impact the education of a student with a hearing impairment?
2. Is it possible that due to the instability of Emily's family she would be better served in a separate class for students with hearing impairments? Can the stability of the family be taken into consideration in a decision of least restrictive environment (LRE)?
3. What can school personnel do or not do to help Emily's family?
4. How can Ms. Juarez and Mr. Christian help Emily handle the daily challenges of school given the many family problems that affect her mood and ability every day?
5. Should Ms. Juarez and Mr. Christian have arranged to have a spare FM system battery available at school? Or is that the responsibility of the parents?
6. *Activity:* Research the functional difference between an FM system and a behind-the-ear hearing aid. What does each amplification system do? When is each the appropriate choice for a student?

 C A S E 34. HARI

Issue: Social diversity

Hari is a ninth grader attending a residential school for the deaf. This case recants the many difficult decisions his parents made over the years and the challenges of hearing parents raising a deaf child.

Hari Koul is a ninth grade student at the State School for the Deaf. He was born profoundly deaf, able to distinguish no sound. The cause for Hari's deafness is unknown. For educators, it is important to understand that Hari is prelingually deaf. That is, unlike a youngster who gains some oral language skills and acquires a hearing impairment *after* progressing through early stages of language development, Hari has experienced no oral language. He has neither spoken nor heard words and sentences. Whatever form of communication his parents chose for him to learn, he was starting from ground zero, a complete lack of language experience. That fact made the task of learning a language or form of communication immensely difficult during Hari's school years.

When Hari's parents first noticed his deafness at age 2, they had him evaluated by a hearing specialist. The evaluation confirmed their fears. The Kouls immediately searched in their community for the best educational and treatment program possible for their son.

The first program the Kouls looked at was the Vonnegut Center, a deaf education school dedicated to the teaching of oral communication. The Vonnegut Center taught young children with hearing impairments to speak

English and read lips, an attempt to normalize the students into the communication system of the hearing world. American Sign Language and signed English were not formal parts of the program.

The second program the Kouls considered was the Havlicek School, a facility that specialized in teaching deaf students total communication. Total communication is an instructional approach that combines oral language and sign language instruction, thereby allowing the student to access the spoken language of the hearing community and the sign language system of the deaf community. Students in the Havlicek program received speech and language therapy to help them learn to speak and read lips. Additionally, the students were taught signed English, a complex and demanding form of sign language in which the specific hand motions and body gestures are produced in conjunction with oral speech.

Since over half of the faculty and staff of the Havlicek School were deaf, the institution was an example of what has been called "deaf culture." In everyday use, the teachers, staff, and students conversed in American Sign Language, a system of communication that operates without spoken language. American Sign Language is not a derivative of English. It stands alone as a complete language. Through this means of communication, the students and employees of the Havlicek School created a community, a culture greatly isolated from the language and ways of mainstream hearing society.

The Kouls decided on the oral program, reasoning that their child would have the best chance to succeed in the hearing world if he could communicate in spoken English. If Hari could learn to speak and could learn to understand oral speech, he would be nearly normal. Wouldn't he? It seemed like the obvious choice at the time.

After two years of intense oral language instruction, 4-year-old Hari had made little gains in acquiring speech or language skills. The director of the Vonnegut Center recommended that Hari may benefit from a total communication program. While the director defended his school's oral program as suitable for most youngsters, he admitted that some deaf children are unable to acquire oral language despite quality instruction.

Mr. and Mrs. Koul shifted Hari over to the total communication program at the Havlicek School. Hari began to learn both signed English and American Sign Language. Hari's parents enrolled in the parent classes offered by the Havlicek School so that they could also learn to sign. They knew that it would be important that they become fluent in this second language (Hari's first language) to communicate with their son.

However, as frequently occurs, Hari blossomed into sign language, eagerly soaking up the language and the opportunity to communicate and connect with others. He was leaping from a world of isolation into a world of relationship. His signing skills developed quickly, while his parents struggled slowly to become even marginally proficient. Within a year, Hari had left his parents far behind in sign language proficiency.

Hari's father had never been a confident student during his school years as a boy in Kashmir. As Hari learned to sign, his father became frustrated at the difficulty of the new language. Gradually, he stopped attending the evening parents' classes at the Havlicek School and started doing overtime shifts at his job at the police department.

As Mr. Koul dropped out of the sign language class, Mrs. Koul felt an intense pressure to be the one member of her family who could talk to Hari. She knew that without her sign language skills, Hari would be a silent exile in their family. Worse, she would be unable to understand her son's hopes, dreams, and fears.

Soon after Hari's fifth birthday, Mrs. Koul gave birth to a baby girl, Aman, the family's second child. As she devoted herself to caring for her newborn, Mrs. Koul stopped working on her sign language skills. She knew that she was letting Hari slip away. With a new baby and a 5-year-old deaf boy needing her love and attention, Mrs. Koul felt pulled in two directions. Over the course of the next six months, Hari's parents' signing skills became rusty. They resorted to a series of basic signs and simple gestures to communicate with their son. Hari became increasingly frustrated with his parents.

On one occasion, Hari came home from a day at the Havlicek School feeling extremely upset. He had gotten into a fight that day with an older boy. He tried furiously to explain how the older boy had picked on him and how he felt helpless. But his hands flew in all directions, making complete sense to him but little to his mother.

"Write it down. Write it down," Hari's mother instructed him, pushing a pencil and paper into his hands. "I can't understand you. You'll have to write it down."

Hari broke the pencil in half and tore up the paper. He raced around the house bellowing odd sounds and crying. Mrs. Koul tried to calm him down. He grabbed a glass vase filled with flowers and held it above his head. Tears streamed down his cheeks as he stared at his mother. She seemed a thousand miles away, lost in another language. She walked forward and put her arms around him. The vase dropped to the floor with a crash as he crumpled into her arms. She held his small frame close to her body. The mother and son fell to the floor where the two of them cried themselves into exhaustion.

Two weeks later, Mr. and Mrs. Koul made the painful decision to send their boy to the State School for the Deaf, a residential school for deaf students located 150 miles from home. They would only see him for one long weekend once a month. Despite the incredible feeling of guilt they felt over sending their boy away, the Kouls knew they had little choice. Their son was growing into a world of language and friendship and learning. That world was based on American Sign Language. He needed to be among people who could speak his language.

At the State School, Hari prospered. During his seven years in attendance, the school has become his home. He has built a large friendship network. He is active in sports and drama. He is thankful that his parents understood that there were opportunities at the State School for the Deaf that he never would have found in his home community and in the mainstream setting of the local school district.

QUESTIONS

1. Often we here someone speak about African American, Asian American, or Cuban American culture. Is "Deaf Culture" a culture? What makes a cultural group? How is this different than a disability group?
2. Is American Sign Language an anti-inclusion communication system? Or is it a justified and useful mode of communicating?
3. Why is the age of onset of a hearing impairment important information in the process of planning a successful intervention program?
4. How does Hari's deafness impact his relationships with his parents?
5. What future options will be open to Hari after high school? What options will be closed?
6. *Activity:* Do library research on the many communication approaches to teaching persons with hearing impairments to communicate (oral, total communication, American Sign Language, etc.) Why are there so many different approaches and how do they differ?

 CASE 35. ANTHONY

Issues: Collaboration/consultation

Anthony is a high-achieving high school student who has a hearing impairment. He is educated completely in general education classes. Mr. Finkle is the special education teacher who consults with general education teachers to help them adapt and modify their instruction to Anthony's strengths. Mr. Finkle meets with Mr. Candlewood, the new English teacher, to introduce him to the rewarding art of teaching Anthony.

Mr. Finkle, the somewhat eccentric teacher of students with hearing impairments at Gergen High School, reached a hand into his mailbox along the wall of the teacher's lounge. He retrieved a piece of yellow note paper on which was scrawled:

> *Mr. F!!!!*
> *Talk to this new English teacher. He doesn't know the score. Also, can you help me with college applications? Essays to write. Also, can you call my Dad? He says he left you three messages. Don't you pick up your messages?*
> *Thanks, Anthony.*
> *PS: Your beloved 76ers lost AGAIN last night. They're so desperate they'll be suiting you up soon.*

On the back of the note, Mr. Finkle jotted down three notes of his own, reminders to himself.

Remember:
1) Set up meeting with new English teacher. Modifications for Anthony Z.
2) Call Mr. Z. Apologize lots.
3) Talk to Anthony about going into teacher's lounge. Pretend to be angry. Be convincing. Off limits and he knows it! Detention next time! That kind of stuff.

He stuffed the note into his right breast pocket, behind the pocket protector, into a deep chasm full of notes of all sizes, colors, and shapes. He placed a rubber band around his left wrist to remind himself to look in his pocket for the reminder note. His wrist jangled with a bundle of aging rubber bands.

As he walked down the hallway toward his office, Mr. Finkle heard a strange voice call his name, "Finkle! Are you Finkle?"

Mr. Finkle turned to see a small, portly gentleman peering over an armful of books at the other end of the hallway.

"Are you Finkle?" the man asked again sharply. His round body bustled toward Mr. Finkle with quick, firm strides. He seemed all business.

"Yes, that's me." As Mr. Finkle moved forward, he hurriedly searched every corner of his memory for traces of this man. Who could this be? Is this a parent? Did I forget an (individualized education program) IEP conference? Mr. Finkle puzzled. He plucked at the rubber bands on both wrists and dug a finger into the stack of reminder notes in his right breast pocket.

"Finkle?" the little round man thrust out his hand in greeting, "Candlewood. New English teacher. Actually, thirty years at Beaman Prep. But new to this school." He grasped Mr. Finkle's hand and whipped it up and down for a full ten seconds. When Mr. Finkle finally retrieved his hand, generally unharmed, the two teachers stepped into Mr. Candlewood's classroom to discuss the education of Anthony Zemecki, a twelfth grade student.

"This Zemecki kid in Senior English tells me he's . . . ah . . . blind. I don't buy it. Tell you why." Mr. Candlewood barked out sentences in a matter of fact tone. "I watched him closely. He reads. He writes. He walks the halls in appropriate fashion. He's no-"

"Mr. Candlewood?" the special educator interrupted meekly. "You're right. He's not blind."

"I knew it. Just another kid trying to pull a fast one on the new teacher. Well, you-"

"Mr. Candlewood?" Mr. Finkle interrupted again, this time more forcefully. "Anthony is not blind. He's deaf."

"Deaf? Then what's he doing here?" objected Mr. Candlewood. "Don't they have a school for kids like that?"

"Well, yes, there is an institute for the deaf, but Anthony is not enrolled there. He's enrolled here at Gergen. And he's an honor roll student."

"Honor roll? How can a deaf kid meet the standards for honor roll?" Mr. Candlewood demanded. "I've only had Zemecki in class for a week. And I'll tell you, he can't cut the mustard. His weekly quiz grade was a 67. That's a D in my book."

"To be more precise, Mr. Candlewood, Anthony Zemecki isn't completely deaf." Mr. Finkle went on under the assumption he had a willing audience. "He has a mild hearing impairment. As a young child, he suffered from repeated cases of otitis media . . . bad ear infections . . . that damaged the internal workings of both ears. He wears two hearing aids, the in-the-ear style that you can't easily see."

Mr. Candlewood seemed visibly perturbed. "You don't say. So you're the special ed teacher, right?"

"Yes, I'm the hearing impairment specialist assigned to Anthony."

"Good. So you'll be taking him out of my class, right? I mean, you are the one who is qualified to teach him. "Mr. Candlewood's stubby fingers ran nervously up and down his tie.

"No, Mr. Candlewood, my job is not to take him out of your class. Anthony has been successful in mainstream classes. He is planning to go to college next year." Mr. Finkle paused momentarily in response to the aghast look on his colleague's face, then continued, "My job is to consult with you about the kinds of instructional modifications you can make so that Anthony can succeed."

"Modifications to my instruction?" Mr. Candlewood leaped up out of his seat. "Are you asking me to give this deaf kid special treatment? I won't do it. I've worked in this field for too long to start letting slackers slide now. No can do."

"No, of course I wouldn't ask you to make it easy on him." Mr. Finkle gently counseled his colleague. "Anthony is an excellent English student who needs a demanding instructor. What I mean by modifications is not a watering down of the curriculum. Not at all." Mr. Candlewood grumbled under his breath slightly as he calmed down and returned to his seat. Mr. Finkle continued his explanation, "What I'm talking about is giving Anthony access to the knowledge of the course. For example, I'll bet you lecture quite a bit."

"Yes, of course, I've been lecturing on English and American literature for three decades." Mr. Candlewood stated proudly.

"And where does Anthony sit while you lecture?"

"Hmmm, let's see." The experienced English teacher pulled out a seating chart and searched for Anthony's name. " Sixth period. Zemecki. There. Back row. By the window."

"Your seating chart is alphabetically arranged, isn't it, Mr. Candlewood?"

"Yes, of course. Makes attendance a breeze."

"Here's the first modification." suggested Mr. Finkle, "Alphabetical order is great, but do it in reverse. Z's in the front. A's in the back. Anthony Zemecki gets a front row seat so he won't miss a single word of your lecture. You do want him to hear every word of your lecture?"

"Of course . . . hmmm," Mr. Candlewood pondered. "That sounds simple enough. Keep the alphabetical order, but put the deaf kid up front. OK. Is that all?"

"One more. This is a big one. Your classroom has to go."

"Go where?"

"It's a problem of signal-to-noise ratio. Students with hearing impairments like Anthony have trouble distinguishing between background noise and the teacher's voice. Your room is especially bad. A tile floor and the air conditioning units for the entire school are humming right next door. Too much background noise."

"What do I do?"

"I can handle it." Mr. Finkle reassured. "Mrs. Simon owes me a favor. I'll get her to switch classes with you for sixth period. Her room has carpeting and the air conditioners are a mile away. OK?"

"You can do that?"

"I can and I will."

Mr. Candlewood reached out his hand. Pleased with the arrangement, Mr. Finkle gladly offered his hand. Mr. Candlewood clenched the hand like a vise and jiggled it about until Mr. Finkle was certain all blood flow had ceased to his fingers. His hand finally returned, Mr. Finkle massaged his crumpled fingers. Then he pulled out a small note pad. He scratched himself a quick reminder:

Remember:
1) Get Simon to trade sixth period room for Candlewood's. Smile when asking. Stand straight or she'll comment on posture.
2) Keep hands in pockets when talking to Candlewood. Dangerous like a crab!

QUESTIONS

1. What additional classroom or instructional modifications can you think of that might help a high school student with a moderate hearing impairment?
2. What challenges does Anthony present to a teacher like Mr. Candlewood who is somewhat old-fashioned and fixed in his ways?
3. What strengths can you identify in Mr. Finkle's style of consulting with the general education teacher? What weaknesses?
4. One of the difficulties with working as a consulting special education teacher who serves one or more secondary schools is self-organization. How might Mr. Finkle improve his organization of his professional communications and activities?
5. One of Mr. Finkle's strongest selling points in his dealings with Mr. Candlewood is that Anthony is an excellent student. How might this consultation have been different if Anthony had a weak academic record or if Anthony were commonly considered to have a behavior problem?
6. *Activity:* Interview a special education teacher who helps high school teachers plan accommodations for students with hearing impairments. What accommodations has he or she found to be most effective?

CHAPTER 10

INDIVIDUALS WITH SEVERE AND MULTIPLE DISABILITIES

DEFINITIONS

The federal (IDEA)* definition of severe disabilities is:

> "children with disabilities who, because of the intensity of their physical, mental, or emotional problems, need highly specialized education, social, psychological, and medical services in order to maximize their full potential for useful and meaningful participation in society and self-fulfillment."

The federal (IDEA)* definition of multiple disabilities means:

> "concomitant impairments (such as mental retardation-blindness, mental retardation-orthopedic impairment, etc.), the combination of which causes such severe educational problems that they cannot be accommodated in special education programs solely for one of the impairments. The term does not include deaf-blindness."

KEY TERMS

attention deficit hyperactivity disorder (ADHD)   A disorder characterized by inattention, hyperactivity, and impulsivity, which may interfere with the child's educational performance.

biologically at-risk   An individual whose parent's biology, such as a genetic defect, place the child at-risk for developing learning or behavior problems.

cerebral palsy   Several conditions grouped under one label in which there is an impairment of the neurological system.

circle of friends   A group formed on a person's (with disabilities) behalf to serve as a social support network.

communication board   A board with large pictures that represent various requests, such as bathroom, drink, eat, go, stop, and so on. Because of poor communication skills, the communication board serves to supplement the individual's language.

---

* *Individuals with Disabilities Education Act Amendment of 1997,* 105th Cong., 1st Sess. (1997).

community-based activities   Functional academics (e.g., counting money) that are taught to students in a community setting such as a grocery store, bus stop, or fast-food restaurant.

environmentally at-risk   A student who lives in an environment that would place him or her at risk for developing learning or behavioral problems.

full inclusion   A program that places children with disabilities, despite the severity of disability, in general education (full inclusion) classes at proportional rates as those disabling conditions are found in the natural population. In this type of program, students typically receive all of their special education and related services in the general education (full inclusion) classroom.

functional skills   A term used to describe simple academic skills, such as counting money or telling time.

microswitches   Simple switches that turn on or off an action in a specially designed computer program.

partial participation   A term used to describe an individual's participation in an activity. Typically the individual contributes to the activity in a limited basis (partial basis).

response analysis   An analysis of student's responses to various stimuli.

E 36. TODD

Issues: Behavior management, transition

This case walks one through the typical day in the life of a student with
disabilities, as seen through the eyes of Todd, a student in the class.

Todd is a 20-year-old with moderate to severe mental and motor impairments caused by cerebral palsy (CP). Todd lives at home with his parents, Susan and Rich, and his brothers, Tom and Tadd. Todd attends his local high school, Susquenata High School, where he works in the school kitchen helping to prepare school lunches. Due to the school's Friendly Circle Project, he has been able to meet other students who are about his age; however, many of these classmates spend time with Todd only during school hours.

Intellectually and motorically, Todd has performed poorly on most assessments. For example, Todd has only earned a full-scale intellectual quotient score of 32 during his most recent reevaluation; and he scored low, a score of 20, on the Vineland Adaptive Behavior Scale. Despite being able to talk, Todd's speech is so severe that at times it is difficult to understand him. Consequently, Todd does most of his communication through signs and a small communication board that he carries with him.

Todd's typical day begins with his mother or father waking him at 6:00 A.M. His parents usually prepare a bowl of cereal for him, and Todd then uses a large spoon with a thick handle to feed himself. He also uses a large straw to drink most liquids. Most of the adaptations in Todd's life have been made because his severe tremors make fine motor skills difficult for him. He has made much progress over his fourteen years of schooling, mostly due to an educational program that has focussed on improving his motor and communication skills.

The special education school bus pulls up in front of his house to transport him to school. As his mother helps him board the bus, she asks the driver to watch Billy, another student with severe disabilities, who has been hitting Todd. The driver tells his mom that she'll keep her eye on him and helps place Todd behind John in a seat away from Billy. She also yells back to Billy, "Keep your hands to yourself. There will be no trouble on my bus." Billy looks on unaware of what is going on around him.

As soon as the bus reaches school, the part-time teacher aide, Janice, boards the bus and greets the students. Todd hops off first and begins to run toward the doors of the school. When she sees him in a full trot, Janice yells at Todd to slow down and to wait for her. As the students enter the building, it becomes obvious that the "special education" students (as they are referred to by the other students) have arrived. John is slapping himself in the face, as he always does when excited. Todd's odd gait and stomping of his feet as he walks announces his arrival. Billy's loud grunting sounds and tense facial expression tells the regular education students that he has arrived. As the regular education students linger around outside of their respective home-rooms, a silence falls over a once noisy hallway at Susquenata High School as Todd and his classmates pass by each classroom. As they walk down the middle of the hallway to their self-contained special education classroom, regular education students move aside in an attempt to get out of their way, reminiscent of the parting of the Red Sea. Day after day, this routine occurs twice—arrival and departure.

Once in the room, Billy immediately heads toward Ms. Queeny, another teacher aide, to give her a hug. Stopping him before he reaches her, Ms. Queeny reminds Billy that he needs to work at shaking hands or saying hello. She also adds, "You're too old to give hugs to women. It's not appropriate." Mrs. Murdock, the teacher, lets out a laugh and shakes her head, knowing that Billy has no idea what "appropriate" means. With eleven students in her class, Mrs. Murdock keeps physically busy throughout much of the day using hand over hand techniques with her students. When the bell rings, as if on cue, the students make their way to their desks. Mrs. Murdock takes roll and then begins calendar with the students. "Who can tell me what day today is?" she asks the class. None of the students respond. After a few seconds she provides the answer by saying, "Today is Tuesday." She writes it on the board and goes on to tell the students that in the afternoon they are going to take a trip to the local grocery store to start their training at stocking shelves. She reminds the students that they have practiced for weeks in the classroom and that now it is the "real thing."

In the classroom, Mrs. Murdock has students work on vocational activities. These activities are meant to simulate a worksite. While some of the tasks are nothing like the real-life tasks, they do represent one step closer on a chain of responses leading to actual tasks. For example, many of her fine motor tasks involve having students drop small pegs into a tin can with a small hole in the lid. Todd is usually involved with these types of activities because one of his individualized educational plan (IEP) goals is to improve fine motor skills. Most mornings are spent doing vocational tasks, leaving the afternoons open for functional skills and gross motor activities.

Finally, after lunch, the bus has arrived to take the class to the grocery store. As Mrs. Murdock and the aide get coats on the students, she reminds them that the purpose of the community-based trip is to show them where they could be working in the future. Fortunately for her, all but two of the eleven students are ambulatory. Motorically, all of her students can perform most gross motor skills such as walking and carrying objects.

Once at the store, they are greeted by the store manager, Mr. Tucker. Mr. Tucker had a son with a disability and now enjoys being involved in the lives of his "special kids." Mr. Tucker leads the group to the stockroom where he has prepared materials for the students to stock. He also introduces Jim to the group and tells them that Jim has worked stocking groceries for him for years. As planned, the students put on aprons and, as directed by the teacher and aide, begin to load boxes on a cart for stocking.

Once in the appropriate aisle, the students begin working in small groups of two or three students unloading the boxes and stocking the items on the shelves. As Todd begins stocking cans of beans on shelves, his tremors from his CP cause him to drop a can every now and then. Ms. Queeny, who is working with Todd's group, has to constantly remind him to keep his mind on his work. Occasionally Todd stops. Pointing to his picture of a toilet, he asks Ms. Queeny to go to the bathroom. She tells him "no" and five minutes later Todd asks again. She tells him, "Todd, you should have gone back at the classroom." Todd does not respond, but keeps pointing to the picture of the toilet. Finally, she agrees and tells the two other students to keep working while she takes Todd to the bathroom.

When Ms. Queeny returns, she finds her students rolling cans of soup down the aisle. At first she yells at them to stop, but they continue until she takes the cans out of their hands. Ms. Queeny also notices another student eating cereal from a box that he opened. She approaches the student, tells him to stop, but he does not. Finally, she takes the box from his hand and tells him to sit down, as a form of time-out. After hearing the yelling from two aisles over, Mrs. Murdock runs over to inspect the students' progress. For the most part, they have done well at stocking shelves. After her inspection, Mrs. Murdock rounds up all of the students and tells them it is time to return to school.

Once back at school, Todd heads toward the cafeteria, knowing it is time for him to work there. Seeing the other workers, Rosa and Wilma, Todd runs to give them a hug. They hug Todd and ask how he is doing. Todd responds with a thumbs up, meaning everything is going well. As the women begin to cook the food, Todd sets out the trays, plates, and silverware in preparation for the first lunch. When the bell rings, students rush in, grab trays and utensils, and hurriedly rush through the food line. All the while, Todd watches them with a smile. One student, who doesn't like Todd, walks past Todd and calls him a "retard." When one of the workers overhears this remark, she quietly says to Todd, "Don't listen to 'em." When the students finish lunch, they return the trays to the dishwashing area, where Todd loads the dishes into the dishwasher. Todd then heads back to the classroom to eat his lunch.

QUESTIONS

1. What do you think will happen to Todd after he graduates? Do you think he will be able to live independently? Work independently?
2. What behavior management would you set up to help Billy control his hitting behavior on the bus?
3. What are the benefits of having a self-contained special education class in a regular education school? What are the benefits for the students with disabilities? What are the benefits for students in regular education?
4. What are some age-appropriate ways to greet people? Is giving a hug considered one of them?
5. What are the benefits of Mrs. Murdock taking her students to the grocery store?
6. How would you handle a student calling Todd a "retard"? What would you do?

7. If this was your classroom, what could you do to ensure that your students were respected by and treated well by other students?
8. *Activity:* Visit a classroom for students with severe mental retardation. What are some skills that they work on in the classroom? What are some of the unusual activities that occur while you are observing?

---

 c**A**s e 37. KATHY

Issue: Inclusion

Kathy is a student with severe disabilities, causing her to participate in life in a different manner than other students her age would. Her parents and others have learned that sometimes small, steady gains are the "best" gains to make in life.

Kathy Klopski is a 12-year-old with multiple disabilities. Kathy is non-ambulatory and can move around only with the use of her motorized wheelchair. She exhibits severe communication and motor deficits and scored within the profound mental retardation range on a recent IQ test. Kathy lives at home with her parents, Carole and Bill Klopski, and her sister, Theresa. Kathy attends the local elementary school and is currently in a self-contained classroom with six other students, all of whom have severe disabilities.

Although she does have a communication board attached to the tray of her wheelchair, it is not of much use because she has a limited vocabulary. To communicate, Kathy uses a combination of gestures (e.g., she makes a fist and twists it to motion that she wants to go to the bathroom) and her communication board. She does not communicate much with other students unless encouraged. For instance, during calendar and morning activity, Kathy will say hello (gesture) to another student only after much prompting from the teacher or aide.

In the classroom, most of the academic activities that Kathy works on are tied to her individualized education program (IEP) goals of improving motor and communication skills. At school, the teacher, Ms. Dawson, has been working on the following skills with Kathy: using appropriate eye contact, increasing the number of gestures used for communication, communicating the greeting hello to another person, using the computer to aid in communication and learning, changing body positions in the wheelchair when sore, independently obtaining objects from the wheelchair, and feeding herself using a spoon. Daily, Ms. Dawson and the teacher aide work on the skills and monitor progress. Through multiple trials (opportunities for response), each person records the percent of correct responses and the time spent working with each child. Before the students leave for the day, Ms. Dawson completes a daily progress report and sends home one activity that should be completed. For example, Kathy's note asked the parent to spend fifteen minutes getting her to respond to the direction of a sound and to touch the object. The parents frequently respond to the teacher about their work with Kathy.

Carole and Bill Klopski are always actively involved in Kathy's life. They are constantly working with Kathy at home in the evenings and often spend weekends working with or getting her involved in community activities through "partial participation." Using partial participation, even though Kathy is not able to perform an activity independently, she is still given the opportunity to participate in the activity. Kathy recently became a Girl Scout with their neighborhood scout group. In addition, she and Carole are also involved in a local "Mothers and Daughters" social group. In the scout group, the scouting leader and organization make numerous accommodations for Kathy. She usually earns badges with the assistance of other scouts. For example, she earned her badge for first aid by watching another student conduct first aid on her and answering "yes" and "no" questions about first aid, even though she answered half of the questions incorrectly. At her "Mothers and Daughters" group, Kathy and her mom volunteer their time at community activities to raise money for various charities. At one recent activity, Kathy's mom made some baked goods and sold them with other mothers at the local shopping center. Kathy was also present and her mother said that her presence there helped to increase bake sales. Despite being known throughout the community, Kathy's limited communication skills make it difficult for others to talk to her or hold a conversation with her.

Kathy's teacher feels that Kathy has made much progress this year. Ms. Dawson has spent quite a bit of time working to get Kathy to respond in an appropriate manner to others, mostly through maintaining eye contact and making a limited number of gestures. Ms. Dawson, concerned with getting her students into the community more often, frequently takes her class on community outings. On one recent trip, they went to an animal farm. At the farm, the children were treated to petting and feeding the animals. As each child petted the animals, Ms. Dawson carefully noted their reactions so that she could report their trip to the parents. On another trip, the students visited a local fruit farm and were taken on a tractor ride around the farm. Later back at the school, the students tasted the different types of fruit and vegetables. Again, Ms. Dawson noted what occurred and reported this information to the parents in her daily notes. Ms. Dawson has a reputation of being an excellent teacher in the district; consequently, parents like Kathy's often request to have their children placed in her room.

During a recent IEP conference with the Klopskis, Ms. Dawson reported to Kathy's parents that she had made much progress this year. She started by telling them how Kathy has learned a new gesture to communicate (i.e., juice) and how Kathy has learned to extend her reach one inch farther since she started in her classroom. She then told them how, through the use of an electronic switch that turns on a tape player, Kathy learned to move her arms up higher in the air. As she reported on Kathy's progress of each objective, Ms. Dawson was proud at how much improvement Kathy had made since entering her room two years earlier. Throughout the meeting, Kathy's parents seemed strangely quiet.

When Ms. Dawson completed her update on Kathy's growth in her class, she turned to the Klopskis and asked what was wrong. Although pleased with her progress, the Klopskis heard of a radical, new program whereby *all* students, regardless of their disability, attend regular education classrooms. Commonly referred to as full inclusion, the concept is new to this district. As the Klopskis broke the news to Ms. Dawson and her supervisor, Mrs. Frew, that they would like Kathy to attend a regular education classroom next year, a silence fell over the room. Kathy's parents went on to explain that they felt that it was more important for Kathy to develop friends, rather than work on skills that she may never use. Next, the Klopskis related to the group of how they recently saw a TV show in which the students with disabilities at a school had developed a "circle of friends" with their regular education peers. They asked Ms. Dawson and Mrs. Frew why there weren't schools like these in the area. Taken back by the question, Ms. Dawson and her supervisor looked at each other and then told the Klopskis that these schools were still experimental. Not satisfied with this response, Kathy's parents demanded that her new IEP be written so that it reflects their request.

In an attempt to help the Klopskis understand the rarity of their request, Mrs. Frew explained how Kathy's goals and objectives were sequenced so that they built upon one another throughout the school year and over her lifetime. According to her, these goals and objectives could best be achieved in a self-contained classroom. Ms. Dawson said how successful the classroom program had been in the past for other students and how in a regular education setting the friendships that she would develop with other students would be only temporary. Mrs. Frew also mentioned that an inclusion classroom would not be feasible and would go against the current teaching philosophy of the district. After hearing these remarks, the Klopskis were steadfast in their position for a full inclusion classroom.

QUESTIONS

1. Inclusion has been defined in many different ways. How would you define "appropriate" inclusion? Why?
2. What are the advantages, if any, of Carole taking Kathy to her "Mothers and Daughters" activities? What are the advantages for Kathy? What are the advantages for others?
3. Should society make accommodations for persons with severe disabilities or should the person with severe disabilities learn to compensate to fit into society? What type of accommodations should society make? What type of compensation strategies could a person with severe disabilities make?
4. Should school districts be mandated to provide "full inclusion" programs? Why or why not?
5. What could you do to resolve the difference between the parents and the school concerning Kathy's attendance in a full inclusion classroom?
6. *Activity:* Conduct an ERIC search on the following terms. Read about each intervention, define each, and describe in detail one example of each: systematic sensory stimulation, microswitches, and partial participation.

CASE 38. PHILLIP

Issues: Behavior management, educational goals/objectives

Having parents that are graduates of a special education program, Phil was born at-risk. Phil is a happy-go-lucky child who really doesn't care what others think of his appearance or behaviors.

Born to Tim and Gale Martin almost ten years ago was little Phillip Martin. When he was born, there was no question that he would be biologically and environmentally at-risk. After all, both Tim and Gale, graduates of District 3 Special Education Program, were classified as having moderate mental retardation in school. When the two met in high school, teachers from the program never expected their relationship to last longer than high school. After they were married, many of their teachers never expected their marriage to last, even though both Tim and Gale had "good" jobs. Tim is a janitor at an elementary school in town and Gale works at a clothing factory in a different part of town. However, the final shock came when their teachers heard of Gale's pregnancy. Although they live in an apartment complex monitored by the social service staff from their high school, the two manage to remain independent. Unable to drive to work, Tim and Gale board the bus each morning and travel to their respective jobs. At night, they take the bus home and usually eat dinner at a fast-food restaurant.

Phillip Martin has been identified as having severe mental retardation. Phillip is a small, overweight boy who looks young for his age. His immature behaviors, such as frequent temper tantrums, add to the illusion of him appearing younger. Phillip also has communication deficits and often communicates through a series of hand gestures and verbalizations. Although he is difficult to understand because he articulates words poorly and speaks softly, his speech can be understood when he speaks loudly.

Phillip currently attends a self-contained special education classroom at Swarthmore Elementary School in Du Pres, Kansas. Phillip is in the classroom with ten other students with varying degrees of moderate to severe mental retardation. Phillip has been a student of the Special Education Program since he was in preschool. Although he has received intense training in basic skills, Phillip is still learning many functional skills, such as telling time, counting, vocational skills, communication skills, and basic functional words. Mr. Bennis, his teacher, has helped Phillip make tremendous progress over the last year, but Phillip still displays many inappropriate behaviors, such as throwing tantrums when frustrated or upset, using a finger gesture to attract attention, and displaying aggressiveness toward other students. In fairness to Phillip, Mr. Bennis feels that some of his problems are exacerbated because of his difficulties with communication.

On a recent evaluation, Phillip received a full-scale IQ score of 36 and an Adaptive Behavior Composite of 32. The following scores depict Phillip's performance:

Pictorial Test of Intelligence = IQ score of 31
Developmental Test of Visual-Motor Integration = 3 years 6 months

Wechsler Intelligence Scale for Children—Revised (WISC-R)

Subtest	IQ Score
Verbal	30
Performance	39
Full scale	36

Vineland Adaptive Behavior Scales

Subtest	Standardized Score
Communication domain	33
Daily living skills domain	52
Socialization domain	44
Motor skills domain	22
Adaptive behavior composite	**32**

The results from the Brigance and other informal inventories indicate the following areas as present levels and concerns for Phillip:

Present Levels

Recognizes functional words (e.g., Danger, Exit, Police, and Caution)
Recognizes numbers 1 to 5
Writes first letters of his name (PHIL)
Follows three step oral directions

Concerns

Other functional words
Writing skills
Recognizing numbers above 5
Working independently
Using appropriate communication skills for needs and dislikes
Using appropriate communication skills in vocational settings

Though Phillip is considered one of the higher functioning students in the classroom, Mr. Bennis has concerns for Phillip's communication and working skills. For example, Phillip has learned and is often reinforced for giving other students "the middle finger." His parents also relate that this behavior is a problem at home. According to them, he frequently sits by the street and gives "the finger" to passing motorists. Angry motorists, unaware of Phillip's disability, either return the gesture or honk their horn in disgust.

In addition, another communication deficit involves his inability to make requests. Rather than trying to gesture or verbalize the name of an object that he wants, Phillip frequently points to an object or gets the object himself (i.e., bathroom, drink, cup, food, etc.). Mr. Bennis has begun to make Phillip verbalize or gesture for the object, however, he is often frustrated because Phillip still continues to point rather than ask. During a recent conversation with Tim and Gale Martin, they related to Mr. Bennis that it is easier to give Phillip what he wants because if he does not get it, he will throw a tantrum.

In the vocational area, Mr. Bennis has found similar communication and behavior problems. For example, when Phillip runs out of an item while working on a vocational task (e.g., assembling flashlight), rather than ask for more items, Phillip sits back in his chair and watches other students. At other times when Phillip does not want to work on a vocational task, rather than saying that he would prefer a different task, Phillip usually throws a tantrum. Rather than have Phillip hurt himself, Mr. Bennis usually lets him work on a different task.

Finally, Phillip has one other behavior problem particularly embarrassing to Mr. Bennis. When in a public setting, Phillip often throws tantrums and when physically assisted to stand up, Phillip often yells loudly. For example on a recent community-based trip to the local drug store, Phillip wanted to go down the toy aisle, however, Mr. Bennis wanted students to attend to the personal hygiene products found three aisles over. When Mr. Bennis approached Phillip and gently grabbed his arm in an attempt to direct him to the personal hygiene aisle, Phillip fell to the floor and yelled, "help, help." When other customers began to gather around, Mr. Bennis became embarrassed and remarked to Phillip "forget you." He then went back to his students who were waiting for him next to personal hygiene products. When Mr. Bennis' lesson was over, he directed the students to the front of the store to catch the bus. As he was heading out the door, he yelled for Phillip to join him or risk missing the bus. Upon hearing this threat, Phillip dropped the toy that he was playing with and ran to the front of the store.

QUESTIONS

1. What could Mr. Bennis do to discourage Phillip from giving other students the finger?
2. What could Mr. Bennis do to decrease the number of (and intensity of) tantrums that Phillip exhibits?
3. Write two behavioral or educational goals with two supporting objectives for each goal.
4. What type of parenting techniques should be used by Phillip's parents? Who should train them with parenting or behavior modification skills?

5. What could Tim and Gale do after they had a child to ensure that environmental factors would not delay the child's cognitive, verbal, or motor development?
6. Years ago, couples with mental retardation were prevented from having children. Knowing that a child would have a 70 to 90 percent chance of being born with moderate to severe mental retardation of parents with mental retardation, what advice or actions should be taken to prevent these parents from having children?
7. *Activity:* Visit a high school classroom that houses students with severe mental retardation. Talk to the teacher and find out what lies ahead (i.e., jobs, living arrangements, etc.) for these students. Report your findings in class.

 C A S E   39. RAYMOND

Issues: Collaboration/consultation

Having a child born with a disability creates enormous stress on a family. Raymond was born with severe cerebral palsy (CP), and his parents must face some tough decisions.

Raymond Miller is a 5-year-old with severe to profound mental retardation. Raymond also has severe cerebral palsy (CP), which keeps him confined to a wheelchair and has restricted his fine motor skills to slow movements. His CP was accompanied with severe oral motor difficulties, which have prevented speech and language development, and have made it impossible for him to eat normally. As a result of his feeding problems, it was necessary for him to have a gastronomy to ingest food. His gastronomy involved a small incision in his stomach through which a feeding tube is inserted.

When Ray was born, he placed a severe strain on the emotional and financial resources of his parents, Tom and Nicole. When their first child, Simon, was born two years earlier, he experienced no difficulties or delays; consequently, it came as a shock to see Raymond born with such severe difficulties. At first, both Tom and Nicole had great difficulty accepting Ray as theirs. But slowly Nicole adjusted to the intense demands needed to raise a child with multiple disabilities; even Simon adjusted to the new baby by helping his mother care for Ray. When Tom was away on long business trips selling power tools, Simon was his mother's helper, running to get baby items around the house. On the other hand, Tom never quite adjusted. Tom could never accept the responsibility that came with raising such a child with special needs. For Tom, he sought escape through his work and often spent an inordinate amount of time away from home. He told Nicole that the extra time at work would provide additional money to take care of Ray's growing medical costs, but for him it was an escape from the intense responsibility of caring for a fragile child.

When Nicole looks back on those early days, she could sense their marriage slowly deteriorating. After the first year, Tom admitted that he was burned out and could not take it anymore. Tom explained that he needed some time off, some more space. With that, he left and was never seen again. Ray, too young to understand, did not care, but Simon took it hard. For weeks after his father left, Simon sat by the door, cried, and asked when his father was coming back. After the first year, Simon accepted that his father was never going to return and that he would have to help his mother raise Ray.

Today, Ray attends a self-contained special education kindergarten classroom at Belle Elementary School in Beltway, Maryland. Ray is in the class with five other students with severe or multiple disabilities. Psychologists have estimated that Ray's intelligence score is about 25, but his teacher, Mrs. Larimore, has told his mother that Ray is a lot smarter than that. Mrs. Larimore says that she can tell by "the fire in his eyes that he is no 25 IQ kid." Perhaps it is her sense of connection with each child in her class that prevents Mrs. Larimore from burning out like so many of her colleagues. Or perhaps it is her deep religious faith that keeps her "high hopes" for each child alive everyday. Whatever her source of energy, Mrs. Larimore is by far one of the most dynamic and optimistic teachers that Belle Elementary School has seen in some time.

Ray usually arrives on the first bus of the morning and is wheeled into his class by the aide, Judy Marlin. As Judy unpacks his knapsack, Mrs. Larimore is busy setting up Ray's first morning activity—a battery operated toy car. During this activity, as Ray raises his hand, a microswitch in the wrist pack (attached to his arm) powers the car. Whenever Ray raises his arm one inch or more above the table, the car turns on and moves forward. Mrs. Larimore likes to start with this activity because she feels that Ray likes this activity. Ray's arm movements also serve as starting points for other more complex actions, such as pointing or signaling for assistance. She is frequently on the lookout for subtle changes in Ray's expression. Mrs. Larimore is currently trying to shape his arm movement into a pointing movement, which she hopes he will use to activate a communication board. Ray is also working on the most basic communication skills, such as making eye contact when spoken to, responding by tapping his finger to "yes" and "no" questions, and touching or grabbing objects (toys) in his environment. Through a response analysis, Mrs. Larimore hopes to shape his subtle motor responses into functional responses.

While the relationship between the school and home could be described as "good," over the past two weeks, things have begun to deteriorate. It began a week ago after Ray came to the school with a sore on the side of his abdomen in the area of the gastronomy. After Judy alerted Mrs. Larimore to it, Mrs. Larimore decided to speak to Nicole about it. Mrs. Larimore requested that Nicole take Ray to the doctor to have it treated. Nicole remarked that she would deal with it in her way. Being deeply religious, Nicole had been applying an ointment that was blessed by the Pope. She then prayed for several hours each day. Mrs. Larimore, taken back by her comment, tried to explain the importance of seeking medical attention for the treatment of the infection before it became serious. With reluctance, Nicole agreed that she would take

Ray to the doctor, but continued to apply the ointment and pray. Soon there-after, Mrs. Larimore noticed that Ray's infection had gotten worse and called again to see what action Nicole had taken. Nicole, feeling that Mrs. Larimore was interfering with raising her child, immediately took offense to her second telephone call. (Nicole had to work double shifts all week and was unable to take Ray to the doctor's office.) Despite Ray's infection turning green, Nicole felt that she could treat it using the religious ointment.

After three more days, Mrs. Larimore saw that the infection was not getting better and asked her supervisor, Mr. Reilly, to call Ray's mother. When Mr. Reilly spoke to Ray's mother, he told her that if she did not take Ray to the doctor that he would call Social Services. Social Services is a government organization that checks into complaints of neglect or abuse. With some reluc-tance Nicole agreed to schedule a doctor's appointment. Mr. Reilly then called Ray's doctor to confirm that Ray had an appointment. When the day of the appointment arrived, Nicole was forced to work a double shift or risk losing her job. She knew Ray's teacher was upset with her, so she rescheduled the appointment for the following week. Unfortunately, Mr. Reilly received word that Ray missed his appointment, and he decided to file a complaint with Social Services. The next day a social worker came to the house and spoke to Nicole. Because Nicole had already scheduled a new appointment, the social worker was unable to take any action against Nicole. Three days later, Ray's doctor told her that the wound was seriously infected and that he would have to admit Ray to the hospital for two days of treatment.

QUESTIONS

1. What are the effects that a child with a severe disability has on a family? Name five possible negative effects that it could have on parents. Name five possible negative effects that it could have on siblings.
2. Why is it essential for Mrs. Larimore to watch for subtle changes in Ray's (any student's) expression? What could this signal?
3. When children with disabilities are born, parents often experience many different emotions. What are some of the emotions that parents might feel and why?
4. What should Mrs. Larimore do to reinforce Ray's subtle responses?
5. How could you get a parent, such as Nicole, to get medical treatment for her child, rather than rely on prayer? What role should prayer play in medical treatments?
6. Should Social Services take any action to get Nicole to provide better care for Ray?
7. Being a single parent is often difficult. What are some problems that a single parent with a student with severe disabilities might encounter when compared to a single parent of a nondisabled child?
8. *Activity:* Talk to the parents of a student with a disability. How did they find out about the disability? How did they deal with this news? What changes occurred in their lives because of their son's or daughter's disability?

C A S E 40. DIXON

Issue: Behavior management

Dixon was born into a rough world. Being raised by his step-father and mother, Dixon soon learns the difficult lesson of abuse. What his step-father calls discipline, others call abuse.

Dixon Zembowski is a 10-year-old with severe mental retardation. During a recent evaluation, Dixon's IQ score was found to be borderline and fell within the moderate to severe mental retardation range. Dixon has severe cognitive deficits and has also been diagnosed as having attention deficit hyperactivity disorder (ADHD). Dixon's attentional and cognitive deficits are accompanied with minor speech and language disorders. Although Dixon has numerous disabilities, he is cognizant of his environment and gets along well with other nondisabled students.

Dixon was born to Zeezee Zembowski when she was only 15 years old. A child of incest, his father is also his maternal grandfather. Growing up, Dixon always thought that Zeezee's husband, Zack, was his father. Zack was a large burly man, who often is mistaken for a linebacker or boxer. The family lives in a subsidized housing unit, referred to locally as "slum town," in the heart of Packardburg, New Jersey. Packardburg was once the industrial giant of the Atlantic coast producing steel for the entire United States, until these products were imported for a much lower cost from foreign countries. Now, Packardburg is a city void of much industry. Zeezee, now 25, works part-time as a waitress at the Blueburg Diner. Zack, who met Zeezee when she was 16, works nightshift (full-time) at Gatlin Springs, installing springs on cars and trucks. Though this is his fourth job in six years, he has managed to hold on to this job for three years.

Zack is Dixon's step-father but he still has much to learn about parenting. On one recent evening, after an afternoon of heavy drinking, he came home just in time to kiss his wife goodbye, as they switched babysitting duties for the night. Zeezee would work until midnight and Zack would leave for work at 10:00 P.M. There were a couple of hours when Dixon was unsupervised, but Mamma Betern, a neighbor, would check on him. By 10 P.M. Dixon was usually asleep. This routine of tag team babysitting seemed to work well. On this night, Dixon was louder than most nights and Zack was more intoxicated than most nights. For Dixon, this was a harmful combination. As Dixon ran around the house with the radio playing loudly, Zack lost his temper. He grabbed Dixon and threw the radio against the wall. When Dixon began to cry, Zack slapped him hard across the face and Dixon immediately began to bleed. Next, Zack sent Dixon to his room.

When Zeezee arrived home, she found a smashed radio on the floor and Dixon asleep in his room on a blood-soaked pillow. Zeezee called Zack at work to ask what had happened. He repeated a line that he has used many times before. "Allz the boy needs is some tough love. I'll make it up to him by walkin' him to school tomorra'." Although not a serious injury, Zeezee knew it was only a matter of time before Dixon would get hurt.

As promised, Zack showed up in time to walk Dixon to school. As Dixon left the house, he gave his mother a kiss and held Zack's larger calloused hand. Dixon was not mad at Zack because he felt that he got what he deserved for not listening to his dad. On the walk to school, Zack told Dixon that he had better behave in school or he would come back to give him a "woopin." When they arrived at the classroom door, they saw Dixon's teacher, Mr. Newman, working. Still an hour from the start of school, Mr. Newman was startled to see Dixon and his large, towering father. Mr. Newman, not a big man, always became nervous when dealing with Zack. On two other occasions, Zack became easily angered and made Mr. Newman fearful, particularly when he was alone with him.

As Zack entered the room, he bellowed "hello."

From across the room, Mr. Newman could smell the beer on Zack's breath.

"Oh! Hi. How are you today?" Mr. Newman nervously replied back.

"Everythin's cool," Zack replied. "Howz my boy doin' in school?"

Mr. Newman, stumbling for a response said, "Well . . . there are times when Dixon displays many inappropriate behaviors, but I feel that these are just developmental delays for Dixon."

"Uh, OK," Zack replied not really knowing what was said.

"Hey Newman, you got anything to eat?" Zack asked, smelling Mr. Newman's bagel cooking in the toaster in the back of the room.

"Yeah, bbbbut I was going to . . . ," before Mr. Newman had finished his sentence, Zack was already next to the toaster eyeing the bagel.

"Go ahead," Newman replied.

Mr. Newman then noticed the swelled lower lip that Dixon had been trying to hide. "What in the world happened to you? Did you fall off your bike?" Mr. Newman asked.

A shy raspy voice replied, "No, I was givin' Daddy trouble."

"Oh, I see," Mr. Newman responded, not certain what to say next.

Swallowing down a bite of bagel, Zack interrupted to ask, "Do you got anything that I can wash this down with?"

"Yeah, there's coffee right behind you. Help yourself," Mr. Newman replied.

Mr. Newman stood there fumbling for a statement that would let Zack know he cared, but also that hitting Dixon was not acceptable

Finally, Zack yelled from the back of the room, "When I was a boy, a few whacks from my daddy did me some good."

"Yeah, but nowadays you can't *hit* kids," Mr. Newman shot back. "Someone might consider this abuse."

"Bull," Zack replied, " I didn't hit him that hard and I was jus' trying to get him to listen."

"That's OK, but you *cannot* hit," Mr. Newman responded.

Mr. Newman knew that Dixon would probably not be able to survive without Zack and Zeezee in his life. As pathetic as a life it was for Dixon, it was, nevertheless, a life. He realized that Dixon and his family were poorly educated and lived in one of the poorer sections of town, yet he wasn't sure if the situation was serious enough to call in Social Services. Or should he just let the situation alone and hope it would get better?

Mr. Newman decided to restate what he had already said, "Zack, I know Dixon is hyper, but you *cannot* hit him. If you have to, send him to his room for a few minutes when his behavior gets out of hand."

"Yeah, I guess I could do that," replied Zack.

Mr. Newman knew that this talk probably wouldn't stop the occasional punishment that Zack used as part of his parenting skills.

Then he remembered a parenting class held on weekends.

"You know Zack, this Saturday morning at the Y (YMCA), they are having classes that would help you deal with Dixon's hyper behavior, and they have free coffee and donuts."

"Coffee and donuts?" Zack repeated.

"Yeah, you may even meet folks like you who have kids with problems," Mr. Newman added.

Mr. Newman felt that Zack was not physically abusing Dixon, just mis-using his parenting skills. Mr. Newman knew that like so many of his students' parents, Zack lacked effective parenting skills. Mr. Newman also felt that Zack was, essentially, a positive influence in Dixon's life. Zack had taken Zeezee away from the abusive household that she grew up in and gave Dixon a father. By the stories told by Dixon, Mr. Newman knew that Zack did *try* to be a "good" father. He spent a lot of time with Dixon. Whether he took him to the park or zoo, Zack did make an attempt to be a father to Dixon. On other occasions, Dixon would arrive at school in new clothes that Zack had bought for him. Still, in the back of Mr. Newman's mind was the burning question, "Would Zack go too far and hurt Dixon?"

QUESTIONS

1. Was it abuse or bad parenting skills that Zack used on Dixon?
2. Should Mr. Newman report this incident as "abuse" to Social Services?
3. How can we help parents be "better parents"? Particularly those raising a child who not only has severe mental retardation, but ADHD?
4. What should Zeezee do to help Zack be a better parent? Does she lack "good" parenting skills?
5. What can be done to give parents (of children with severe disabilities) a break when the pressures of life become too much?
6. Who is responsible for teaching Zack parenting skills? Dixon's teacher? A church minister? Should the state provide free programs? The local university?
7. *Activity:* Check with public service organizations (school districts, YMCA, YWCA, churches, etc.) in your area. Find out if they offer parenting classes. What areas are discussed during the class? Are these classes open to parents who have children with disabilities? Are there special classes for these parents?

CHAPTER 11

INDIVIDUALS WHO ARE GIFTED, TALENTED, OR CREATIVE

DEFINITIONS

The term "gifted" refers primarily to students who are academically gifted, demonstrating superior achievement in academic performance and on measures of intellectual ability.

"Talented" students excel in areas that go beyond traditional academics, including theater, leadership, music, and art.

"Creative" students demonstrate unique abilities in divergent thinking, idiosyncratic expression, problem solving, and artistic production.

The Gifted and Talented Children's Act of 1978 describes these students as:

> ". . . possessing demonstrated or potential abilities that give evidence of
> high performance in areas such as intellectual, creative, specific academic,
> or leadership ability, or in performing and visual arts. . . ."*

KEY TERMS

intelligence quotient (IQ)   A singular construct of general cognitive functioning.

multiple intelligence theory   A concept of intelligence developed by psychologist Howard Gardner that proposes seven kinds of intelligence: visual/spatial, musical, verbal, logical/mathematical, interpersonal, intrapersonal, and bodily/kinesthetic.

---

* *Gifted and Talented Children's Act of 1978*, Educational Amendment of 1978, p. L 95-561, Title IX.

C A S E   41. Luis

Issues: Educational goals/objectives

After some initial concerns about their 5-year-old son Luis's delayed speech, Mr. and Dr. Pacheco are surprised to find that their son is highly intelligent. He has an incredible memory for details and a penchant for learning foreign languages. Soon the Pachecos find themselves seeking the best gifted and talented programming for their son.

When Luis was 5 years old, his parents became concerned about his language and speech development. While their son seemed extremely inquisitive, sometimes playing on the computer for hours, looking through the pictures on the CD-ROM encyclopedia, he rarely spoke. When he did speak, it was only in single word utterances and short phrases.

Mr. and Dr. Pacheco worked at the local university. Dr. Pacheco was a history professor and her husband managed the pharmacy in the university hospital. They decided to take Luis for an examination at the Child Development Center, a division of the university hospital. The complete evaluation was scheduled to take three days, but after only 45 minutes the developmental neurologist, Dr. Williams, brought young Luis back to his parents in the waiting room.

"I don't think we need to assess this boy's speech problem," Dr. Williams explained with a smile. "Luis will tell you why."

The Pachecos looked oddly at the physician and then at their son. Luis began to speak like never before.

"A developmental evaluation is unnecessary. My language skills are not deficient," the child announced.

The Pachecos nearly fainted. But why, they wondered, had he spoken so little if he could put together sentences of such vocabulary?

The developmental evaluation team completed their assessment and were unable to answer the Pachecos' query. What they did find was that little Luis scored 170 on the IQ test, in the high superior range. The child could read at a seventh grade level and perform math calculations at an early sixth grade level. Undoubtedly, he had not only been enjoying the encyclopedia pictures but had taught himself to read the written text. He demonstrated an incredible memory for facts, ranging topically from major league baseball to Greek philosophy. Luis had memorized every Cy Young award winner in the American and National Leagues. He had used the Internet to gain access to a number of great novels, including works by Mark Twain, Edgar Allen Poe, and Ernest Hemingway. With accuracy and enthusiasm he told one evaluator the story of Huck Finn's travels down the Mississippi River. He also asked why someone so brilliant as Hemingway committed suicide.

Luis displayed a particular gift for language. In addition to his interests in literature, he had an ability to pick up foreign languages. Although his parents spoke very little Spanish at home, Luis could carry on a fair conversation in his parents' native tongue. His exposure to other foreign languages had come primarily in the form of printed text with little opportunity to hear conversational speaking. Therefore, his skills had been limited to reading and writing. For example, although the evaluation team had no standardized measures of French reading comprehension, they found through informal procedures that Luis was nearly as adept in reading these languages as he was in English.

The evaluation team at the Child Development Center recommended that Luis be switched immediately from his kindergarten class to a program for gifted students. They specifically recommended that Luis be placed in a program to foster interests and abilities in the areas of languages and literature. These strengths, the committee stated, should be supported within the context of a well-rounded, highly advanced academic program. The committee listed a number of excellent private schools for gifted youngsters, including two nationally recognized boarding schools.

Mr. and Dr. Pacheco immediately were faced with figuring out what education would be best for their child. They were concerned about the possibility of pushing their son too much, of shortening his childhood by forcing him away from the playful joys of a five-year-old's world toward the serious knowledge and work of adulthood. Also, they didn't want Luis to think of himself as different, as weird or strange, as better or more important than his peers. They wanted him to somehow remain an average kid while pursuing studies that met his expansive needs.

Luis's parents arranged a meeting with the gifted education supervisor in the public schools to find out about the various programs. The supervisor supported their desire to keep Luis in as many regular education classes as possible, but she admitted that the curriculum in those classes would be much too easy for Luis. Additionally, some of her comments left the Pachecos wondering if even the separate classes for gifted students might be inadequate in meeting Luis's needs. The public school gifted programs seemed to merely move the youngsters ahead to higher level textbooks without providing additional opportunities for exploration, discovery, and self-expression. It seemed to them that Luis didn't just need to work in middle school textbooks. He needed a rich setting full of resources, opportunities, and support.

Next, the Pachecos arranged to visit the classroom of a primary level gifted teacher who had a reputation for being creative and dynamic. When they entered the classroom, both parents knew immediately that this would be a good place for their child. The teacher, Ms. Maher, explained that the class curriculum was based on multiple intelligence theory. The learning activities were designed to develop each child in seven specific intelligences: interpersonal, intrapersonal, logical-mathematical, linguistic, musical, spatial, and bodily-kinesthetic.

The classroom was arranged into complex, multisubject area exploration centers designed to develop these seven intelligences. The room was buzzing with activity as students worked in groups of two and three on a variety of complex projects. One center featured two computers linked to the Internet. A second center was a science laboratory with a microscope, small plants, and rows of experiments growing in petri dishes. On the wall behind the dishes were charts where the students were plotting data. In a third area, students were painting the background for a dramatic play they were producing. The room overflowed with investigation and creation.

Ms. Maher introduced Mr. and Dr. Pacheco to the students. Then each student in turn came up and respectfully introduced himself or herself in as many languages as possible. One child introduced herself in three languages, including a Native American dialect.

Finding such a wonderful classroom for Luis solved one problem but left another unaddressed. How could the Pachecos arrange for Luis to spend as much time as possible with typical children without losing out on the obvious array of opportunities in Ms. Maher's classroom? Ms. Maher explained that most of her students were only mainstreamed for music, art, and physical education. Some students didn't even go out for these classes. Luis's parents drove home that day feeling glad that they had found Ms. Maher's classroom but puzzled by the issue of inclusion versus separation for their gifted child.

QUESTIONS

1. What would Luis gain by being in Ms. Maher's gifted class? What would he gain by being in a regular first grade class?
2. How is it possible that a boy with an apparent developmental delay in the area of language is advanced in this area? How could Luis's language abilities have developed so quickly if he didn't speak often with his parents?
3. Keeping in mind that individualized education programs (IEPs) should involve input from students, parents, and family members, write one annual goal and three short-term objectives that might be suitable for Luis in the area of language arts.
4. How does Ms. Maher's classroom compare to other primary grade classrooms you are familiar with? Is this approach only suitable in gifted education or would it be appropriate in other classrooms?
5. Luis's parents fear that their boy may be viewed as strange or weird by youngsters his age. Are their fears well-founded? How do children view gifted and high-achieving students? How does society view gifted academicians?
6. *Activity:* Find a school in your local area that employs multiple intelligence theory as the basis of their program. (You should be able to find one.) Visit the school and talk to the teachers to find out about this unique educational approach.

CASE 42. WARREN

Issue: Educational goals/objectives

Warren is an elementary school student with a unique talent. He plays an incredible blues harmonica. His parents go to great lengths to support the development of his musical abilities. They also work with his local school district to arrange for opportunities through the school music programs.

Neither of Warren's parents played a musical instrument, and Warren had never displayed an unusual interest or ability in the area. So it didn't seem too surprising that when Warren's mother gave him a harmonica for his seventh birthday, he spent the afternoon blowing in the wrong side of the instrument. What else would a little boy do?

Then his mother turned the harmonica around and Warren's talents as a blues harmonica player have flourished. His parents arranged for lessons at the downtown music store. Warren practiced for hours each day, having more fun than he had ever had, imitating his father's Little Walter and Sonnyboy Williamson CD's with amazing accuracy. After three months, Warren's harmonica teacher informed his mother that Warren could no longer benefit from lessons because the boy had already surpassed his teacher's abilities. By age 8, he had been invited to play a local benefit concert with blues legend B. B. King. By age 9, his unique talent had carried him from his small hometown in North Carolina to Los Angeles to play major nightclubs.

Warren's parents made the difficult decision to split the family temporarily to encourage Warren's musical growth. Warren's mother travelled to California to be with her fourth grade son while her husband remained in North Carolina to continue his career as an industrial sales representative. It was difficult for the family, but they felt it was necessary to give Warren opportunities that his town could not offer.

In Los Angeles, Warren attended public school each day, earning As and Bs in a general education program. Despite his musical talent, neither his teacher nor his parents ever initiated a referral for a gifted, talented, and creative diagnosis and placement. It seemed that the public school did not need to provide specific instruction or nurturing in Warren's area of talent—blues harmonica—because Warren and his family had already gone to great extremes to do so.

As an elementary school student moonlighting in late night blues clubs, Warren put in a long day. He worked hard each day at school, completed his homework immediately after school, took a long afternoon nap to rest up for the evening, and hit the stage each night to play the blues into the early morning hours. It was exhausting and exciting.

After five months of the musical big time, Warren and his mother were ready to return to the small time, ready to get back home to the family life and small town they loved. Warren's father was glad to have them back, too.

When Warren returned to his old elementary school in North Carolina, Warren's classroom teacher told his parents that Warren would probably qualify for admission to the state school for the arts. The state operated a public boarding school for students with significant talents in the areas of music and visual and performing arts. When Warren's parents pursued this idea, they discovered that the school was only for high school students. Warren was too young to attend. With this, Warren's mother and father sighed in relief. They didn't have to make the difficult decision about whether to send Warren to live at a school two hours away from home. It was an opportunity lost but a boost to their family stability.

Warren's teacher referred him for an evaluation for giftedness. The assessment demonstrated that Warren had above average general intelligence and academic skills. His Stanford-Binet full-scale score was 119. Academic achievement grade level scores were as follows: Reading Comprehension—4.1; Mathematics—4.4; Written Expression—4.7. On the Bender Visual-Motor Gestalt test, Warren scored a standard score of 135, attesting to his superior visual motor skills and fine motor dexterity.

The most dramatic overachievement displayed by the evaluation was in the area of music. Warren demonstrated an extremely heightened sensitivity to rhythms and tones. He could immediately match the notes and timing of any recorded musical passage with either his voice or the harmonica. He could also creatively improvise an endless variety of melodic runs to match any piece of music the evaluator could find.

The question still remained: How could Warren's unique talents be supported so that he would feel no limitations on his musical development? The responsibility for answering this question seemed to rest on both the parents and the public schools. A meeting was arranged between his parents, Warren's teacher, the school principal, the director of special education, and the director of gifted programs. The school officials offered to allow Warren to play with the high school jazz band as a supplement to his usual fourth grade curriculum. Additionally, the jazz band teacher would provide forty minutes per week of one-to-one instruction in music theory and practice, allowing Warren to further his knowledge and abilities in the jazz/blues genre while expanding into other traditions and styles of music.

Warren and his parents knew that this was the best possible arrangement given the limited resources of their local schools. They knew it wouldn't take long before Warren would become bored with the limited talents of the high school jazz musicians. They knew that Warren would need periodic moves to Los Angeles or Chicago to play with professional musicians. They set a tentative plan of taking Warren to a major city each summer, using the school vacation to concentrate on Warren's musical education. Even this plan, his parents wondered, may not suffice for long. They knew that at some point the family may need to relocate to foster Warren's talents.

QUESTIONS

1. Keeping in mind that individualized education programs (IEPs) should involve input from students, parents, and family members, write one annual goal and three short-term objectives that might be appropriate for Warren's IEP.
2. What family issues do you see Warren's family confronting because of his musical gift? How can school teachers, administrators, and counselors help this family deal with these issues?
3. It seems that the public schools may not have the ability to teach Warren music at the instructional level that his abilities require. Is the school system obligated to meet his musical education needs? If Warren were a highly advanced mathematician whose skills were advanced far beyond those of the public school math teachers' skills, would the public school have an obligation to teach him at his instructional level?
4. Can Warren be categorized as gifted with a full-scale IQ of 119? Why or why not?
5. Does Warren benefit more from playing his harmonica with talented musicians in Los Angeles or from living with his family and going to school in a small town in North Carolina?
6. *Activity:* Go to the library to find out how many states have special boarding schools for gifted students. Do you have one in your state? What specific subject areas and creative talents do these programs foster?

 C A S E 43. DARLENE ✶

Issues: Collaboration/consultation

Darlene is an extraordinary mathematician who, despite being placed in the advanced math class in sixth grade, finds herself bored. The assignments are too easy and Darlene loses interest. Her grades have dropped, masking her gifted abilities. Her mother struggles to get her daughter the gifted educational services she needs.

Darlene was first identified as a gifted mathematician in the third grade. Mr. Chislenko, her classroom teacher, observed her to be the best mathematics student in the class, standing head and shoulders above the rest. As her peers worked on learning multiplication and division facts, Darlene was learning to do square roots and complex, multifunction word problems. At first, Mr. Chislenko prepared two math lessons each day, one for Darlene and one for the rest of the class. In other subject areas, Darlene's skills fit more suitably within the highest achieving group in the class. This allowed her to work in a reading group and participate in whole class instruction in social studies and science. But when it came to math, tying Darlene down to the standard curriculum of her peers would have only been frustrating and boring to her.

After a while, Mr. Chislenko felt overwhelmed. The girl was learning so much so fast that no general classroom teacher of twenty-eight students could keep up with her. Besides, after eight years of teaching primary grade math, he was beginning to doubt his ability to teach higher level mathematics concepts and calculations. He consulted with the new gifted teacher, Ms. Harrison, who helped design an advanced, independent curriculum that allowed Darlene to remain in the general class while progressing ahead at her own speed. Ms. Harrison was a first year teacher full of exciting ideas. In addition to constructing an individualized curriculum, she also paired Darlene with one of her "official" gifted students to work on a cooperative project in the mathematical area of basic physics.

When Darlene moved to the middle school in grade 6, this special programming unfortunately and suddenly ended. Darlene was placed in a top-level math class, but she was bored because she had learned the material three years earlier. She sat quietly in class, doodling in her notebook and seeming disinterested and even lazy to her teacher. Due to Darlene's inattentiveness and lack of effort, her first two quiz grades were low Bs.

Darlene's mother Mildred called Mr. Rodriguez, the school principal, to ask why her daughter was not receiving supplementary instruction in mathematics. Mr. Rodriguez, upon consultation of the school records, found no indication that Darlene was gifted. She had never been referred or identified as gifted. Additionally, he commented, after talking to her sixth grade math teacher, she is performing at only an average level in her current math class. This certainly was not a gifted student, claimed Mr. Rodriguez.

Angered by her discussion with the principal, Mildred drove down to Darlene's old elementary school to see Ms. Harrison. When she explained the situation, Ms. Harrison felt terrible. She apologized for not following through to make sure Darlene received the math instruction she needed in her new middle school. She assured Mildred that she would talk to Mr. Rodriguez to solve the problem.

When Ms. Harrison explained the history of the situation to Mr. Rodriguez on the telephone, he criticized her for providing special services to a child without an official gifted designation. The proper procedure would have been to refer Darlene for evaluation. If she qualified for the gifted services, then Ms. Harrison could have pulled Darlene out for special instruction or collaborated with the classroom teacher on an inclusive educational plan. Ms. Harrison felt hurt at this criticism, but she kept her focus on the purpose of her phone call, the arrangement of the necessary services. Mr. Rodriguez said that he would start the referral process immediately. If she did qualify as gifted, she would receive special services in approximately three to four months.

Three to four months of stultifying boredom in the wrong math class did not sound right to either Ms. Harrison or Mildred. The two of them decided that they needed to advocate for Darlene's needs by asking that Mrs. Winn, the middle school gifted teacher, provide an advanced, individualized curriculum for Darlene during those months of waiting for the official gifted label to be processed.

Mildred arranged a meeting with Mr. Rodriguez and Mrs. Winn. Mildred brought along Ms. Harrison to provide support to her case for Darlene's giftedness. Ms. Harrison brought Darlene's mathematics assessment portfolio—a large file of work samples and products gathered in a number of math skill areas over the course of her fifth grade year—to demonstrate the student's ample capabilities.

During the meeting, Ms. Harrison presented the portfolio and described Darlene's work over the prior academic year. Her advanced skills surprised the principal and the sixth grade math teacher. She had shown no such ability by their observations. While Mr. Rodriguez admitted that Darlene appeared to be a sharp mathematician who would qualify for gifted services, he said that he could not violate standard procedure by providing such services before the gifted designation had been made. Mrs. Winn remained quiet throughout the meeting.

As Mildred and Ms. Harrison left empty-handed and dissatisfied, they wondered aloud about what that quiet teacher had been thinking as her principal had restricted her from providing services. It is possible that she wanted to volunteer but felt she couldn't oppose her principal. Mildred suggested that she sneak behind the principal's back to talk with this silent gifted instructor. Perhaps they could arrange something to meet Darlene's needs while the official wheels turned slowly forward. Ms. Harrison knew she needed to back out of this sticky situation at this point. But she also wanted to support Mildred's efforts. As Mildred finished describing her plan to secretly seek out the middle school gifted teacher, Ms. Harrison smiled and said, "You never know what two women working together can do." Mildred smiled back and they laughed.

QUESTIONS

1. What mistakes did Ms. Harrison make? How could she have avoided these mistakes?

2. Was the middle school principal right in not allowing Darlene to work with the gifted teacher until she had been fully assessed and designated as gifted? Explain.

3. This case contains examples of both exemplary and questionable consultation and collaboration practices. What practices do you think were good? What practices do you think could be improved?

4. Ms. Harrison and Mr. Chislenko kept Darlene in the regular classroom while providing an alternative mathematics curriculum. Would Darlene have been better served by receiving math instruction in Mr. Chislenko's gifted classroom?

5. Ms. Harrison and Mildred have formed a close bond by working together as advocates on Darlene's behalf. How might this form of closeness between parent and teacher be viewed by school professionals? Do teachers and administrators typically support or frown upon such intimacy? What do you think about this relationship?

6. *Activity:* Do library research under the topic of collaboration and consultation in special education. What approaches are currently supported in the professional literature? What are the purposes for these approaches?

 C A S E 44. ANYSSA

Issue: Social diversity

Anyssa is an African American high school student who has demonstrated outstanding academic and leadership talents. After her school district reformed their narrow criteria for admission to the gifted and talented program, Anyssa qualifies and receives a rich and expansive education.

Anyssa is an honor roll student in the tenth grade. She is also African American. Despite demonstrating outstanding academic and leadership abilities through her middle school years, she was not nominated for the gifted and talented program until the spring of her eighth grade year. The results of the evaluation placed Anyssa below the range of IQs and achievement scores accepted into the program. Both she and her parents were disappointed at this rejection because they felt that the extra resources and opportunities of the program would have benefitted Anyssa greatly.

When Anyssa entered tenth grade, a change in school district policy provided her a chance to be accepted into the gifted and talented program in her high school. For years the Malden School District gifted and talented program had included proportionally few girls and even fewer students of color. District leaders examined the criteria used to assess and identify gifted and talented students and found that many exceptional students were not being identified. The evaluation system placed great weight on IQ score as the primary factor. This system followed a narrow concept of what intelligence is, a concept based on IQ testing alone. The District decided to use a broader approach to assessing giftedness based on Howard Gardner's multiple intelligence theory. MI theory posits seven different intelligences: visual/spatial, musical, verbal, logical/mathematical, interpersonal, intrapersonal and bodily/kinesthetic. The District developed ways of assessing each of the seven intelligences, realizing that this would open doors to students previously excluded under the traditional IQ tests.

The second part of the district's problem of the underrepresentation of girls and students of color was created by the pattern of student nominations made by general classroom teachers. Teachers had been nominating white males for the gifted program far more often than they nominated girls or students of color. The district decided to combat this prejudice by holding workshops to help classroom teachers understand the many forms giftedness may take and to encourage high achievement among many types of students.

As the criteria and attitudes changed, the doors opened for girls like Anyssa and a number of other African American and Hispanic American students to join the gifted and talented roster.

Anyssa is a strong academic student in all areas, earning mostly As in college-preparatory math, English, social studies, foreign language, and science classes. Her favorite academic subject is American history. She plans on majoring in history in college and then going on to law school. She has a strong work ethic and participates extremely well in problem-solving groups.

Above all, Anyssa's unique strength comes in the area of leadership. By grade 10, Anyssa has risen to become the vice president of the student council. She spearheaded a movement to include student representatives on the influential School Advisory Committee, a governing group made up of school personnel, parents, and community leaders. Thanks in great part to Anyssa's tactical efforts, one student from each grade level sits on that board, including Anyssa who represents her grade 10 student colleagues.

Anyssa is active outside of school, too. She is the founder and coordinator of her church youth group's "Feed the Homeless" task force. She and other church members raise funds and collect food for an outreach mission and shelter located in the inner city. Next summer, Anyssa will attend a leadership institute at her state's Governor's School, a 2-month program to develop political knowledge and leadership skills among the state's most talented high school students.

Anyssa's day-to-day school program consists of Advanced Placement academic courses designed to prepare her and her peers for advanced college courses. After lunch, Anyssa attends a daily meeting of the gifted students, a time used by her teacher for many purposes, including peer support and preparation for a regional gifted student competition called Odyssey of the Mind. At 2:00 each afternoon, Anyssa and her friend Peter drive to the nearby university to take a course in college calculus. After the lecture, she and Peter typically go to the university library to work on calculus or to conduct research for their other high school courses.

Anyssa's parents are delighted with her educational progress. Her mother is a special education teacher who teaches students with developmental disabilities at the same high school Anyssa attends. Anyssa and her mother have initiated the Buddy Program, an effort to link special education students with their general education peers in friendship opportunities.

Anyssa's father is a successful dentist in the local community. He grew up in a poor, rural community and attended underfunded, segregated public schools. He feels encouraged that the gifted and talented program provides great support and opportunities to his daughter, the type of encouragement he would have liked to receive when he was a high school student a quarter century earlier.

Anyssa's only sibling is her younger brother, Bobby, an eighth grader. His sister's success has been difficult for him to handle. He is an average student who sets extremely high goals for himself, striving to equal or even surpass his sister in any way he can. This intensity has brought him much frustration. Despite his parents' encouragement to be his own person and not compare himself to his high-achieving older sister, Bobby can't seem to help himself. His parents have noticed that Bobby's one extraordinary talent is creative writing. They are trying to place less emphasis on Bobby being a straight A student while supporting his developing craft of language. When his sister attends the Governor's School next summer, Bobby will go to Vermont for a student writing camp.

QUESTIONS

1. The Malden School District changed their assessment process for admission to their gifted programs. Partly, they did this because they believed that the standardized measures of intelligence and achievement were unfair to students of color. Is this true? Are IQ tests biased? Are achievement tests biased?

2. The Malden School District also found that white boys were referred by teachers to the gifted program proportionally more often than girls or students of color. Why might this occur? Do you think this problem is common?

3. Is "leadership skills" typically considered an area in which a student may be gifted? Do you think that "leadership skills" is a legitimate area of giftedness?

4. How can teachers help Bobby deal with his feelings of frustration while also encouraging him to achieve?

5. Is it important that gifted programs be socially diverse? Or does this emphasis on diversity only inhibit schools from admitting students who are "truly" gifted?

6. *Activity:* Contact the special education or gifted education directors in local school districts. Ask them for the giftedness criteria their district currently uses. Ask if their districts have made any changes in the criteria over the years to open gifted programs to a more diverse student population.

CASE 45. JANICE

Issue: Transition

*Janice is a talented high school student with an addiction to alcohol.
Her drinking problem built up over many painful months after her
father died. When she finally receives treatment and joins Alcoholics
Anonymous, she is surprised at what she finds.*

In the first two months of her senior year, Janice's dream of attending Duke
University was thrown into jeopardy. Suddenly Janice, the clean-cut, well-
behaved, studious girl admired by so many, stumbled and fell. It was quite a
fall, landing her in the Adolescent Unit at Crestwood Psychiatric Hospital.
Her mother, Paula, committed her for a 30-day treatment program after a series
of wild incidents involving Janice and alcohol.

Janice first tasted alcohol at age 11. Her father had struggled for years
with an addiction to alcohol. He travelled in and out of twelve-step groups,
alternating extending periods of hopeful sobriety and disheartening months
of binges and blackouts. Janice downed a third of a bottle of Scotch on the day
her father died in an automobile accident. Ironically, he had not been drinking
at the time. The months after her father's death were difficult. Alcohol seemed
like a trusted friend, something that reminded her of her father and made the
pain of the loss hang frozen in the air. With her older brother away at college,
Janice and her mother were alone to deal with the loss of her father. Janice
watched her mother curl up into a fearful ball, becoming quiet and withdrawn
after her father's death. She sought no comfort from her daughter, and she
offered none to her. The house grew cold and tense, and Janice found that
drinking made her feel alive and relaxed. Typically, she smuggled the liquor
into the house and hid the bottles in her bedroom closet. Her mother stopped
coming upstairs anyway. Janice would drink herself into a dull stupor at night
after her mother had gone to bed.

Over the course of twelve months, this pattern of drinking had increased
and expanded. Janice's late night drinking had progressed from one or two
nights on a weekend to include many school nights. After doing her homework, she would wait until her mother called "'night!" up the stairs. She would
call "'night!" back and pour her first drink. Her mother never suspected a
thing. Janice knew that as long as she kept up her A average and maintained
respectable standing in the gifted and talented program at her high school, no
one would have cause for concern.

As school began in the fall of her senior year and as alcohol grew in
importance in her life, Janice expanded her drinking beyond the four walls of
her bedroom. She started sneaking out at night, taking a spring water bottle
filled with gin, and riding around town. She climbed out her bedroom window and shimmied down a tree trunk to the ground below. She pedaled her
moped until she was a safe distance from her sleeping mother's ears, then she

cranked the engine and raced off into the night. The streets were quiet and Janice felt relaxed. The intense pressures of keeping up her valedictorian standing and of living in the same house with her depressed mother seemed to drift away as she rode and sipped from the bottle.

Janice's midnight drives finally impinged on her school performance. She started not going home to bed at the end of the drive. Instead, she'd park her moped in the forest on the edge of town. She'd climb into the park ranger's tool shed, a tiny little shack filled with rakes and shovels, and fall asleep. Waking up at maybe 9:00 or 10:00 the next morning, Janice would ride home to sleep away the school day on the couch.

After four of these sleep-out incidents over the course of two weeks, Ms. Zelinski, the coordinator of the high school gifted program, set up a meeting with Janice and her mother, Paula. Ms. Zelinski had worked with Janice since freshmen year. She knew her well and cared about her very much. She had a gut feeling that Janice had a substance abuse problem. She had seen this sort of thing before.

In the meeting, Janice denied having a drinking problem. She claimed that she liked to ride her moped late at night "to blow off steam." She promised her teacher that she would do better. Paula offered little input at the meeting. She spoke softly of being worried about her daughter. When asked by Ms. Zelinski if she had seen any evidence of Janice's drinking, she said that she hadn't noticed anything. In her mind, Janice was mature and could take care of herself. As the mother and daughter left, Ms. Zelinski thought to herself that poor Janice had been taking care of herself for years. Maybe the girl couldn't do it anymore.

That thought proved true. A week later, the school principal, Dr. Bhargava, called Janice into his office for a pep talk. He was worried that his school's star pupil was not putting enough effort into her studies. Dr. Bhargava explained to Janice that success takes continuous hard work. He lectured Janice, encouraging her to pull herself together and work hard to keep her number 1 class rank through the end of the school year. The next day, Janice skipped school and broke into Dr. Bhargava's home. She found the keys to his wife's BMW and smashed it through the garage door. That night around 11:30 the police found her in a field on the edge of town. She was drunk and asleep in a badly dented BMW.

Dr. Bhargava offered not to press criminal charges if Janice paid for the damage and entered a treatment facility. Paula immediately signed her daughter into Crestwood Psychiatric Hospital.

As part of her substance abuse treatment, Janice was required to attend Alcoholics Anonymous (AA) meetings four evenings a week. The meetings were held in the basement of a nearby church. A small van drove Janice and two other hospital patients to the meetings. At first, she resented attending these silly meetings with a bunch of old drunks. She had no drinking problem. It was her father who was the alcoholic, who neglected his daughter because he was devoted to booze. She wouldn't let them convince her that it was her problem. She knew better than that.

In AA, Janice learned that she would be set up with a sponsor, an older, more experienced member of the group who had gone through it and could counsel her along to sobriety and personal growth. One evening, Janice was surprised when she heard a familiar voice behind her say, "Excuse me. I think I'm your sponsor." Janice turned to find Ms. Zelinski!

"Ms. Z? What're you doing here?" Janice felt ashamed that her teacher had caught her attending an AA meeting. "Ms. Z. This isn't me. I mean, they're making me go to this. I don't want you to think. . . ." Suddenly it struck her that her teacher was also attending the meeting. "Ms. Zelinski. You're a drunk?"

"Ex-drunk. And proud of it. And also, I believe I am your sponsor." She smiled and gave her student a hug.

"All right!" Janice exclaimed with relief. "At least *you* won't try to convince me I'm an alcoholic."

Ms. Zelinski's face became solemn. "Janice. You and I share a serious problem. That's why we're here. I'm your sponsor because I'm doing something about my problem. And now, if I have anything to say about it, you will, too."

QUESTIONS

1. What factors in Janice's home and school life contributed to her developing into an alcoholic?
2. Janice hid her substance abuse by keeping up what we might call "the gifted student image." In our society, what is the common image of what a gifted student is like? In what ways is this image true and not true?
3. Explain the relationship between Janice's state of mental health and the health of her family system. How are the well-being and performance of an individual and a social system like a family or classroom group connected?
4. Unlike Ms. Zelinski, most teachers do not sponsor their alcoholic students in Alcoholics Anonymous. How can teachers identify and help students addicted to alcohol or drugs?
5. Janice is coming to the end of high school and getting ready to transition to college. Why is this a stressful time for many students? How can teachers help students deal with this stress?
6. *Activity:* Contact a local chapter of Alcoholics Anonymous or a nearby alcohol treatment facility. Arrange for a knowledgeable speaker from one of these groups to speak to your class about teenage substance abuse problems and treatment.

CHAPTER 12

INDIVIDUALS WITH PHYSICAL AND OTHER HEALTH IMPAIRMENTS

DEFINITIONS

The IDEA* definition of "orthopedic impairments" is:

" . . . a severe orthopedic impairment which adversely affects a child's performance. The term includes impairment caused by congenital anomaly (e.g., clubfoot, absence of some member, etc.), impairments caused by disease (e.g., poliomyelitis, bone tuberculosis, etc.), and impairments from other causes (e.g., cerebral palsy, amputations, and fractures or burns which cause contractures)."

The IDEA* definition of "health impairments" is:

" . . . limited strength, vitality, or alertness, due to chronic or acute health problems such as a heart condition, tuberculosis, rheumatic fever, nephritis, asthma, sickle cell anemia, hemophilia, epilepsy, lead poisoning, leukemia, or diabetes, which adversely affect a child's educational performance."

KEY TERMS

accommodations   An adaptation or adjustment made in the child's environment to assist him/her. For example, one type of accommodation might be to allow a student with learning disabilities additional time to complete a test.

acquired immune deficiency syndrome (AIDS)   A syndrome that may be fatal because of the body's inability to fight infections.

cerebral palsy   Several conditions grouped under one label in which there is an impairment of the neurological system.

grand mal seizures   Seizures characterized by involuntary violent shaking or jerking of the muscles. It is often accompanied by loss of consciousness.

hemiplegia   Paralysis in the upper and lower limbs on the same side of the body.

---

* *Individuals with Disabilities Education Act Amendment of 1997*, 105th Cong., 1st Sess. (1997).

human immunodeficiency virus (HIV)   A virus that impairs the body's ability to fight off infections.

hydrocephaly   A condition in which excessive fluid accumulates in the brain of a child. If not corrected, this condition could result in injury to the brain.

myoelectric limb   An artificial limb that moves in response to impulses in the existing portion of the limb.

petit mal seizures   Small, barely noticeable seizures in which the individual may appear "tuned out" but is experiencing a seizure.

prosthetic limb   An artificial limb that "appears" lifelike.

quadriplegia   Damage in the spinal cord that causes all four limbs to be nonfunctional.

spina bifida   A condition in which the spine fails to close around the spinal cord.

T cells   A type of cell that fights infections in the human body.

46. Jean

Issue: Transition

Every parent dreams of having the "perfect" child. When Jean was born, her imperfection caused her parents to take a "new" look at life as they helped Jean live with her disability.

When Mary was pregnant with Jean, she and her husband, Tim, were elated. This was their first child and anticipation filled the air as Mary's due date drew closer. Aunts and uncles were also elated at the thought of adding another child to the growing family. Soon Mary's labor pains began and both parents rushed to the maternity ward of the hospital in preparation for Jean's birth. As soon as she was born, doctors and nurses rushed her into a separate section of the birthing room. As the parents looked on, it became apparent to them that something was terribly wrong.

Later that evening, a crying Tim called his sisters and broke the news. Jean was born without part of her arm. She was born with an elbow and about two inches of forearm. Tim's sisters didn't know how to react. They congratulated him, but they also expressed their sorrow. Many comments were made about how happy Tim should be that Jean was still a healthy child, but nothing could erase the feelings of guilt and despair that Tim felt.

Over the next two years, it was amazing to watch Jean adapt, despite her missing limb. She learned to balance a drinking cup under her chin by using her good hand and limb. She was also able to pick up toys in the same manner. Because the lack of a limb caused a slight imbalance in body weight (i.e., one side of the body weighed less than the other side), Jean did not reach some developmental milestones at the same rate as peers her age. This slower rate of development was a concern to her parents; however, they were happy with the knowledge that from a cognitive standpoint, Jean was advanced for her age. Although frustrating at times, Jean was learning to live her life without a limb.

Since her birth, Tim and Mary had been in contact with doctors who specialized in amputee injuries. Many of these specialists were considered the "best" in the region. Despite that the 2-hour drive to see these specialists at Children's Hospital was often expensive and time consuming, both parents felt confident that Jean was receiving excellent care. During the visits to the hospital, the doctors assured Tim and Mary that Jean would grow like an "average" child. During Jean's first visit, the doctors discussed with the parents the options concerning a prosthetic arm. They told the parents that children like Jean did not receive a prosthetic device until they were 2 years old and that the type of prosthetic device often was determined by the length of bone and functioning of the muscle available on the affected limb. For Jean, this meant that she would probably get a prosthetic arm by the time she was $2^{1}/_{2}$ years old, but she would have to settle for a mechanical prosthetic arm, not a lifelike, myoelectric arm.

As promised, at the age of $2^{1}/_{2}$ years old, Jean received her prosthetic arm and received physical therapy from the hospital to expedite the efficient use of it. Jean became proficient at using her mechanical hook and claw arm, and within a short time began using it to perform fine motor tasks, such as coloring with crayons, cutting with scissors, and picking up small objects. Despite Jean's progress, her parents still had many questions, such as "When would she receive her myoelectric arm?" "What special techniques should we use to raise her?" "What should we tell her when other people stare at her arm?"

By the age of 3, Jean and her parents became conscience of Jean's disability, especially when in public places. At the playground, they noticed that other children stared at Jean's prosthetic arm and some children seemed to be afraid to approach Jean. At the store, adults stared at her arm and often expressed sympathy toward Jean's disability. In other social situations, some parents who were curious about Jean's prosthetic arm were not sure how to discuss the topic during conversations. These incidents caused Tim and Mary to debate how best to approach each situation and often resulted in both parents coming up with different solutions. In turn, their different approaches often caused conflict between them.

Over the next few years, Jean grew and developed in a normal manner. By now, Jean was 6 years old and ready to attend her local school. For parents of nondisabled children, this is often a time of new anxieties, yet for Jean's parents, these same concerns were often compounded by her disability. For example, on the first day of school, should the teacher inform the other children of Jean's disability or should she let Jean's classmates find out about it in time? Or, during gross motor activities such as dodgeball, should the teacher have special rules for Jean? These situations concerned Tim and Mary and it was only after many parent/teacher conferences that both parents and the teacher felt at ease with Jean's disability.

Jean is now 9 years old and her parents still make the 2-hour trips to Children's Hospital where Jean periodically receives a new prosthetic arm as her bones outgrow the old one. During one recent visit, her parents requested a myoelectric arm, but were told that the costs were prohibitive and that Jean was not able to use one due to the length of her forearm. While at the doctor's office, Jean saw other adults with prosthetic limbs and she asked her parents quite a few questions, as she pondered her future with a prosthetic arm.

QUESTIONS

1. How should Jean's parents approach children who stare or are afraid of Jean's prosthetic arm?
2. How should Jean's parents approach her teacher concerning Jean's disability?
3. Because Jean has a disability, should her parents adjust their parenting style and allow Jean to display more inappropriate behavior? Why?

4. How would Tim or Mary's concerns be different if Jean was born with a learning disability rather than a physical disability?
5. What physical or cosmetic adjustments could be made so that Jean's disability is less visible?
6. To help Jean transition from one social setting to another, what accommodations should her parents make?
7. When considering the system "society," there are differences between what society "says" and what it "does" with regard to people such as Jean. Discuss how society views persons with physical disabilities and how these views translate into actions.
8. *Activity:* Visit a store that carries prosthetic devices and record several different prothestics and their use or function.

 C A S E 47. DUDLEY

Issues: Instructional methods/techniques, transition

Dudley was born with cerebral palsey (CP). Now a college student, Dudley has had to learn how to deal with the odd stares and puzzled reactions from strangers. In some cases he has touched the lives of others in a positive, unforgettable way, yet for others, they will soon not forget the guy named Dudley.

Dudley, a college student, has cerebral palsy (CP). He is currently a sophomore attending Blue Valley University in the Midwest. He is majoring in mathematics education and plans to become an elementary mathematics teacher. He works part-time at the university library where he reshelves books, locates missing books, and works at the information desk.

Dudley has a mild form of CP, whereby only his right side is affected by the disability (a condition known as hemiplegia). For him this means that he walks with a limp, his foot drags slightly, and his right arm is slightly spastic (stiff or tense). From his appearance and actions, you would swear that he was like any other college student, until you learn that the smoothness of his gait and arm movements came only after years of practice and intense muscle control. He does not know the cause of his CP, nor does he care. His mother, Susi, admits that she smoked heavily during her pregnancy and sometimes blames herself for his disability. Despite her admission, Dudley will gladly tell you that he doesn't care and that "you deal with the hand that you are dealt." Besides, with no possible cure in the near future, Dudley has accepted his disability and has moved ahead with his life. Interestingly, during some of Dudley's dreams, he imagines himself as being nondisabled.

Dudley knows that he could have been afflicted with a more severe form of CP. From his trips to the Easter Seal Center and special programs for the disabled, he has seen and spoken to other children and young adults with more severe forms. He has seen children with mental retardation and severe motor disorders (such as paraplegia and quadriplegia). From these experiences, he has developed a sense of appreciation for his abilities, while at the same time realizing the limits of his disability.

His high school years were tougher on him than on most students. Dudley easily recalls the bad memories of being rejected by girls because they thought he was abnormal, the embarrassment of being given alternative physical education activities because he was unable to participate in certain motor games, and the reduced sense of worth because some teachers often felt sorry for him and therefore excused him from doing certain assignments. Dudley was sorrowful at times as he watched friends and classmates make the sports teams. He made friends who stood by his side through the tough times. In addition, because Dudley focused much of his time and energy into school, he became an excellent student, frequently making the honor roll.

Upon graduating, Dudley had a university chosen and a career in mind. He wanted to be a teacher. From an early age he had wanted to be a teacher, mostly because of his positive experiences with the educational system. His dream was to teach math to children and to show all children, those with and without disabilities, that they can overcome a disability if they focus their energy on their goals. With this spirit, he entered Blue Valley University and majored in education.

Now at the age of 20, Dudley is in his second year of college and enjoying life. While at the university, he remains active. He has been living on his own at the student dormitory, working part-time at the library to supplement his income. Recently, he volunteered to work five hours a week at the local group home for persons with disabilities. In the process, Dudley made new friends who often ask how his disability has affected his life.

Despite his friendships with his classmates, Dudley is frequently in arguments with one or more of them over issues involving his disability. For instance, on one recent winter day as he was exiting the library, one of his friends, Rusty, grabbed him by the arm to help him walk across some ice. Dudley immediately became embarrassed, then angry at his friend for trying to assist him. After this incident, no matter how many attempts were made by Rusty to engage him in friendly conversation, Dudley ignored him and avoided him whenever possible.

On another day, his friend, Erin, insisted on helping Dudley during lunch. Seeing that Dudley was having difficulty carrying a tray of food, Erin insisted on carrying his tray. Dudley was so mad at her that he dropped his tray and ran out of the cafeteria in anger. Even after Erin's numerous apologies, Dudley refused to speak to her. Like anyone else, stubbornness is one quality that prevents him from resolving many issues in his life.

Dudley also has some other minor problems with classes. In advanced math, he asked the professor, Dr. Janson, if he could hand in assignments late, due to his slow writing skills from his disability. The professor responded that because Dudley had the syllabus, which listed all of the assignments and due dates, he would be penalized, like the other students, for turning in late assignments.

Knowing that there was a university disability advocate, Mrs. Williamson, on campus, Dudley called a meeting with the professor and advocate to discuss the accommodations that the professor had refused to make. Not wanting to anger the professor, Mrs. Williamson tried to suggest ways that the professor could accommodate Dudley. Feeling that Mrs. Williamson was dancing around the accommodation issue, Dudley demanded to know what Dr. Janson was going to do. Unfortunately, Dudley's demands were met quickly with Dr. Janson's sharp reply of "nothing." Storming out of the meeting, Dudley went back to his dorm to sulk. The next day, Dudley dropped the class and tried to take another course to substitute for it, but couldn't.

In Dudley's spare time, he likes to go to the coffee and book shop in the mall to read and relax. On one recent outing, Dudley was confronted by a stranger who noticed him walking oddly and suggested that he was drunk. Upon hearing this, Dudley pushed the woman and began to lash out at her. Within minutes, mall security escorted Dudley out of the mall and told him never to return.

QUESTIONS

1. How do you think Dudley should approach new people who are curious about his disability, but are afraid to ask?
2. How do you think Dudley should have handled the situation with Rusty trying to help him across the ice? With Erin?
3. What should Dudley have done when his professor refused to allow him to turn in assignments late?
4. Do you think dropping Dr. Janson's class was the appropriate action for Dudley to take in response to his meeting with his professor?
5. When considering the system "society," there are differences between what society "says" and what it "does." Discuss how society views persons with physical disabilities and how these views translate into actions.
6. As the physical education teacher, choose an activity or game and describe three modifications that could be made to it that would allow Dudley to participate in it, yet still retain his self-respect.
7. *Activity:* Talk to a person with a physical disability and find out what effect their disability has played in their life. Ask them what role others could play to assist them in public.

CASE 48. LATASHA

Issue: Behavior management

Latasha was born HIV positive. In a small, conservative town, word of her disease quickly spreads and causes fear for some. Yet, Latasha is able to teach others to see her "person" first and her disability second.

Latasha, who is 6-years-old, was born with human immunodeficiency virus (HIV). When she was originally diagnosed with HIV at the age of 2, the virus was in its latent stage. Her mother, Sasa, has since died from complications brought on by acquired immunodeficiency syndrome (AIDS). It wasn't until her mother became very sick that doctors even knew she had AIDS. Once they discovered the virus in her, they immediately tested Latasha. Now living with her grandmother, Latasha is in the middle stage of HIV.

It was not until the virus had reached this middle stage that Latasha began to feel ill. To that point, when she was tested to determine her level of immune cells, the test were always positive, high levels of T cells. The medication, Hivid, that she was taking three times a day had been warding off the virus by the inhibition of viral DNA synthesis. However, her latest CD4 cell count indicated that her level had dropped dramatically, below 300 cells, and for someone Latasha's age, normal CD4 cell count is 1,700 per milliliter of blood. She had been able to keep up with her schoolwork, but as her cell count dropped, she became more fatigued and less able to work for long periods. It was also at this point that her doctors placed her on the medication Bactrim, an antibacterial drug to help her fight off bacterial infections.

When school officials first found out that Latasha had the HIV infection, they wanted anyone coming in contact with her to take special precautions, such as wearing rubber gloves. However, after the initial scare and once they were fully informed about the virus, officials at her school decided to ease these restrictions. This initial panic also reverberated through Latasha's classroom, as teachers and children were literally afraid to go near Latasha for fear of becoming infected. Even her first grade teacher, Mr. Jackson, was initially frightened to touch Latasha for fear of spreading the virus. These first days were rough for Latasha.

To this point, with her virus in check (latency), her grandmother felt that Latasha's illness was nobody' business. It was only once that HIV had progressed to its middle stage that her grandmother decided to share the news. On the first day that her grandmother informed the school of Latasha's condition, school officials hurriedly contacted several local schools to see what precautions should be taken and restricted Latasha's participation until they received information from these schools. As word spread through the school, Latasha began to feel like an outcast, as students would stare at her or avoid eye contact. In addition, her illness made her tired throughout the day.

Parents of children in her school began to become concerned. Within days, the principal's office was inundated with questions about the safety of their children. Later that week, school officials called for an emergency school staff meeting to respond to the new blitz of concerns and threats. Parents and children from the school were invited to the meeting. At that meeting, many parents were outraged to learn about the lax policy concerning children with infectious diseases. Many of the parents threatened lawsuits, while others threatened to pull their children out of school. Everywhere that Latasha went, she felt that she was living under a microscope. Once when she went into a local fast-food restaurant, customers stared and made hushed comments. In such a small town gossip and rumors spread fast, often preventing the truth from coming to the forefront.

In school, students would call her names behind her back, at times calling her "sick girl." The pressure became too much for Latasha, as she was frequently involved in arguments with other students. On one occasion, another girl threw her book at Latasha when Latasha got too close to her. When this happened, Latasha jumped up and began to punch and spit on the girl. On another occasion, when another student mistakenly took Latasha's book, Latasha retaliated by gluing his locker shut. Latasha also pushed a classmate down a flight of steps after the student bumped into her. With each of these incidents, Mr. Jackson decided that Latasha should not be punished because he felt that she had "enough problems" dealing with her HIV infection.

Latasha's problems continued until the visit of "Illusion Lou," a National League Football player who had recently revealed that he had AIDS. Lou came to her town, Minortown, Illinois, to promote his new book, *Living and Dying with AIDS.* Lou had already appeared in several national television specials about AIDS before his visit to Latasha's town. When Latasha met Lou, it was in front of the camera on the local news channel. During their meeting, Lou spoke about compassion and understanding for persons with infectious diseases. Lou's visit to town seemed to ease some of the fears. While his appearance helped to educate parents and students, many in the community still avoided Latasha. As literature on AIDS was spread through town and local doctors began to educate members of the community at meetings, many people began to change their attitude toward Latasha. In the meantime, Mr. Jackson read up on the illness and began to educate children in the school. As he saw that she was becoming too fatigued to work for long periods, he decided to start the evaluation process and recommended that she receive special services.

Immediately, school officials determined that her illness was adversely affecting her educational performance and recommended that she receive additional instruction. In addition to her fatigue, Latasha also had to fight off fevers and constant diarrhea. As teachers and students began to work with her, Latasha gained in popularity. Where she had once found anger and fear, she found comfort and understanding. Still, there were those who never accepted her and continued to harass her.

A few weeks later, her HIV moved to its final stage—AIDS. By now her CD4 count was less than 100 cells per milliliter of blood and Latasha was bedridden, too weak to walk. During this last stage, she also suffered from seizures and blurred vision. When she contracted a severe case of pneumonia, friends and family knew that her death was imminent. After her death two weeks later, the entire community held a vigil in her memory. School officials vowed to not have her die in vain and dedicated a wing of the school library in her name. That section of the library now houses books, letters, and literature on HIV/AIDS.

QUESTIONS

1. How does our society view adults with AIDS? Are children with AIDS treated differently by society? If so, in what way?
2. Why is HIV/AIDS considered a disability?
3. Did Latasha's grandmother contact school officials too late?
4. Considering the community's initial reaction to the news that Latasha had HIV, what could have been done to prevent this negative reaction?
5. How would you deal with Latasha's frequent arguments and fights? Would you use behavioral interventions? Would you provide counseling? Or, would you use both?
6. At what point would you expect a child with HIV to receive special services and why?
7. As a teacher of a child with HIV, what steps should you take to prepare your students to receive this information?
8. What role should nurses, doctors, and other health officials play in AIDS education?
9. *Activity:* Read a recent article about AIDS or AIDS education. Share this information in a discussion with classmates.

 CASE 49. ERIC

Issues: Inclusion, transition

Eric's physical disability is obvious, as his wheelchair makes it evident that he cannot use his legs. Unfortunately for Eric, most strangers define who he is based upon his disability. While this problem has plagued Eric since he was a child, he is constantly battling the negative stereotypes, often to no avail.

Eric is a 35-year-old man with spina bifida. Eric was born with a form of spina bifida called myelomeningocele that has caused a variety of motor problems for him. The location of the defect on Eric's spine has resulted in paralysis of his legs. The two biggest effects of the illness are his inability to walk and his lack of bladder and bowel control. Restricted to a wheelchair, he is among the few that did not also develop hydrocephalus—a condition in which there is an excessive amount of fluid in the brain—resulting in mental retardation. Fortunately for Eric, he was born with above-average intelligence and has never shown signs of developing hydrocephalus.

When Eric was born, his parents, Rob and Kim, suspected that there might be something wrong with him. Later, doctors confirmed that he had a neural tube defect. Even though it was too early to predict the extent of his disability, his doctors suggested that his parents might want to consider placing him in an institution for children with disabilities. Or they could care for Eric at home for a few years and "wait and see" if his disability was severe enough to require institutional care.

As they cared for Eric, his parents noticed that he reached some of the same developmental milestones as students who were not disabled, with the exception of gross motor skills. When they saw that his lower body was not developing due to damage of the nerves in his spine (i.e., spina bifida), they considered sending him to the experts at Walbash Children's Institute, but decided against it after touring the institute. During their tour of the facility, they saw individuals with severe disabilities who were not well cared for.

When Eric reached school age, the school district insisted that he be placed in a classroom for students with severe disabilities. His parents disagreed and wanted him in the regular first grade class. They argued with the district and claimed that he did not need any special education services because he was such a "smart" kid. What his parents didn't understand was that the class for students with physical disabilities provided individualized instruction and also provided specialized services for those children in wheelchairs (e.g., physical therapy, occupational therapy). Reluctantly, Eric's parents agreed and so began Eric's long career in special education.

Today, Eric lives in his own apartment in the city and uses the county's public transportation system to travel to and from work, even though he owns a customized van. His job as a clerk at the county courthouse keeps him busy during the week and his workouts at the gym keep him active on weekends. He has made many friends who provide him with support. Although he is mobile, there are times when he has difficulty accessing the same activities that nondisabled individuals do.

For example, one weekend Eric was interested in working on the genealogy of his family. To find information about his ancestors, Eric needed to visit a local historical building that kept records of the town's people. This particular building, the Brown House, was operated by a local family and was located in the historic section of the city. This part of the city was like walking back in time, with cobblestone streets and narrow entrance ways into each building. When Eric arrived, he drove his van into the parking lot and used his motorized ramp to lower himself down onto the street. When he did this, he noticed his first obstacle, cobblestone streets and sidewalks. As he wheeled himself to the Brown House, he had to stop a few times to rest and often had to free his wheels when they got caught between cobblestones. When he finally arrived at the Brown House, he found that there was no wheelchair ramp. As he sat at the entrance to the steps, he contemplated what to do. When one of the Brown House tour guides noticed him outside, she came out and offered him some assistance. Eric replied, "Only if you can carry me up this flight of steps." Realizing that the situation was more difficult than she could handle, the guide summoned her supervisor. Again, her supervisor (another woman) came out and talked to Eric, but there was nothing that they could do to help him. They couldn't carry him up the steps and even if he would allow them, he would be embarrassed. Dejected, Eric wheeled back to the van and drove home. That night he became depressed because another one of his great ideas had gone down the drain.

A few days later, Eric had the idea of visiting a beautiful outlook in a park. That morning Eric packed his lunch and his camera and took off for the scenic view of Wasshoppin's Hawk Bluff. Hawk Bluff was famous not only for its beautiful view of the valley, but also for its annual hawk migration. On warm days, visitors can view hundreds of hawks flying overhead as they make their annual migration north. For the past week, Eric had heard people in his office talking about the sight of watching hundreds of different hawks soaring in the air. On the 2-hour drive to the park, Eric could picture in his mind the hawks flying over head and looking down at the valley. When he finally arrived, he was relieved that the long drive was over and was excited about his arrival. As he wheeled his way through the paved parking lot, he noticed rough terrain, which led up to the bluff. He was then told by one of the park's guides that he shouldn't even try to make the quarter mile hike up to the bluff lookout. Eric, never one who liked to be told no, wheeled himself up the path. Repeatedly, Eric got stuck on the narrow, rocky path, preventing other people from going farther and angering park guides responsible for maintaining the flow of persons to and from the outlook. At about half way up the path, Eric got stuck for the last time. As he pulled his wheel out from between two large rocks, he noticed that his wheelchair brakes had broken because of his travel on the rocky surface. Eric turned around and headed back down the path. His drive home was the longest two hours that he had ever spent in his van. When he arrived at home, he again sat alone and depressed. He called in sick for the entire week because he was too depressed to go and listen to his coworkers' stories about Wasshoppin's Hawk Bluff.

QUESTIONS

1. How does our society view adults with physical disabilities, particularly if the person is in a wheelchair?
2. In the 1950s and 1960s, when a child was born with a disability, most doctors took a "wait and see" attitude. Parents were told to take care of the child at home and to wait to see how she/he was doing. How has this attitude changed?
3. In the 1950s and 1960s, for those children with obvious disabilities, another choice that doctors gave parents was to institutionalize. How has this attitude changed over the years?

4. Were Eric's parents wrong by wanting him to attend a regular education classroom, rather than a special education classroom? What are some advantages and disadvantages of placing Eric in a regular education classroom for the entire day without special education services? What are some advantages and disadvantages of placing Eric in a special education classroom for an entire day?

5. What could you do to create an inclusion classroom for Eric and other students in first grade?

6. Should the owner of the Brown House be required to build a ramp (estimated cost = $10,000) that would allow wheelchair users access to it? Should the streets of this historic portion of the city be modified so that persons with physical disabilities could more easily travel on them?

7. What could you say to Eric when his disability prevents him from carrying out his planned activities?

8. What should Eric do about his depression? Is it appropriate for him to feel depressed?

9. What changes (physically and philosophically) can our society make to change into an "inclusion" society?

10. *Activity:* Travel around your town and city and choose three different sites (e.g., a store, an office, a post office). Describe the physical layout of each site and tell whether accommodations have been made for persons with physical disabilities. If no accommodations have been made, describe what should be done to create a "friendly" environment for persons with physical disabilities.

 C**A**S E 50. ELIZABETH

Issues: Collaboration/consultation

High school is tough enough for a teenager, but Elizabeth's seizure disorder makes it tougher. Her grand mal seizures make it obvious that she has a disability, but her petit mal seizures often cause others to look upon her with skepticism.

Elizabeth is a 16-year-old girl who suffers from seizure disorder. Elizabeth suffers from two types of seizures, grand mal (or tonic-clonic) and petit mal (or absence) seizures. A grand mal seizure involves losing consciousness and is immediately followed by rapid body convulsions. This type of seizure leaves her body drained of energy and typically takes about two days for her to recuperate. A petit mal seizure, less conspicuous, involves losing consciousness for only a brief time, up to fifteen seconds. Usually after a petit mal seizure, Elizabeth can resume the activity that she was previously working on. In most cases, people around her do not realize that the seizure has occurred. This type of seizure occurs frequently throughout the day (up to twenty times), whereas grand mal seizures occur less frequently (three to four times a year).

As Elizabeth will tell you, before having a grand mal seizure she can usually predict that it will occur. Elizabeth says that she gets an unusually bitter taste in her mouth prior to a grand mal seizure. For Elizabeth, the worst part of this type of seizure is the embarrassment that she feels when she regains consciousness and the short-term memory loss that often occurs with the seizure. Because her petit mal seizures aren't as noticeable, she isn't as embarrassed, but her temporary loss of consciousness often interferes with learning. Many of her teachers remark how they have to repeat things to Elizabeth on her bad days (those days with many petit mal seizures).

To help control her grand mal seizures, Elizabeth takes Nembutal, a barbiturate, three times a day, and to help control her petite mal seizures, she takes Klonopin, twice a day. To a large extent this controls her grand mal seizures, but it does not control her petit mal seizures. The medication has several side effects, one of which is drowsiness. Elizabeth feels that she could be a better student if she didn't have so many petit mal seizures and if she didn't have to fight off drowsiness all day. Many of Elizabeth's teachers feel that she is a smart student and agree that if she had better control of her seizures she would probably be an excellent student.

Currently, Elizabeth is in tenth grade and attends Hoban High School. Most of her teachers are understanding about the disability, but a few of her teachers don't believe that she has petit mal seizures. Instead, they feel that Elizabeth isn't listening or that she is lazy. On one recent occasion, her history teacher, Mr. Orville, confronted her in class about her disability. It began during one of his lectures about the Civil War. As he was rambling on about the Civil War, with his war stories interspersed, he noticed that several students, Elizabeth included, weren't paying attention. Frustrated, he decided to give a pop quiz. When several students protested, he quickly informed them that he was the teacher and if they did not pass his quiz, they would have to do a book report. During the next class, Mr. Orville announced the names of the students who did not pass the quiz and informed them of the due date for their book report. Despite paying attention that day, Elizabeth did not pass his quiz. When Elizabeth approached Mr. Orville to explain that she had several petit mal seizures during that class, he told her that he did not want to hear any excuses about doing poorly on the quiz and that she, like the other students, had to write a report. When she commented again about her disability, Mr. Orville shook his head and walked away. Not wanting to irritate him further, Elizabeth returned to her seat.

The next day, Elizabeth went to the special education teacher, Mr. Rosenthal, to explain what had happened and to see if he could help. Mr. Rosenthal was an understanding teacher. He listened to Elizabeth explain her problems and then thought about how to approach Mr. Orville about this situation. Mr. Rosenthal decided that it would be best to approach Mr. Orville with documentation of Elizabeth's medical records and explain to him the complexities of seizure disorders. He also decided to bring along his special education law book to inform Mr. Orville of Elizabeth's rights. When Mr. Orville saw Mr. Rosenthal entering his room with her records and his law book, he immediately became angry. He told Mr. Rosenthal that he was insulted and that Mr. Rosenthal should mind his own business. As Mr. Rosenthal insisted that he listen to him, Mr. Orville walked out of the room, complaining that he had more important things to do. Mr. Rosenthal then went to the principal's office and demanded that something be done.

QUESTIONS

1. How does our society view adults with disabilities that at first may not be obvious (learning disabilities or petit mal seizures) compared to disabilities that are often obvious (severe motor disabilities) at first glance?
2. What information would be helpful for teachers that work with Elizabeth?
3. Was there a better way for Elizabeth to handle her situation with her history teacher?
4. Was there a better way for Mr. Rosenthal to approach Mr. Orville about Elizabeth's problems?
5. How would you establish a "collaborative" environment with regular education teachers in the school?
6. How should teachers and medical personnel be involved in the treatment of Elizabeth's disability?
7. At what point should Elizabeth receive special education services?
8. Should the other students be informed of her seizures? If so, how would you approach the topic and what would you say?
9. *Activity:* Examine books and other resources to find out what you should do for a student who has a grand mal seizure. Are there certain medical precautions that you should take? What should you do during the seizure? What should you do after the seizure to comfort the student?

CHAPTER 13

INDIVIDUALS WITH OTHER LOW INCIDENCE DISABILITIES

DEFINITIONS

This chapter contains cases about children with three different disabilities: autism, traumatic brain injury (TBI), and deaf-blindness.

Autism is defined in the Individuals with Disabilities Education Act (IDEA)* as:

> ". . . a developmental disability significantly affecting verbal and nonverbal communication and interaction, generally evident before age 3, that adversely affects educational performance. Other characteristics associated with autism are engagement in repetitive activities and stereotyped movements, resistance to environmental change or changes in daily routines, and unusual responses to sensory experiences. The term does not apply if a child's educational performance is adversely affected primarily because the child has a serious emotional disturbance."

IDEA* defines traumatic brain injury (TBI) as:

> ". . . an acquired injury to the brain caused by an external physical force, resulting in total or partial functional disability or psychosocial impairment, or both, that adversely affects a child's educational performance. The term applies to open or closed head injuries resulting in impairments in one or more of the following areas, such as cognition; language; memory; attention; reasoning; abstract thinking; judgment; problem solving; sensory, perceptual, and motor abilities; psychosocial behavior; physical functions; information processing; and speech. The term does not apply to brain injuries that are congenital or degenerative, or brain injuries induced by birth trauma."

Deaf-blindness is a dual sensory disability combining a hearing impairment and a visual impairment. See the introductions to Chapter 8 for a complete definition of visual impairments and Chapter 9 for hearing impairments. A wide variety of persons have deaf-blindness. A person who is deaf and blind may have two disabilities caused by a single condition, such as Usher Syndrome. The person may have multiple mental and physical disabilities. Or the person may be of average or even gifted intellectual ability.

---

* *Individuals with Disabilities Education Act Amendment of 1997*, 105th Cong., 1st Sess. (1997).

KEY TERMS

cognitive functioning   General or overall intellectual activity including reasoning, attention, memory, and language.

echolalia   Speech consisting of literally repeating something heard.

facilitated communication   A mode of communication involving a typewriter or computer used with persons with autism or other disabilities whereby a facilitator holds or supports the individual's hand or arm, allowing that person to effectively press a letter or sign. The facilitator typically provides resistance to the arm and finger, leaving it to the person with a disability to push their hand and finger toward the right key.

frontal lobes   Region of the brain considered the center of emotional control and home to our personality. The frontal lobes are also involved in motor function, problem solving, spontaneity, memory, language, initiation, judgement, impulse control, and social and sexual behavior.

seizure disorder   A brain dysfunction (such as epilepsy) characterized by repeated episodes of seizures.

stereotypical speech   A characteristic, seemingly dispassionate and detached speaking style common to persons with autism.

tonic-clonic seizure   A seizure involving the entire body, usually characterized by muscular rigidity, violent muscular contractions, and loss of consciousness, caused by abnormal electrical activity in the nerve cells of the brain. Also called grand mal seizure.

Usher syndrome   A genetic disorder with hearing loss and retinitis pigmentosa, which causes a progressive loss of vision.

CASE 51. NGHIA

Issue: Behavior management

During a visit to the pediatrician, the doctor notices a possible delay in Nghia's language development. His parents, Le and Mai, take him for a full developmental evaluation. As Nghia approaches his third birthday, he is diagnosed with autism and begins a program of behavior therapy designed to improve his language and social-behavioral development.

After ten months of unsuccessful treatment with a fertility specialist, Le and Mai were heartbroken. It seemed that they would never be able to have a child of their own. Knowing they would feel unfulfilled without children, they decided to adopt. After investigating a variety of options, they found that they could adopt an infant from their homeland through an adoption agency that specialized in Vietnamese children. Working with this adoption agency, they adopted little Nghia, a healthy, 9-week-old Vietnamese infant with deep, dark eyes and a round smile. Le and Mai were overjoyed.

The first sign of a problem was that little Nghia didn't seem to be learning to talk. As a normally growing infant, his expressive language skills were either delayed or nonexistent. Mai had stayed home to care for Nghia while Le worked operating the two beauty salons the family owned. One day, when Nghia was almost 28 months old, Mai took Nghia to the pediatrician for an ear infection. After examining Nghia's ears, Dr. Stackhouse tried to strike up a conversation with little Nghia.

"Nghia, do you have a favorite food?"

Nghia looked away from the doctor and mumbled some jumble of sounds over and over.

The doctor repeated his question. "Nghia, what's your favorite food?"

"Mmmm," replied the boy.

"Oh, I love M & Ms. Do you like Hershey's Kisses?"

Again, Nghia turned away from the doctor as he spoke. He tilted his face up toward the ceiling light above and said, "Kisses. Kisses."

"Nghia, I want you to tell me your favorite story. Can you tell me a story?"

"Story. Mmmmmm." Nghia continued to stare away as if he were hardly aware that someone was speaking to him.

"Can you tell me a story?" Dr. Stackhouse continued.

No response. Nghia began humming to himself.

Dr. Stackhouse looked concerned. "Mai, does he usually talk like this?"

"He says words now and then. They don't make sense yet, but he's very young. " Mai looked at the physician's face and suddenly became worried. "Is something wrong?"

"Well, I'm not sure. Does Nghia speak in full sentences at home? Not giant sentences but simple sentences. 'I want teddy bear. Give me carrots.' Does he use sentences?"

"No," Mai thought for a moment, "Not yet. Last week he used the word 'video' when he wanted to watch his favorite movie. He learns a few words every week."

"Does he carry on conversations? You know, where you say something, he responds, and so on, back and forth?"

"Not yet. He mostly says back part of what I say to him. He's not retarded, is he? Oh God, I . . . ," Mai's eyes teared up and she turned away.

Dr. Stackhouse tried to comfort her. "I don't know if he has a cognitive disability. That is possible. I'm particularly concerned about his language development. He doesn't use words as well as or as often as other boys his age. He should be talking up a storm by now."

"Maybe he's just shy," Mai offered hopefully. "His father is shy."

Dr. Stackhouse pulled out a piece of paper and scribbled out a note. He handed it to Mai. "I think Nghia needs a complete evaluation, speech and language, everything. This is the number of Developmental Associates, a practice of developmental pediatricians, speech therapists, and child psychologists. I want you to call this number. The office is just around the corner past the Burger King. These people specialize in diagnosing and treating problems like this. They're the best I know."

Mai followed Dr. Stackhouse's recommendation. The evaluation team concluded that Nghia had a mild form of autism. His expressive and receptive languages were significantly delayed. He was exhibiting what the doctors called "stereotypical speech," the odd repetition of phrases and sounds that don't seem to make much sense. His habit of repeating back the last few words of what another person had said to him was called "echolalia," a common symptom of autism. Additionally, Nghia was beginning to manifest other autistic behaviors; a lack of eye contact when spoken to, social withdrawal, and a tendency to focus for long periods of time on lights and other objects.

After the evaluation, Nghia and Mai began seeing a child psychologist, Dr. Winger, who taught Mai how to use behavior modification techniques with Nghia at home. They set two specific goals: (1) to teach Nghia to make eye contact with someone who was speaking with him, and (2) to increase how often and how much Nghia talked. Dr. Winger wanted to catch Nghia early and promote his speech production and his social interaction skills before bad habits became permanent parts of the child's style of social behavior. Mai and Le were to briefly correct Nghia every time he failed to make eye contact and shower him with praise and hugs every time he was successful. Similarly, on the language goal, the plan called for Mai and Le to provide praise and attention when Nghia spoke.

Over the next few months, his parents worked diligently on these two goals and Nghia made strong progress. He quickly learned to face his mother or father when carrying on a conversation. Mai charted his language production on a wall chart to demonstrate Nghia's growth in the number of words spoken. His increases were dramatic and exciting. Yet, Mai noticed that while Nghia spoke more words, he still did not speak in sentences.

There was a more troubling problem that Mai and Le brought to Dr. Winger's attention. Le had noticed that Nghia was losing hair along his forehead. It didn't make sense. How could a 3-year-old be losing his hair? A receding hairline?

Dr. Winger instructed Nghia's parents to observe him in bed at night. He may have been pulling his hair out as he lay in bed or even as he slept. They did observe Nghia and found that Dr. Winger was right. Their son was pulling his hair out!

"Some children with autism develop the habit of yanking out their hair. It could be frustration or anxiety, but no one really knows. It's nothing to be too alarmed about. We can set up a plan to change this behavior just as we've set up plans to change other behaviors."

"OK," Mai spoke up optimistically, "What do we do?"

QUESTIONS

1. Design a behavior modification plan to stop Nghia from pulling his hair out.
2. Why did the child therapist set a goal to increase the quantity of words spoken by Nghia without trying to encourage him to speak in full sentences? Was this a strategic error?
3. Behavior modification attempts to modify specific behaviors. It confronts the symptoms of autism without addressing the source of these behavioral symptoms. Why doesn't the treatment go to the source of the symptoms?
4. What are the possible ways the emotional stability and quality of relationships in this family system might be impacted by Nghia and his autism?
5. Young couples often proudly display their first child and receive much support from friends and neighbors in the way of comments about how the youngster is cute, talkative, curious, or smart. How might friends and neighbors view Nghia? How might these reactions affect the feelings and behavior of Nghia's parents?
6. *Activity:* Visit a preschool program for youngsters with autism. Observe the children and the ways the staff members work with them. Talk to the staff to learn about the goals and methods they use to teach these children.

 CASE 52. TAKIA

Issues: Instructional methods/techniques

Takia is a lively 15-year-old girl. She has autism and has limited language abilities. Early behavioral difficulties have subsided greatly. Her mother enjoys and loves Takia, but she wishes they could communicate in a more complete way. Her mother is considering using a communication technique called facilitated communication.

Two distinct aspects of Takia's personality are evident to anyone who knows her. Takia loves to dance and she has a terrific sense of humor. When she first wakes up in the morning, her mother puts a Clint Black CD on the stereo and cranks the volume up so that the house quakes with the sounds of country music. "No! No!" Takia cries as she runs around the house with her pillow wrapped around her head. Takia laughs and rushes to the CD rack. She grabs her favorite CD, the only CD she ever listens to: Led Zeppelin 2. She hands this to her mother and begs, "Please. Whole lotta love!" Her mother then kisses her, tells her she "whole lotta loves her," and puts on the CD. Once Zeppelin is playing, Takia dances, kicking her feet high and waving her arms in the air. The smile never leaves her face.

At 15, Takia has attended the Trevor Winston School since kindergarten. The Winston School is a special school for students with autism, developmental disabilities, and multiple disabilities. Takia scored 49 on a general intelligence test when she was 4 years old. She was diagnosed as having a developmental disability requiring a significant degree of support. Subsequent evaluations over the years have produced similar cognitive functioning scores, but her primary diagnosis was changed to autism at age 6 due to the nature of her communication skills and behavior patterns.

Takia rarely speaks. When she does, it is almost always stereotypical speech, the repetition of words or phrases that Takia has somehow gathered from other places and other situations. As she starts her school day by coloring a picture of a mountainside landscape, Takia blurts out, "Incoming! Incoming!" Later, as she walks through the lunch line with her tray, she imitates Dustin Hoffman from the movie *Tootsie* shouting "Taxi! Taxi!" first in a high feminine voice and then in a low masculine voice. These words seem to jump out of her without reason or intention, as if Takia is not in control. Takia's mother, Aleesha, and her teacher, Ms. Downs, don't know why she fixates on certain lines from movies or television commercials. She rarely watches television, but much of her apparently random speech seems to come from that medium.

Some of Takia's communication is obviously purposeful. She says "Hi" to nearly everyone she sees. She has learned to ask to use the bathroom and to ask for food. There are days when she asks for food continuously. She also says "Mom" and "Daddy" to identify her parents and "Jeff" and "Sis" for her brother and sister.

Takia displays many of the behaviors common for persons with autism. She likes to keep a string or thread in her pocket that she often dangles and swings in front of her face. Her body slowly begins to sway with the string and sometimes she murmurs a repetitive, wordless chant. If uninterrupted, she can do this for an hour or more.

She also becomes obsessed with specific details and routines. She demands that her mother wash her each morning with the blue washcloth. When the blue washcloth is in the laundry basket and her mother uses a yellow cloth, Takia screams and swings her arms in the air. Sometimes she smacks herself in the face with the heel of her hand. When she was small, Takia could be held when she threw a tantrum. As she has grown larger than the rather petite

Alecsha, this has become increasingly difficult. Her parents tend to keep strict, daily routines that seem to comfort Takia and decrease the chances of tantrums and the self-hitting.

Over the years, tantrums and self-hitting have been less of a problem at school. After a brief initial period in which Takia resisted the time schedule and activities of her class, she has become more than accustomed to the school procedures. She now demands that Ms. Downs and the teacher's aide keep the school classroom operating like clockwork. Her parents and teacher have begun to question whether the school routine, while obviously providing comfort and order to Takia's day, might not also be limiting her growth by not challenging her or presenting her with new experiences. Her parents and teacher have begun discussing how Takia can be exposed to new opportunities, environments, and situations that will help her learn more than robotic routines.

Aleesha is pleased with her relationship with her daughter, but she wishes that she and Takia could communicate in a better way. The most exciting and controversial possibility Aleesha has found is called facilitated communication. Aleesha first heard about facilitated communication in a television report in which an autistic child sat at a computer keyboard and a teacher held the boy's outstretched hand. The boy and his teacher somehow typed letters into the computer to communicate what the boy wanted to say. The method was supposed to help the boy communicate because he only spoke in nonsensical phrases. Very slowly, despite that the boy often didn't seem to be looking at the keyboard, the boy and his teacher produced a sentence for the reporter: "R U ON TV60 MINUTS?" The reporter told the boy that he worked for a local station. The boy and the teacher then typed, "WEN WILLTHIS B ON?" The reporter told them it would air that night at 6:00.

The boy's mother told tearfully of how she finally had found her son who had been concealed, how facilitated communication gave her a chance to know her son. At the close of the news segment, the reporter said that this communication method was drawing a lot of criticism. It was being called a hoax and the facilitators were being accused of putting words in the students' mouths. After all, these were students with severe disabilities, most with very low IQs and little or no speech abilities. Suddenly they were writing meaningful sentences?

Despite having many questions about how this teaching method worked or didn't work, Aleesha wanted to give it a try. She felt like there was more to her daughter than most people thought, more than the test scores would show. She wondered if their might not be a fascinating little girl trapped under this odd disability called autism. Maybe she could find this girl and start some sort of relationship, some sort of mother-daughter bond that certainly didn't exist now.

Ms. Downs, though knowing little about facilitated communication, was willing to try the method. But she insisted that she and Aleesha first learn this method and receive training as facilitators. No teaching method had a chance if it were put into practice without knowledge and competence.

The mother and teacher agreed and their learning process began. They scoured the local university library to find books and educational journal articles by the leading facilitated communication practitioners. They also discovered where the various training centers were located and called them to find out how to be fully trained as a facilitator. As they searched the library, each noted that the critics of facilitated communication far outweighed the proponents, at least within the published books and articles by professionals. This caused the mother-teacher duo to move ahead with great caution but move ahead nonetheless.

QUESTIONS

1. Keeping in mind that individualized education programs (IEPs) should involve input from students, parents, and family members, write one annual goal and three short-term objectives that might be appropriate in the area of social skills. Focus on helping Takia become more able to emotionally handle changes in her school environment and routine.
2. What can be done to reduce Takia's self-hitting behavior at home?
3. In this case, the teacher is supporting the mother's interest in facilitated communication. Should she do this or should teachers only support the use of teaching methods that have been scientifically demonstrated to be effective?
4. What are the possible benefits and detriments to students and teachers of having a highly regimented classroom routine?
5. If the facilitated communication intervention is successful, what impact might this have on Takia's relationships at school and at home?
6. *Activity:* Organize a classroom debate on the topic of facilitated communication. One side supports the use of facilitated communication and one side doesn't. Access the current educational literature on the topic in the library to build your arguments.

 C A S E 53. EUGENE ✱

Issues: Educational goals/objectives

Mr. Grossman is puzzled by recent changes in his 12-year-old son Eugene's academic performance. He soon discovers that his son suffered a head injury but had never told his father. Father and son seek medical and educational support.

Mr. Grossman paced between the dining room and living room with the portable telephone at his ear. His face wore a look of concern as he listened to his 12-year-old son's English teacher describe the boy's recent poor performance in her class. Mr. Grossman was worried as perhaps only a single father of an only son can worry.

"Eugene has been a strong English student all year," Mrs. Wong, the teacher, explained, "but in the past three weeks or so he's seemed like a different kid. His writing is awkward, full of grammatical errors that he hasn't made all year. During class discussions, he is usually a leader who offers tremendous insights into characters and themes. Lately he doesn't even seem to understand the short stories we're reading."

"Why would his work suddenly drop off like that?" Mr. Grossman asked. "I mean, since his mom died last year, I'm all he's got, and I work a lot. I probably could help him more with school. But he's never needed help. You know?"

"I can understand why he's never needed help, Mr. Grossman. Eugene's an excellent student. But something has changed. Is there some personal problem or stress that Eugene is struggling with right now?"

Mr. Grossman paused for a moment. "No. Well, I don't think so. He has quite a crush on this one girl in school. Maybe he's preoccupied."

"I think it must be something more than that," Mrs. Wong observed. "I've seen my share of adolescent love. I sense that something much bigger is wrong. Will you talk to Eugene about this, Mr. Grossman?"

"OK, I'll sit him down tonight and talk with you tomorrow."

That night after dinner, Eugene and his Dad talked while they watched a college basketball game on television. As they talked, Mr. Grossman noticed for the first time that his son seemed to hesitate and struggle to explain himself, as if the words didn't flow easily. Also it seemed as if Eugene did not hear or process some of what Mr. Grossman explained. It was the strangest conversation Mr. Grossman had ever had. He felt guilty for not noticing earlier that his son was experiencing some form of difficulty with thinking and communicating.

Eugene then admitted that he had fallen while rock climbing during a weekend Boy Scout trip earlier in the month. He had avoided telling his father out of fear that his father would not let him go on the next rock climbing outing. Though Eugene was wearing a helmet when he fell, the blow to the head had knocked him out momentarily. He awoke with a strong pain in the back and left side of his head. Only one other boy witnessed the fall. By the time the boy had arrived at Eugene's side, Eugene was conscious and able to pretend he was unhurt. As a result of the fall, Eugene felt a temporary sense of confusion and light-headedness for the rest of the weekend.

In the weeks since the injury to his head, Eugene had experienced occasional headaches. He felt fine while walking but clumsy and unbalanced if he ran. He had skipped every gym class because he was unable to play basketball without falling down. The scariest part to Eugene was the way many of his usual abilities in using the English language (reading, writing, talking, listening) had been interrupted or sidetracked. As Eugene described it, "If I've got something to say, I don't remember the words. Or maybe the words come out jumbled. And sometimes when I read, I suddenly feel like I'm an alien trying to read the words, you know, another planet's words. It's like I'm not me."

Mr. Grossman took Eugene to their family doctor for an examination. The family doctor referred them to a neurologist who specialized in working with children with brain injuries. The neurologist described Eugene's injury as a closed head injury, a severe blow to the head that did not open the skull but caused internal trauma by bouncing the brain against the inside of the skull. Eugene probably suffered a concussion at the time of the fall. His difficulties with language skills, memory, balance, and gross motor coordination were the result of the trauma suffered by the brain. The language problems were due to injury of the left temporal lobe, the lower left hemisphere of the brain that controls many language functions. The balance and coordination difficulties were caused by damage to the cerebellum, the lower rear portion of the brain that regulates many physical agility functions.

Mr. Grossman and Eugene were worried about whether Eugene's normal abilities would return with time or if the damage was permanent. The neurologist was unable to say what would happen. He predicted that some of the symptoms of the brain trauma would go away gradually as the healing process progressed. He also predicted that Eugene would probably have to work hard to achieve the same level of language ability that he had before the accident. Eugene could become a high-achieving reader and writer once again, but it would take extra effort on his part to reteach himself many skills.

Mr. Grossman relayed this information to Mrs. Wong. She informed Mr. Grossman that extra help in rehabilitating Eugene's academic skills might be available through special education. Eugene might qualify under the category of traumatic brain injury. She agreed to make the referral so that Eugene could be tested for admission to this school program.

One week after the examination by the neurologist, Eugene dropped his lunch tray in the school cafeteria and dropped down on the floor. His arms squeezed tight against his chest and his feet pulled up behind his back. He quivered and shook on the floor while his friends called out for someone to help. After the longest two minutes, Eugene's body relaxed and became still on the floor. He had suffered a tonic-clonic seizure, a brief episode of abnormal neurological functioning in which he lost control of his body, lost consciousness, and experienced a convulsion across his entire body. An ambulance took Eugene to the hospital. His neurologist ran a series of tests and placed him on Dilantin, a medication to control seizures. He diagnosed Eugene as having a seizure disorder brought on by the blow to the head.

The school's diagnostic evaluation did confirm that Eugene qualified for special education services. He was placed in two special classes each day, a language arts class where Eugene could work to rebuild his lost language skills and a study skills class where he could receive assistance in handling the heavy reading and writing requirements of his many content area subjects. Additionally, Eugene was placed in a biweekly adaptive physical education class designed to help him address physical coordination and balance problems. Within weeks, these motor problems went away and Eugene happily returned to his regular physical education class. The language problems will not be so easy to solve. Eugene continues to work hard with his teachers to improve his reading comprehension and written expression skills.

QUESTIONS

1. This vignette does not tell how a boy like Eugene might respond emotionally to the loss of abilities and the changes in his academic program. How do you think he would be affected?

2. That Mr. Grossman didn't know that his son was injured on a rock climbing trip raises the question about how much information educators might not know about their students. How much of what has occurred or currently occurs in a student's life do teachers typically know about? What do teachers need to know to provide a quality education for a child?

3. Describe the quality and nature of the relationships in Eugene's family system. What is unique about a family consisting of only a father and son? How can this family either help or limit Eugene's educational progress?

4. Keeping in mind that individualized education programs (IEPs) should involve input from students, parents, and family members, write one annual goal and three short-term objectives that might be appropriate for Eugene, a seventh grade student, in the area of study skills.

5. Imagine you are Eugene stepping off the school bus and walking inside the school for his first day of class after the day he fell to the cafeteria floor with a tonic-clonic seizure. How do you (Eugene) feel? How might the other students view you and treat you after such a seizure?

6. *Activity:* Research the topic of seizure disorders. Learn the different types of seizures and what you should do if a student has each type of seizure in your class.

 C A S E *54.* ANGELA

Issues: Collaboration/consultation

Angela is a second grade student who suffered a brain injury in a bicycle accident. Her mother, her teacher, and her neurologist meet to discuss how the injury will affect Angela and her education as she prepares to return to school.

Miss Wooden had been a special educator for nineteen years, but she knew little about the dramatic affect a severe blow to the head could have on a child. She entered the doors of the rehabilitation hospital ready for her meeting with the neurologist and other specialists working with Angela during the child's recovery. Soon Angela would be discharged and would return to elementary school. Miss Wooden was in charge of assessing and understanding Angela's educational needs and arranging for those needs to be met either in the general or the special education classroom.

Angela had not been a special education student before the accident, before she had fallen from her bicycle and struck her forehead on the pavement. She had been a typical second grader. In anticipation of the hospital meeting, Miss Wooden talked with Angela's teacher, Mr. Paul, to learn as much as possible. Angela had been doing average second grade work. Her standardized achievement test scores from early in the year placed her academic skills from the 54th to the 65th percentile in comparison to her grade level peers. Mr. Paul described her as an able student with a particular fondness for memorizing and reciting children's poems and songs for her classmates. Her memory was sharp and her performances were lyrical treats for everyone. He also explained that Angela sometimes had difficulties organizing herself and her schoolwork. Sometimes she forgot or lost homework sheets and notes sent home to her parents. She usually followed teacher directions well and remained on task until her work was completed.

Socially, Angela was outgoing and exuberant. She was funny and well-liked, possibly the most popular girl in the class. She enjoyed playground games such as kickball and basketball. What she most enjoyed were board games; Monopoly, Risk, checkers, and chess. At recess, she often asked Mr. Paul if she and a pal could take a board game out on the playground.

Miss Wooden was anxious as she entered the small meeting room at the rehabilitation hospital. As she sat alone waiting for the meeting to begin, waiting to find out about this little girl who had suffered such severe and complex injuries in the accident, she looked at a giant picture of the human central nervous system that hung on the wall. All the nerves looked like great rivers running through the body. Within minutes Miss Wooden was joined by Angela's mother, Mrs. Bakameyer. Miss Wooden quickly found that she and Mrs. Bakameyer had much in common. They traded stories about singing in their church choirs and riding horses in the country.

Finally, a neurologist named Dr. Hu entered the room. The mother and the teacher began the barrage of questions. Dr. Hu patiently listened and answered their queries. She talked about a little girl who was simultaneously the same Angela and a new, different Angela. The doctor described the injury as primarily affecting the frontal lobes region of the brain. The injury impacted Angela cognitively and affectively, in her patterns and processes of thought and emotion. Luckily, the accident did not harm her vision, hearing, language, or mobility.

Angela's thought processes had been altered in many ways, impairing her ability to solve logical problems, handle directions involving sequences, and reason through complex situations. Her concentration had weakened dramatically, limiting her to short ten-minute bursts of focused attention on a given task.

Educational testing completed by the hospital teacher demonstrated that many academic skills had decreased considerably while some remained intact. For example, in the area of reading, Angela's comprehension ability had slipped to a mid-first grade level. In contrast, her decoding skills remained at her previous high second grade level. In mathematics, she retained her ability to accurately perform basic operations like addition and subtraction, but her capabilities in figuring word problems or in following a sequence of operations had diminished significantly.

Additionally, the evaluator noted that throughout the testing Angela was frustrated and critical of herself. She had a strong awareness of her sudden loss of ability and this visibly angered her. At one point, she pounded the table, cried, and refused to continue. The testing had to be completed on the next day.

Although all these losses in cognitive functioning had been clearly documented and measured, Dr. Hu emphasized that no one could be sure about what damage was permanent and what faculties Angela would regain in the following months or years. Angela's brain had suffered a significant trauma, the short-term effects of which were known. The long-term effects were another story. The neurologist anticipated that given the mild to moderate nature of Angela's injury, her brain would heal and adapt, allowing her to gradually recapture many old abilities and develop new ones in the upcoming years. Dr. Hu said that her weak concentration would most definitely improve. In other areas, she would make progress. Due to the complex nature of brain injuries and recovery, which areas and the rate of progress remained a mystery.

After all this information, Mrs. Bakameyer still had one crucial question. She spoke hesitantly, "How will Angela . . . you know . . . I mean . . . feel . . . How will she feel?"

Dr. Hu paused. She spoke cautiously when discussing the emotional effects of the injury. The neurologist explained that Angela's typical pattern of emotions had been disrupted in two ways. First, the physical impact to the brain had damaged the frontal lobes, the portion of the brain where emotions are thought to be produced. Second, the overall emotional trauma of the entire episode in Angela's life had caused her and would continue to cause her and her parents much grief and anguish. She had suffered a frightening personal loss.

During her hospital stay, Angela had suffered from depression, often crying in her bed at night. She had also been irritable and nasty to staff members and other children. Her mother had most keenly noticed the change in temperament from her usual joy and playfulness to gloom and quick anger. This was understandable given her sudden loss and her fear for her future, noted the staff psychologist. At this time though, one could not be certain which emotional and behavioral changes were rooted in the damage done to the frontal lobes and which were a typical little girl's reaction to a traumatic event. Either way, the key for professionals would be patience and understanding in working with her.

As they parted at the doorway, Miss Wooden and Mrs. Bakameyer hugged and promised to talk again soon to make educational plans for Angela. Miss Wooden left the meeting feeling invigorated and somewhat overwhelmed with the professional task before her. She sat in her car making notes on her legal pad. She drew a large chart like the one following. She began brainstorming a plan of action focusing on what Angela would need and what interventions she, Mrs. Bakameyer, Mr. Paul, and other school professionals could develop to address those needs.

	Social/Emotional	Instructional
What are Angela's needs?		
What intervention and supports can we provide to meet those needs?		

QUESTIONS

1. Fill in Miss Wooden's brainstorming chart. Make some notes regarding Angela's needs and possible educational supports that you would bring to the meeting with Mr. Paul and Mrs. Bakameyer.
2. What classroom placement or arrangement of placements will best serve Angela? How can Miss Wooden, Mrs. Bakameyer, Mr. Paul and other school professionals work together to provide her with the services and supports she needs?
3. Persons who experience a traumatic loss often go through a process of grief. What do you think this grieving process might entail? How can Angela's mother and teachers support her grief and recovery process?
4. Changes in Angela's cognitive and affective functioning will impact not only her school performance but her relationships with peers and family members. How might the family and classroom systems be changed by Angela's brain injury? What can be done to help these systems remain stable and supportive?
5. While Angela's reading decoding skills remain strong, her reading comprehension abilities need specific instructional intervention. What reading activities can be done with Angela to help her reading comprehension?
6. *Activity:* One historical root in the field of learning disabilities grew out the 1930s and 1940s work of researchers Strauss and Werner. They focused on the learning and attentional problems of persons who had suffered brain injuries. Access this research in your library. What do persons with learning disabilities and persons with brain injuries have in common? How are they different?

CASE 55. SALLY

Issue: Transition

Sally is trying to make the difficult transition from high school to college, a stressful time further complicated when she is diagnosed with Usher Syndrome, an illness that combines impairments of hearing and vision. Sally has had a hearing impairment for almost all of her life. Then she began to lose her vision during her adolescent years. Her world and her hopes for the future seemed to be fading into darkness.

Mrs. Pershing looked up from the newspaper with an expression of surprise. She heard a sound coming from the kitchen, but she thought she was the only one in the house.

"Sally? Is that you?" Mrs. Pershing called out.

"Uh-huh."

"I thought you'd already gone to your graduation party," said Mrs. Pershing as she rushed into the dark kitchen. She found Sally sitting in her winter coat at the kitchen table, car keys in her hand, and tears running down her face.

"I can't go!" Sally exclaimed in a sobbing voice.

"Why not?" her mother comforted her with a soft hug, "What's wrong?"

"I can't . . . When I drive at night, my eyes . . . they just . . ." Sally's voice trailed off. Her mother flipped on the kitchen light.

"Your eyes? What's wrong?"

"There's something wrong with my eyes," Sally explained. "At night, I can't see the road. I can't see the road anymore, Mom."

Two days later, Sally and Mrs. Pershing went to Dr. Littlefield, an ophthalmologist at the university optometry school, who performed a complex series of tests. Dr. Littlefield noticed that Sally wore behind-the-ear hearing aids, a common amplification device consisting of a small plastic casing that rests behind the ear and a molded plastic piece that fits in the ear. The casing and the molding are connected by a small plastic tube that carries amplified sound into the ear.

Sally explained to Dr. Littlefield that she was born with a moderate hearing impairment. She was first fitted with a hearing aid at age 18 months after her mother observed that she rarely looked at the face of the person speaking to her. Also, Sally's early vocalizations sounded more like shrieks and grunts than the usual infant imitations of vowel and consonant sounds. With the help of this assistive device, Sally began making strong progress in language and social skill development. In her primary grade years, she performed well in the regular education classes while using speech-language therapy and a private reading tutor. By the fifth grade, she no longer needed the extra school supports. Sally recently graduated in the top fifth of her high school class and planned to attend a state university in the fall.

As Dr. Littlefield performed the examination, Sally feared the worst. Not only was she unable to see the roads at night, but her eyesight had been deteriorating for months. Even at school, she had found that her field of vision was becoming smaller, as if the edges of the picture were fading from the light into the shadows. She had told no one. Now she feared for her college future. Was this problem temporary? Would she go blind? She waited anxiously for Dr. Littlefield's diagnosis.

After finishing the tests, Dr. Littlefield spoke slowly and deliberately to Sally and her mother. "I've completed my assessment. The results are clear. Sally has a condition called Usher Syndrome. She is suffering from a progressive loss of vision which is connected to her hearing impairment. It's a fairly rare condition that effects the ears and the eyes. A person with Usher Syndrome is born with a moderate to severe sensorineural hearing impairment. This hearing loss seems to be the only symptom until later in life, often during the teen years or the twenties, when the patient begins to lose vision. This vision loss is called retinitis pigmentosa. Sally, you have the classic symptoms: night blindness, tunnel vision, decreased acuity, difficulty with the glare of lights."

"Am I going blind?" Sally blurted, her face red with fear. Her mother held her hand and tried to remain calm. Sally and the family had struggled for years with one major disability. Much of her adaptation to her hearing impairment had involved an increased reliance on her vision. For example, because she often could not understand spoken language, Sally communicated with her family and close friends through sign language. Now, after so much success and at the brink of a bright future at college, she was losing her ability to see the signs that allowed her to communicate with others.

"Your vision problems will get worse," Dr. Littlefield replied. "With Usher Syndrome, the vision gradually deteriorates. There is no way to know exactly when the deterioration will stop. I believe that you will lose most of your visual functioning."

"I'll be blind." Sally stated firmly.

"Yes," admitted the physician, "While you may retain some vision, you'll be functionally blind."

Over time, while Usher Syndrome caused physical limitations, the emotional toll on Sally and her family was perhaps the greatest result. With her ability to use sign language limited, Sally felt socially isolated. She fell into a deep depression, often refusing to get out of bed and attend school.

On Dr. Littlefield's recommendation, Sally's parents took her to a weekly therapy group for persons with Usher Syndrome. In the group, Sally met other teenagers and young adults. At first, attending the group only further depressed her. Most of the other group members were much farther along in the process of visual deterioration. They used long canes and guide dogs to help them get around. Four of the group members could no longer visually read the hand signs done by persons sitting across the room. They set their hands on the hands of the signing person to read what was being said to them.

Sally was shocked to catch a painful and personal glimpse of her future. After attending two group meetings, Sally refused to attend any more. She decided that her vision would not become progressively worse, that she would not end up with a guide dog like the other group members.

But with time, Sally's anger and denial began to subside. Her tunnel vision and night blindness were becoming more pronounced. She could not pretend otherwise. After a month, her mother finally persuaded her to return to the therapy group. In the group, Sally gradually developed close friendships. The other group members provided support, comfort, and hope to her. They told her that she could still go to college. With the proper support services and modifications, a deaf-blind person could succeed in college.

Sally and her mother arranged for her matriculation to the university to be delayed one year to allow Sally to more fully adapt to her new disability. She practiced reading hand signs by placing her hands on the signer's hands. She continued to go to the group meetings, gradually becoming a leader who in turn provided support and comfort to other newly diagnosed patients.

Sally and her mother met with the university director of disability services to plan for her education. The director explained that the university was devoted to providing full access for Sally. Not all professors would be equally open and sensitive to the needs of students with disabilities, but the Office of Disability Services would intervene when necessary to help a student receive the legally required support and assistance. Sally could tape record lectures. The university would provide a sign language interpreter to communicate the professors' lectures directly into her hands. Also, students like Sally who had low vision could use special equipment to help in reading textbooks. By placing the book face down on the flat screen, the words appeared enlarged on the computer screen. The university also had many textbooks on audiotape for listening purposes. After this meeting, Sally and her mother felt reassured that Sally's college future could still be bright.

QUESTIONS

1. If Sally were a tenth grade student at the time of her diagnosis with Usher Syndrome, what adaptations and supports could her high school provide to allow her to continue in regular education classes?
2. The diagnosis of Usher Syndrome (or other disabling conditions) often brings great emotional pain to the patient. What is the emotional process that Sally goes through? What supports are necessary for a person to cope with such a major loss?
3. How do you feel when you see a person in the community who walks with a cane or guide dog? How are these persons typically viewed in our society?

4. Sally received a hearing aid at age 18 months. What difference do you think it would make in her education and life if she had received that device at age 3 or 4 years?
5. What supports and services would be available to help Sally succeed at your university? Is your university fully prepared to provide full access to a deaf and blind student?
6. *Activity:* Go to the library to research Usher Syndrome. What recent developments have been made in the diagnosis and treatment of this condition?

CHAPTER 14

Individuals At-Risk
for School Failure

Definition

The term "at-risk" does not describe a special education disability category. It is a term used in discussing students viewed as having a low probability of graduating from high school. Typically, a child is considered "at-risk" because of certain personal, environmental, or sociocultural characteristics often connected to nongraduation. Primary among these characteristics are: (1) economic poverty; (2) membership in a minority racial or ethnic group; (3) background without English language proficiency; (4) single parent household; (5) significant medical conditions that inhibit learning or school participation; and (6) significant environmental hazards such as poor nutrition, abuse, and parental drug addiction. The key to a student being "at-risk" is not whether these life conditions exist but the role these characteristics play in a student's life and schooling.

Key Terms

articulation disorder   A condition characterized by a pattern of habitual mispronunciation.

Wechsler Intelligence Scale for Children—3rd edition (WISC-III)   A standardized, norm-referenced measure of individual intelligence.

E 56. CYNTHIA AND UNBORN CHILD

Issue: Social diversity

Cynthia is a homeless teen who is pregnant and addicted to crack cocaine. She ran away from home to escape her father's sexual abuse. She struggles to deal with her addiction, her pregnancy, and the harsh life on the streets.

Cynthia presses down on her bulging belly with a silver Mercedes hood ornament. The ornament looks sort of like a shiny peace sign. Cynthia wears it on a string around her neck. It gives her comfort. Her belly is bloated with a growing fetus, perhaps five months along and becoming hard to deny to herself and to the other homeless residents of Sinclair Park. Cynthia has a nervous habit of pushing down on the unborn infant with the hope of sending the child into a developmental reverse, shrinking and receding to a time when Cynthia wandered the streets alone, thin and less burdened.

Sometimes people ask Cynthia who the father of her child is. She never answers this question, not only because she doesn't know, but because the likely answer is her father. She left home recently to escape his violence. Her memory of sixteen years of life is frozen beneath her daily sacrifice to this man. What memory remains does not include a time when she lived free from sexual violation. She does recall warm times with her mother, but these recollections are overwhelmed by her anger at the way her mother pretended her father wasn't doing what he was doing. When Cynthia went to her to ask her help, she told the girl to stop wearing revealing skirts around the house.

Cynthia's recent months huddled in alleyways and riding shelter buses were supposed to be freedom, a way of escaping her abusive father and denying mother. But she seems to have only moved from one form of violence to another.

Cynthia finds temporary freedom in crack cocaine, a powerful spirit lifter that turns anyone into an immortal. When she can't scrape together the cash or can't trade her body for a few fresh hits, she takes whatever she can. Typically, this means alcohol. Cheap, fortified wine can soften the fall.

She puts the Mercedes ornament under her shirt so she can feel it against her skin. She is feeling empty and her body quivers with what she calls "the urging." The fierce need for the drug organizes and provides direction for her entire life. Anything she does or thinks or feels is merely a side detail of little meaning. Like a religious zealot, a street evangelist with an urgent cause, she is devoted. The drug calls her and envelopes her in every way.

Though penniless, Cynthia knocks on the familiar door. An eye peers out the window to see who it is and a man's voice hollers for her to go away. She begs for just a little. The voices inside laugh. No money, no rock. And they won't give her anything for her baby-bearing body. It is a familiar dance.

Cynthia sits on the steps and cries. Every few minutes she knocks again and begs again. She might have thought about catching the 11:15 shelter bus from the park. It would be the last call for a bowl of soup and a warm cot. But she doesn't think of nourishment or sleep. She doesn't think of her health or that of her unborn baby, at least not in medical terms. To her, health is a smoke and the brief, drug-induced feeling that all is well. She falls asleep on the steps with an eye to the door, praying that God might open the crack house door and give her health.

In the morning, Cynthia awakes sprawled across a chair in a crowded hospital emergency room. The shelter bus driver spotted her on the doorstep the night before and brought her in. After sitting in the chair for six hours, a nurse places her in a wheelchair and wheels her back to an examining room. The doctor rushes in, looks her over briefly, and moves along to the next patient. Cynthia is suffering from anemia and dehydration, both caused by a pattern of malnutrition. She has eaten two meals in the past four days.

A nurse talks with Cynthia while she awaits the bus to arrive from the shelter. She pushes a bottle of multivitamins into Cynthia's purse.

"Take one of these every day. Can you do that?"

"Yeah, OK," Cynthia responds without looking up.

"You should be home fighting with your parents and worrying about who's going to ask you to the prom," the nurse quips. "Where's your family?"

"I'm an orphan," Cynthia lies, her thoughts going to her dad and mom as the words rolled awkwardly off her lips. Then she asserts herself defiantly, "I had a mom once, a long time ago, but thank God I never had a father. I wouldn't want one."

"Okay. So you don't want to talk about it. I can understand," the nurse reasoned softly. "Family or not, you and your baby need food. If you don't eat more, that baby will be sick."

"I try to eat, but mostly I'm not hungry." Cynthia looks away. She knows the nurse is trying to be helpful, but she can't deal with this right now.

"The crack will steal your appetite, along with everything else. The shelter has a substance dependency program that can help you. Have you tried to kick it?"

Cynthia looks up at the nurse with suspicion. She has a half moment to decide whether to admit the crack addiction or to stonewall this lady. "It can't be kicked. I tried and it just. . . ." She begins to cry. She turns away and swipes the tear before it hits her cheek. "When's that bus coming? It should be here by now."

"I'll call the shelter and tell the director to sign you up for the program. They'll put you on the waiting list, probably two months or so. You have to remember to eat in the mean time. Your baby needs the food. OK?"

"Yeah. Yeah. OK. I'll remember to eat." Cynthia hardens herself and forces the pain away. She knows she has to learn not to feel things. You can't be vulnerable like that if you're going to make it out there. "Where is that bus? It really should be here by now."

QUESTIONS

1.   What physiological effects might Cynthia's substance abuse and malnutrition have on her baby? How might these effects inhibit this child's abilities to learn?
2.   Why do some women live under and some children are born into such harsh conditions? What political or social changes must take place to address this problem?
3.   If you have a student in your class whose family is homeless, what can you and your school do to help the student and family?
4.   This account is empathetic to Cynthia's plight. She is primarily described as a victim. Her child will also be a victim of conditions beyond her/his control. Do you think Cynthia is a victim? How might she gain control over her life?
5.   How should public schools view and address the many social problems in America? Does school play a role? If so, what?
6.   *Activity:* Visit a homeless shelter or a soup kitchen. Observe who is served by the facility. How many women, children, and families rely on that charitable facility? If students and the instructor feel comfortable with the idea, talk to some of the persons to learn about their lives, hardships, and hopes.

 CASE 57. STEVE

Issues: Instructional methods/techniques

Steve and his mother, Phyllis, have moved a great distance so Steve could live close to his father. They feel socially isolated in a strange town and stressed by a difficult economic situation. Steve is a first grader already feeling like he can't fit in and find success in school. Steve's teacher says he has attention deficit hyperactivity disorder (ADHD) and should go to a doctor, a recommendation that brings further confusion and stress to Phyllis.

Six-year-old Steve and his mother, Phyllis, live in a trailer nine miles outside of town. They moved here recently from another state after their apartment and all their possessions burned in a fire. Steve's father offered to allow them to use a trailer without paying rent. After the fire, Steve and Phyllis stayed with family members, but Phyllis knew that her family, despite their gracious kindness, could hardly afford to continue to support the two. Steve's father offered a quick solution. He also spoke of spending more time with his son, an attractive prospect for Phyllis who had been raising her son singlehandedly and could use the help. The offer of the free trailer lured Phyllis to quit her bartending job, leave her hometown, and move across two states.

Now, as Steve attends first grade, Phyllis is struggling. She feels depressed living in this new place with no friends and a trailer only half-filled with somebody else's furniture. She has a job waiting tables at Denny's, but she hasn't been able to get to work in four days. Her idle '77 Dodge needs over $600 in repairs and she can't begin to sort out how to find that kind of money.

Steve is trying hard to learn the alphabet. The letters seem strange to him. Some of them look alike, so he can't remember which one is which. They have sounds that go with them, but the sounds only go with them sometimes and not other times. It's very confusing. He has an idea of what reading is because he has watched his mother read detective novels, but she's usually too busy to read to him. The other students in the class already know this stuff. It's hard to struggle each day with learning a P and a B when the kid next to you is reading a whole book about cats and dogs.

Young Steve also knows he is wearing the wrong clothes. His clothes were burned in the fire. Now he owns two pairs of ill-fitting pants and a handful of tee shirts from the Salvation Army. Some of the boys on the bus call him Rag Boy. He feels intense shame and tries to ignore them like his mother tells him.

Steve can't put his problems into words. He can't conceptualize the problems. But he can feel it each day as he goes to school. He can feel the uneasiness, the tension, the fear, the sense that he is not worth much in this new school. He feels like the other students belong there and he doesn't. They know how to do this school thing while he's lost in a foreign land. It's like learning to read is a giant jigsaw puzzle made up of a million pieces. The other kids not only put together the puzzle but they seem to have joyfully memorized the puzzle pieces. Steve is staring at the unopened puzzle box, wondering how all those pieces could make that colorful picture of the mountain and the trees.

Although Steve has always been a mild-mannered, sweet little boy, there is trouble brewing in his life. To Steve, despite the nice way the teacher often acts, he knows he's not wanted here. He can feel it in her tone of voice and the way her eyes roll in her head when he makes a mistake. He knows this place isn't for him. When students get stars for doing good, he doesn't get one. When students get praised for being smart, his name is not mentioned. He is gradually learning his letters and a few words, academic lessons that come with time. But he is also learning that he lives at the bottom of the school food chain, a life lesson that comes quickly and painfully. He is learning well to be an underachiever.

Each morning, he begs his mother to keep him home from school. She sends him to school anyway. By December of the first grade, Steve's mild manner gives way to angry outbursts. He throws his crayons across the room and calls his teacher a "fat goose who ate all the other fat gooses." He bites another student who cut in front of him at the water fountain.

Steve's teacher calls his mother and says that Steve has attention deficit hyperactivity disorder. He has displayed all the symptoms: lack of attention to school tasks, impulsive and disruptive behavior, wandering around the room. To Steve's mother, this sounds like a different child than the one she sends to school each morning. At home, Steve plays quietly while his mother watches TV or reads a book. He rarely gets angry. If he does, he doesn't act out or disobey his mother. If anything, he's been too good, a too well-behaved child. But here the teacher was saying that Steve misbehaves in school and that he has ADHD. She must know what she's talking about since she's the teacher. Besides, Phyllis had a friend back in Delaware whose boy was given Ritalin and his behavior was cleaned up immediately.

Despite agreeing with the teacher that Ritalin would be helpful, Phyllis doesn't immediately take Steve to a doctor. Her medicare card for Steve's health services has expired and she must apply for a new one. At this time, she is not sure where to go or how to reapply, so she has put off taking Steve to the doctor. Besides, how would she get there? She has arranged for his teacher to send home a note about his behavior every day. She has started restricting Steve to his room for the afternoon on days when he receives a bad report. It is unclear at this time whether this intervention will effectively improve Steve's classroom behavior.

QUESTIONS

1. What is the relationship between Steve's recent school behavior problems and the literacy instruction he is receiving?
2. What possible approaches to teaching reading and writing might be tried with Steve?
3. How does poverty effect the way Steve feels about himself? How does poverty effect the opportunities he and his mother have for making a good and happy life for themselves?
4. Do you think that the behavior change plan started by Steve's mother will improve his school behavior? If not, suggest a better approach.
5. How have the social systems in which Steve lives influenced his feelings and behavior?
6. *Activity:* Go to the library and use the ERIC system to find pertinent research on the topic of early literacy learning. Specifically, explore this question: What early childhood experiences help or hamper a young student's learning to read and write?

 C A S E 58. TODD ✗

Issues: Consultation/collaboration

When Ms. Genovese, a special education resource class teacher, hears that a new student will be added to her caseload, she launches a full-scale investigation. She tries to gather as much information as possible about Todd, a sixth grader struggling with language and academic difficulties. She consults with Todd's mother and a number of professionals.

The story of Todd, like so many cases, is not merely a fixed parcel of information. It is fragmented, incomplete, and foggy, and involves some detective work on the part of the teacher. To put together a picture of the child she will teach, Ms. Genovese seeks information and opinions from many sources.

Ms. Genovese, the cross-categorical resource class teacher, likes to know as much as possible about a student as early as possible. As a member of the special services assessment committee at her school, she learned about Todd's referral for special services and followed the evaluation process closely.

First, Ms. Genovese attended a sixth grade team meeting to find out more about Todd from his teachers. These teachers described Todd as inconsistent in grasping concepts. Sometimes he catches on immediately and sometimes he seems to be slow, resistant, and unconcerned. They observed him to be strong in reading decoding skills, fair in initial reading comprehension, but weak in remembering what he reads a day or a week later. He also seems incredibly disorganized. His social studies teacher called Todd's school backpack "the black hole of incomplete assignments." He has lost two textbooks and a school band trumpet this year. Todd rarely turns in his homework, yet he often claims to have done the work. Additionally, his team noted that Todd gets teased by his peers for poor pronunciation. While his speech is intelligible, he seems to slur or mumble as if his lips are heavy or frozen.

Next, Ms. Genovese consulted the school records to learn that Todd was an average or high average student through the first three grades. Difficulties in reading and content areas (social studies, science) seemed to start in the fourth grade and increase. Ms. Genovese knew that this pattern is not uncommon. In the first three grades, children primarily learn decoding skills and weak reading comprehension may not be noticeable. From fourth grade on, the emphasis placed on reading for understanding in a variety of activities increases and those students who comprehend poorly begin to stand out. Todd seemed to fit this pattern. Yet, his inconsistent performance, disorganized style, and speech difficulties cannot be so easily explained.

Included in the school records was the recent psychoeducational evaluation that failed to attest to a learning disability. The school psychologist noted that while Todd's reading and writing achievement scores were almost two grades behind his grade level peers, his Wechsler Intelligence Scale for Children (WISC-III) scores were commensurate with such achievement. He scored five points above the cut off for the Mild Developmental Disability category. The psychologist remarked that this evaluation probably presented a low assessment of this student's abilities and potential as Todd seemed extremely nervous and hesitant throughout the testing.

Ms. Genovese called the school psychologist to inquire about the possibility of a language or communication disorder based on Todd's speech and reading problems. The psychologist described Todd's articulation as muddled and agreed to order a further evaluation by a speech and language specialist.

Additional evaluation data provided by the speech and language specialist produced a diagnosis of communication disorder, including a significant deficit in receptive language and an expressive language problem called an articulation disorder. The specialist observed that Todd's facial muscles along the left half of his face seemed weak and ineffective, producing a speech pattern similar to that of a survivor of a stroke. A neurological dysfunction of unknown origin may have been disrupting or delaying the signals between the brain, facial nerves, and facial muscles. This neurological dysfunction may have also been the source of Todd's problems with receptive language, understanding new concepts, remembering what he learns from day to day, and organizing his materials. After reading the report, Ms. Genovese sought out this evaluator to ask about further testing for neurological problems. She learned that her school system would not conduct psychoneurological or neurological examinations. Ms. Genovese and the speech and language specialist concluded that the theory of a neurological source of Todd's difficulties could not be confirmed.

In the individualized education program (IEP) meeting, Ms. Genovese learned much of Todd's history from his grandmother and guardian, Mrs. Langer. Todd had lived under many roofs in his short 12 years. His father died of a drug overdose when Todd was an infant. Mrs. Langer suspected neglect and malnutrition during these early years, but she is sure that Todd was not physically or sexually abused. She also stated that Todd may have been exposed to drugs and alcohol during his mother's pregnancy.

Todd's mother gave up custody to the state foster care system when he was 4 after she was sent to prison on drug possession charges. After two years and five foster homes, Todd's paternal grandmother, living over a thousand miles away, heard that Todd was in foster care. She immediately sought and was given custody of the then 7-year-old Todd. He has lived in a stable and loving home with her and her husband, Wallace, since then.

Mrs. Langer reported that though Todd's mother had been out of prison for two years, the boy had no contact with her. However, recently Todd's mother called Mrs. Langer and asked to see Todd. The visit went well, prompting Todd to immediately, continuously, and to this day plead to live with his mother. Todd's mother has been attending Alcoholics Anonymous meetings and claims to have three months of sobriety. Mrs. Langer seemed ambivalent about Todd possibly returning to his mother's custody if she has cleaned up her life.

When asked about possible neurological illness or damage, Mrs. Langer reported that when Todd was 3 he attended a day care center that the state investigated and closed down due to excessively high levels of a toxic substance. Mrs. Langer couldn't recall what the substance was, but she did remember Todd being examined by a doctor who said that the substance could possibly cause brain damage or learning problems. Mrs. Langer thought the substance might be asbestos, but Ms. Genovese doubted that asbestos could cause brain or nerve damage.

QUESTIONS

1. Is it necessary for a special education teacher to understand the source(s) of a student's learning or behavior problems to help that student? Why or why not?
2. This case reveals information from a number of social systems. As Todd has developed over the years, explain how each system has influenced his life.
3. When a child such as Todd experiences many changes in his home environment, switching among a variety of caretakers, how might that impact his personality, behavior, and learning?
4. How can exposure to toxic substances affect a child's learning?
5. If you were Todd's special education teacher, what would you foresee to be the greatest challenge in teaching him?
6. *Activity:* Interview a neurologist to learn about how neurological damage or problems can influence a child's learning and behavior.

 C A S E 59. GUILLARMO

Issue: Social diversity

Guillarmo lives on a Navajo reservation with his father and brothers. He attends a high school off the reservation. His grades and behavior have deteriorated as he has developed a thriving business. His father is worried because he wants Guillarmo to be the first family member to graduate from high school.

Sixteen-year-old Guillarmo lives with his father, Ray, and two older brothers, Juan and Manny, on a Navajo reservation in rural Arizona. Neither Juan nor Manny is a high school graduate. They work part-time jobs for a local roofing contractor, not a surprise on a reservation with a 38 percent unemployment rate. Ray tries to tell them to go, leave the reservation, find a life in the big world. But they stay at home where the ways are familiar and the people are their longtime friends.

Ray is a full-blooded Navajo who drives a truck for a large distribution company. He is typically on the road three nights per week. Ray describes himself as a man who has tried to bring up three boys as best he could. His wife died when the three boys were young, so he has raised his sons by himself, bringing them up within the values of his heritage. He has always hoped that his sons would do better than he did, finish high school, maybe even go to college. He has taught his boys to work hard and make a sincere effort at everything they do. It has been a great disappointment to him to see his two older boys leave high school without diplomas. He views Guillarmo as the last chance for any member of his family to earn a high school diploma. Guillarmo has lost interest in school in the past year. He has also been involved in some violent incidents. Ray has tried to talk to Guillarmo, but his son merely tells him, "Don't worry. Don't worry. Everything is OK." Ray is worried. He has scheduled a meeting with the school guidance counselor to discuss Guillarmo's school difficulties.

The reservation has a small, one-room schoolhouse for students of all grades. Most of the older students attend the high school in Brownington, opting to take the long bus ride each morning and evening. Although they are mocked by some of the locals, Guillarmo and his Navajo peers take advantage of the opportunity to attend the only high school available in the southern half of the county.

Tensions between the reservation and Brownington have increased in recent years as the tourist industry has grown and traditional Native American crafts have become popular. As visitors began coming to Brownington, residents of the town began making small crafts (jewelry, clothing, and pottery) in the Native American style. The increase in the profitability of such crafts has stirred a fierce resentment among the Navajo artisans of authentic Native American wares. They claim the local shopkeepers are stocking imitation Navajo items made by white artisans and designers instead of selling authentic pieces. The Navajos set up their own crafts shops but the forty-mile drive from the main highway to the reservation is too far for most tourists. Overall, as Brownington has experienced an economic revival, the nearby reservation has gained little from the tourism.

In the midst of this economic activity is Guillarmo, a talented tenth grader, who has begun an occupation requiring long hours in marketing and sales. One could say that Guillarmo has placed his education on hold to focus on his business full time. While his grades have dropped to the C, D, and F ranges, his business profits have risen at least 50 percent in the last month. He started out working his business alone and he now employs four salespersons. He maintains communication with these salespersons through the use of cellular telephones and pagers, an important task because his sales staff is not always trustworthy. Guillarmo handles the vast recordkeeping on a small laptop computer, logging in all inventory and financial data on a daily basis. He is extremely organized and persistent in his work.

Guillarmo's teachers see another side of him. They are concerned about his future because he seems unmotivated in school, never doing his homework or studying for tests. They sometimes describe him as lazy and lacking ability. He has been described as "needing an attitude adjustment." Moreover, some of the teachers fear him. Three times he has been suspended this year for beating up classmates. The teachers know that these were not merely playground tussles. The beatings were extremely violent, sending each of the victims to the hospital with bruises and cuts. To the teachers and principal, Guillarmo seems to be the leader of some sort of Navajo gang, a small but tough group whose habitual intimidation of other students occasionally takes violent form.

The principal and the school superintendent have organized a task force of school personnel and community leaders to address what they describe as "the growing problem of gang violence." There are no Navajo tribe members on this twelve-person panel.

Recently, Guillarmo's successful business has landed him in the county juvenile detention for two weeks. He was charged with possession of marijuana and cocaine with intention to distribute. He is now free on bond until his trial date in three months. He has hired an excellent lawyer and together they are meeting to plan his defense. Guillarmo continues to attend high school regularly, primarily because the school is his main marketing site for his products.

QUESTIONS

1. What impact do the local social conflicts have on Guillarmo and his high school? How can the high school deal with this?
2. Guillarmo's teachers describe him as lacking academic ability. Is this true? Why or why not?
3. What is the history of public education for Native Americans? How are they educated today?
4. If you were part of the task force on gang violence, what recommendations for action would you make?
5. If you were one of Guillarmo's teachers, how would you attempt to help him become more invested in school?
6. *Activity:* Research the current state of special education for Native Americans. What are the pressing current issues and problems? What is being done about these problems?

 C A S E 60. TALIA

Issue: Transition

Talia is a high school student who lives in a racially isolated and economically depressed city. Her school district is severely underfunded. Few graduates of her high school go on to college. Although Talia is an able student, her career dreams and academic motivation have been gradually slipping away.

It has been five years since Talia decided she was not smart enough to go to college. It has been three years since she decided she was not smart enough to graduate from high school. It has been one year since she decided that she wanted to have a baby. None of these decisions are rightfully called "deci-sions" because Talia made them without adequate contemplation or consid-eration. To Talia, each of these situations fell upon her like inevitable drops of rain from the cloudy sky. She merely stood still long enough to catch them.

Now Talia is an eleventh grader at Frederick Douglass High School. It is only December, but she has already missed more than the yearly limit of absences. She will fail for the year. The school guidance counselor would have called to find out why Talia is absent so often, but Talia's family doesn't have a phone. They live in a low-income housing project on the east side of the river. That same counselor would like to drive out to visit Talia's house to talk to her. He has placed her fifty-sixth on his list of urgent home visits. He is the only guidance counselor for two urban high schools, a total case load of over 6,000 students.

Since Talia's problems and life-limiting "decisions" are not unique on the east side of the river, it is important to understand her high school and her city.

East City is a large metropolitan area whose only recent claim to fame is destitute poverty. Nearly half of all families in East City live below the poverty level. While the average household income in America is around $35,000 annually, East City's average is $15,000. The unemployment rate is over 20 per-cent. African Americans make up over 95 percent of the population of East City. Talia is an Africa American.

Two years ago the East City government went bankrupt, prompting a severe rollback of essential services such as trash collection, fire and emer-gency medical services, police protection, and public education. The local government is controlled by a court-ordered comptroller whose formidable task is to bring the budget out of fiscal deficit. The progress is slow as the local economy is almost nonexistent.

Like most school districts in America, East City's school budget is pri-marily funded by property taxes. The land in East City is worth little on the real estate market, therefore the amount of tax dollars brought in is low by comparison with other districts. As a result, the per student expenditure in East City is among the lowest in the nation. For example, suburban schools across the river in West City spend an average of two to three times as many dollars per student as East City spends.

This lack of school funds can be dramatically viewed in the East City classrooms. At Frederick Douglass High School, where Talia occasionally attends, the average class size is thirty-eight students. The roof of the school building leaks. On a rainy day, the principal and janitor distribute over fifty buckets through the hallways and classrooms. The heat in the auditorium has not worked in six years. Other classrooms are overheated due to an ongoing malfunction in the thermostat system. Teachers on the second floor spend the winter months with windows wide open to bring the temperature down to a livable level.

The textbooks at Frederick Douglass High School are twenty to twenty-five years old. Recent scientific discoveries are nonexistent in these antiquated texts. History students are not able to read about the fall of the Berlin wall because their texts do not reach the end of Communist era in the Soviet Union. Ironically, these African American history students also read of only famous white Americans since the movement to include women and persons of color in school textbooks has occurred only recently, that is, in the last two decades.

The quality of teaching at Talia's high school is also questionable. Many of the teachers talk of being "burned out" or overwhelmed by the immense challenges they face. Many of their students are unmotivated and hopeless about their futures. The teachers try to instill a love of learning and a bright outlook toward the future, but they feel they are fighting a losing battle. As one teacher says, "When a kid lives in a rundown place and goes to schools that are rundown and even the bus drive home goes through only rundown places, it's hard to convince him that studying physics will change anything." Of the 45 percent of students who stick around long enough graduate from high school, a rare few go to college.

Of crucial importance to Talia is the quality of science education in her school district and in her high school. Secretly, since age 5, Talia has wanted to be a scientist. She loves to try to figure out what makes things tick, how and why things work. But she has received little opportunity to build her knowledge and skills.

As talented new science teachers, fresh graduates from the local universities, eagerly seek their first teaching jobs, they rarely apply in the East City schools. Perhaps understandably, they flock to the more affluent districts known for having "good schools," where teachers have ample resources and opportunities to serve college-bound students. Most of these new science teachers are white. Few feel uncomfortable teaching in an all black school on what they call the "wrong side of the river."

Science classes in East City do not include laboratory experiments because there are no laboratory supplies. Most of the teachers can't even remember a day when science classes included real experiments.

There was a time when Talia viewed herself as a college-bound student. But she has gradually flowed with a receding tide. She finds herself looking with envy at the two girls in her class who have beautiful babies. Each left high school to have a child. There seems to be such a fulfillment in holding a baby of your own, a fulfillment Talia doesn't find in school.

Talia knows that her family of five—mother, Talia, two younger sisters, and three-year-old cousin Timmy—can hardly afford another mouth to feed and body to clothe. Her mother would scream if she knew Talia was thinking about having a baby. She reasons to herself that it might happen accidentally. It wouldn't be hard to fool her boyfriend because he never took care of the birth control. She could claim it was a mistake. On some nights, Talia lies in bed dreaming about a baby girl.

QUESTIONS

1. How does economic and social inequality impact public education? What could be done to remedy this?
2. Would you teach in an East City school? Why or why not?
3. What can science teachers do to improve instruction when the school district does not provide experimental equipment and supplies?
4. Are there girls like Talia or is this an unrealistic portrayal?
5. What can be done to help Talia as she moves into adult life? What programs or interventions does your community have that might be helpful?
6. *Activity:* Read Jonathan Kozol's *Savage Inequalities,* a study of how economic inequality in America translates into educational inequality. Discuss issues of race, social class, and opportunity.